Designing
Brand
Identity

Published by John Wiley & Sons, Inc., Hoboken, New Jersey
Published simultaneously in Canada

For general information on our other products and services or for technical support, please contact our Customer Care Department within the United States at (800) 762-2974, outside the United States at (317) 572-3993 or fax (317) 572-4002.

Wiley also publishes its books in a variety of electronic formats. Some content that appears in print may not be available in electronic books. For more information about Wiley products, visit our web site at www.wiley.com.

Library of Congress Cataloging-in-Publication Data:

Wheeler, Alina
   Designing brand identity: an essential guide for the whole branding team
   by Alina Wheeler.—3rd ed.

   p. cm.
   Includes bibliographical references and index.

   ISBN 978-0-470-40142-2 (cloth)

   1. Brand name products. 2. Branding (Marketing). 3. Trademarks—Design.
   4. Advertising—Brand name products. I. Title.

HD69.B7W44 2009

658.8'27—dc22   2009018429

Printed in the United States of America

10 9 8 7 6 5

Alina Wheeler

Designing
Brand
Identity

third edition

an essential guide for the whole branding team

WILEY

John Wiley & Sons, Inc.

Hello

No one does it alone (in branding and in life). This is a resource for the whole branding team—from the CEO to the creative director to the designer and brand strategist. I want to make it easy to quickly grasp the fundamentals and be inspired by best practices; I want to make it easy to seize every opportunity to delight customers and attract prospects; and I want to make it easy to build brand equity.

The tools have changed. The fundamentals have not. The questions are the same whether you're on Facebook or in Shanghai: Who are you? Who needs to know? How will they find out?

Why should they care? The process to achieve remarkable results is the same whether you are an entrepreneur with an audacious big idea, or a global company with hundreds of brands and thousands of employees.

Books, like brands, are built over time. Creating this resource has been my personal Mount Everest. Love, indeed, does conquer all. My husband Eddy's boundless energy and laughter always make the impossible possible. Tessa and Tearson are my shooting stars. Skylight is my Shangri-la.

Thank you to my colleagues who shared their time + wisdom

Abbott Miller
Aiden Morrison
Alan Brew
Alan Jacobson
Alan Siegel
Albert Cassorla
Alex Clark
Al Ries
Alvin Diec
Amanda Bach
Amanda Neville
Andrew Cutler
Andrew Welsh
Angora Chinchilla
Antonio R. Oliviera
Anna Bentson
Anne Moses
Ann Willoughby
Arnold Miller
Aubrey Balkind
Bart Crosby
Becky Wingate
Beth Mallo
Betty Nelson
Blake Deutsch
Blake Howard
Bob Mueller
Bob Warkulwiz
Bonita Albertson
Brad Kear
Brendan deVallance
Brian Fingeret
Brian Tierney
Bruce Berkowitz
Carla Hall
Carla Miller
Carol Moog
Carol Novello
Cathy Feierstein
Charlene O'Grady
Cherise Davis
Chris Ecklund
Chris Hacker
Chris Marshall
Chris Pullman
Clark Malcolm
Clay Timon
Clement Mok
Colin Drummond
Colleen Newquist
Cortney Cannon
Craig Bernhardt
Craig Johnson
Craig Schlanser
Dan Marcolina
Dana Arnett

Dani Pumilia
Danny Altman
Dave Luck, Mac Daddy
David Becker
David Kendall
David Milch
David Rose
David Roth
David Turner
Davis Masten
Dean Crutchfield
Deborah Perloe
Delphine Hirasuna
Dick Ritter
DK Holland
Donna MacFarland
Dr. Barbara Riley
Dr. Delyte Frost
Dr. Dennis Dunn
Dr. Ginny Vanderslice
Dr. Karol Wasylyshyn
Dustin Britt
Ed Williamson
Ellen Shapiro
Emily Cohen
Erich Sippel
Fo Wilson
Gael Towey
Geoff Verney
George Graves
Gerry Stankus
Gillian Wallis
Ginnie Gehshan
Hans-U. Allemann
Heather Guidice
Heidi Caldwell
Heidi Cody
Helen Keyes
Hilary Jay
Hilly Charrington
Howard Fish
Ian Stephens
Ivan Chermayeff
J.T. Miller
Jacey Lucas
Jack Cassidy
Jack Summerford
Jaeho Ko
Jamie Koval
Janice Fudyma
Jay Coen Gilbert
Jay Ehret
Jayoung Jaylee
Jean Pierre Jordan
Jeffrey Gorder
Jenie De'Ath
Jen Jagielski
Jenny Profy
Jerry Selber
Jessica Berwind
Jessica Robles Worch
Jessica Rogers

Jim Bittetto
Jinal Shah
Joan Carlson
Joanna Ham
Joanne Chan
Jody Friedman
Joe Duffy
Joe Pine
Joe Ray
Joel Grear
Joel Katz
John Bowles
John Coyne
John Gleason
John Hildenbiddle
John Kerr
John Klotnia
Jon Bjornson
Jon Schleuning
Juan Ramírez
Karin Hibma
Kate Dautrich
Kate Fitzgibbon
Kathleen Hatfield
Kathleen Koch
Kathy Mueller
Katie Caldwell
Katie Clark
Katie Wharton
Kelly Dunning
Ken Carbone
Keith Helemtag
Kent Hunter
Kit Hinrichs
Kurt Koepfle
Kurt Monigle
Larry Keeley
Laura DesEnfants
Le Roux Jooste
Lee Soonmee
Linda B. Matthiesen
Linda Wingate
Lisa Kovitz
Lori Kapner
Louise Fili
Lynn Beebe
Malcolm Grear
Marc Mikulich
Margie Gorman
Maribel Nix
Marie Morrison
Marie Taylor
Marilyn Sifford
Marius Ursache
Marjorie Guthrie
Mark Lomeli
Mark Selikson
Martha Witte
Mary Sauers
Mary Storm-Baranyai
Matt Coffman
Matthew Bartholomew

Meejoo Kwon
Melinda Lawson
Melissa Lapid
Meredith Nierman
Michael Bierut
Michael Cronan
Michael Donovan
Michael Flanagan
Michael Grillo
Michael Hirschhorn
Michal Levy
Mike Flanagan
Mike Reinhardt
Mike Schacherer
Milton Glaser
Mindy Romero
Moira Cullen
Monica Little
Nancy Donner
Nancye Greene
Nate Eimer
Ned Drew
Nick Bosch
Noelle Andrews
Pamela Thompson
Parag Murudkar
Pat Baldrige
Pat Duci
Paula Scher
Peggy Calabrese
Per Mollerup
Peter Emery
Peter Wise
Phil Gatto
Q Cassetti
R. Jacobs-Meadway
Rafi Spero
Ranjith Kumaran
riCardo Crespo
Rich Bacher
Richard Felton
Richard Kauffman
Richard Saul Wurman
Rick Bacher
Rob Wallace
Robbin Phillips
Rodney Abbot
Roger Whitehouse
Ronnie Lipton
Rosemary Murphy
Roy Pessis
Russ Napolitano
Ruth Abrahams
Sagi Haviv
Sally Hudson
Sarah Brinkman
Sarah Swaine
Scott Tatter
Sean Adams
Sean Haggerty
Sol Sender
Spike Jones

Stefan Liute
Steff Geissbuhler
Stella Gassaway
Stephen Doyle
Stephen Sapka
Steve Frykholm
Steve Perry
Steve Sandstrom
Steve Storti
Sunny Hong
Susan Avarde
Sylvia Harris
Tom Birk
Tom Geismar
Tom Watson
Tricia Davidson
Trish Thompson
Will Burke
Woody Pirtle

3rd Edition
Thank you for your creativity and brilliance.
Jon Bjornson
strategic design advisor

Perpetual gratitude
My publishing team at Wiley:
Amanda Miller
VP + publisher
Margaret Cummins
senior editor
Justin Mayhew
senior marketing manager
Penny Makras
marketing manager
Diana Cisek
production director
Lauren Poplawski
senior editorial assistant

My brother who asked when the film is coming out
All Wheelers
Suzanne Young
Lissa Reidel
Marty Neumeier
Dennis Alter
Tomasz Fryzel
Stephen Shackleford
Richard Cress
Mark Wills
Amy Grove Bigham
Stellarvisions
Gretchen Dykstra
Cathy Jooste
Marc Goldberg
Heather Norcini
Liz Merrill
My favorite cousin
Quest sisters
Sullivan

Contents

Designing Brand Identity is a quick reference guide. All subject matter is organized by spread for ease of access in the blinding speed of business and life. No power source needed—just your desire and passion to be the best.

Part 1 presents the fundamental concepts needed to jumpstart the brand identity process and create a shared vocabulary for the entire team.

Process

Part 2 presents a universal brand identity process regardless of the project's scope and nature. This section answers the question "Why does it take so long?"

Best Practices

Part 3 showcases best practices. Local and global, public and private, these projects inspire and exemplify original, flexible, lasting solutions.

Image and perception help drive value;
without an image there is no perception.

Scott M. Davis
Brand Asset Management

1 Basics

Part 1 illuminates the difference between brand and brand identity, and what it takes to be the best. Don't bypass the fundamentals in the speed of a new project. Establish a shared vocabulary for the entire branding team.

What is brand?

As competition creates infinite choices, companies look for ways to connect emotionally with customers, become irreplaceable, and create lifelong relationships. A strong brand stands out in a densely crowded marketplace. People fall in love with brands, trust them, and believe in their superiority. How a brand is perceived affects its success, regardless of whether it's a start-up, a nonprofit, or a product.

A brand is a person's gut feeling about a product, service, or company.

Marty Neumeier
The Brand Gap

Who are you? Who needs to know? How will they find out? Why should they care?

Brands have three primary functions*

Navigation

Brands help consumers choose from a bewildering array of choices.

Reassurance

Brands communicate the intrinsic quality of the product or service and reassure customers that they have made the right choice.

Engagement

Brands use distinctive imagery, language, and associations to encourage customers to identify with the brand.

*David Haigh, CEO, Brand Finance

It is never too late to be what you could have been.

George Eliot

Brand touchpoints

Each touchpoint is an opportunity to increase awareness and build customer loyalty.

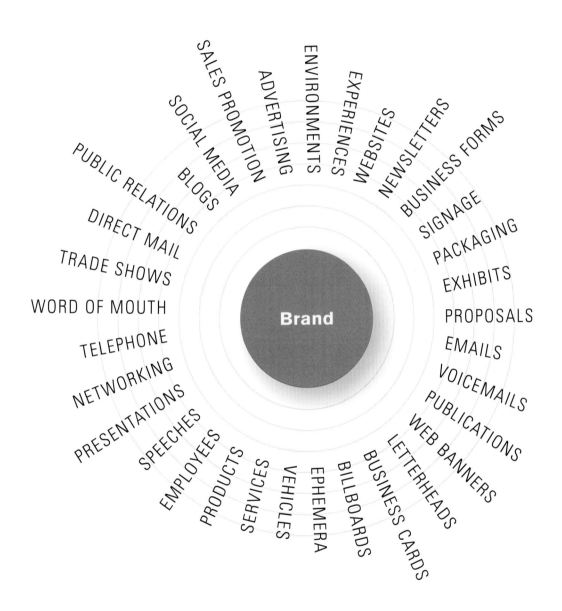

The best brands marry intelligence and insight with imagination and craft.

Connie Birdsall
Creative Director, Lippincott

Brand basics

What is brand identity?

Brand identity is tangible and appeals to the senses. You can see it, touch it, hold it, hear it, watch it move. Brand identity fuels recognition, amplifies differentiation, and makes big ideas and meaning accessible. Brand identity takes disparate elements and unifies them into whole systems.

Trademarks are the shortest, fastest, most ubiquitous form of communication available.

One eye sees. The other feels.

Paul Klee

Design plays an essential role in creating and building brands. Design differentiates and embodies the intangibles—emotion, context, and essence—that matter most to consumers.

Moira Cullen
Senior Director, Global Design
The Hershey Company

Brand identity implies an asset. Corporate identity sounds too much like an expense. This is an important distinction.

On an average day consumers are exposed to six thousand advertisements and, each year, to more than twenty-five thousand new products... Brands help consumers cut through the proliferation of choices available in every product and service category.

Scott M. Davis
Brand Asset Management

My cell phone is my life. Tessa Wheeler

LONDON
IT RAINS MORE IN ROME

I make art.
heavybubble.com

zipcar.com

© Ed Wheeler Photography

HELLO
my name is

What is branding?

Branding is a disciplined process used to build awareness and extend customer loyalty. It requires a mandate from the top and readiness to invest in the future. Branding is about seizing every opportunity to express why people should choose one brand over another. A desire to lead, outpace the competition, and give employees the best tools to reach customers are the reasons why companies leverage branding.

Types of branding

Co-branding: partnering with another brand to achieve reach

Digital branding: web, social media, search engine optimization, driving commerce on the web

Personal branding: the way an individual builds their reputation

Cause branding: aligning your brand with a charitable cause; or corporate social responsibility

Country branding: efforts to attract tourists and businesses

Victory belongs to the most persevering.

Napoleon Bonaparte

Emotional branding is a dynamic cocktail of anthropology, imagination, sensory experiences, and visionary approach to change.

Marc Gobé
Emotional Branding

We continue to invest in our core strengths. First, we don't skimp on understanding the consumer. Second is innovation... And third is branding... We're delivering more messages to our consumers.

A. G. Lafley
CEO, P&G
Business Week, 2009

Process: .... 1 : conducting research .... 2 : clarifying strategy .... 3 : designing identity ....

When to start the process

New company, new product

I'm starting a new business. I need a business card and a website.

We've developed a new product and it needs a name and a logo yesterday.

We need to raise millions of dollars. The campaign needs to have its own identity.

We're going public in the fall.

We need to raise venture capital, even though we do not have our first customer.

Name change

Our name no longer fits who we are and the businesses we are in.

We need to change our name because of a trademark conflict.

Our name has negative connotations in the new markets we are serving.

Our name misleads customers.

We merged.

Revitalize a brand

We want to reposition and renew the global brand.

We're no longer in the business we were in when we founded our company.

We need to communicate more clearly about who we are.

We're going global—we need help to enter new world markets.

No one knows who we are.

Our stock is devalued.

We want to appeal to a new and more affluent market.

Revitalize a brand identity

We are a great company with cutting-edge products. We look behind the times.

Will our identity work on the web?

Our identity does not position us shoulder to shoulder with our competitors.

We have 80 divisions and inconsistent nomenclature.

I am embarrassed when I give out my business card.

Everyone in the world recognizes our icon, but admit it—she needs a face-lift.

We love our symbol—it is known by our market. The problem is you cannot read our logotype.

Create an integrated system

We do not present a consistent face to our customers.

We lack visual consistency and we need a new brand architecture to deal with acquisitions.

Our packaging is not distinctive. Our competitors look better than we do, and their sales are going up.

All of our marketing looks like it comes from different companies.

We need to look strong and communicate that we are one global company.

Every division does its own thing when marketing. This is inefficient, frustrating, and not cost-effective. Everyone is reinventing the wheel.

When companies merge

We want to send a clear message to our stakeholders that this is a merger of equals.

We want to communicate that $1 + 1 = 4$.

We want to build on the brand equity of the merging companies.

We need to send a strong signal to the world that we are the new industry leader.

We need a new name.

How do we evaluate our acquisition's brand and fold it into our brand architecture?

Two industry leaders are merging. How do we manage our new identity?

4 : creating touchpoints

5 : managing assets

Who are stakeholders?

Seizing every opportunity to build brand champions requires identifying the constituencies that affect success. Reputation and goodwill extend far beyond a brand's target customers. Employees are now called "internal customers" because their power is far reaching. Gaining insight into stakeholder characteristics, behavior, needs, and perceptions yields a high return.

A tribe is a group of people connected to one another, connected to a leader, and connected to an idea... People want connection and growth and something new.

Seth Godin
Tribes

Brand is not what you say it is. It's what they say it is.

Marty Neumeier
The Brand Gap

Gen X or Gen Y?

Market researchers use the same terms for classifying generation gaps, but don't agree on the dates.

Generation	Born
Seniors	before 1946
Boomers	1946-1965
Gen X	1966-1980
Gen Y	1981-1995

People need emotional navigation.

Colin Drummond
Crispin Porter + Bogusky

The fundamentals of brand building, from listening to and learning from customers, to relevantly meeting their needs, have been magnified in a world of digital communications and consumer empowerment.

Allen Adamson
Brand Digital

As the branding process unfolds, research about stakeholders will inform a broad range of solutions from positioning to the tilt of brand messages, to the launch strategy and plan.

Evangelism means convincing people to believe in your product or ideas as much as you do, by using fervor, zeal, guts, and cunning to mobilize your customers and staff into becoming as passionate about a cause as you are.

Guy Kawasaki

A lot of companies sabotage themselves by failing to consider the far-reaching impact of their stakeholders.

Lissa Reidel
Marketing Consultant

Why invest?

The best identity programs embody and advance the company's brand by supporting desired perceptions. Identity expresses itself in every touchpoint of the brand and becomes intrinsic to a company's culture—a constant symbol of its core values and its heritage.

Brands now appear regularly on balance sheets in many companies. The intangible value of the brand is often much greater than the corporation's tangible assets.

Wally Olins
The Brand Book

Steady investment in design is rewarded by lasting competitiveness.

Design Council UK

When you affect behavior, you can impact performance.

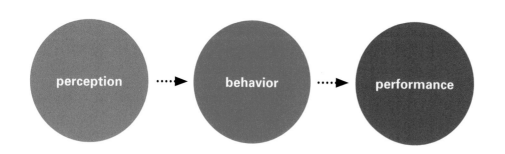

In *Brand Leadership* by David A. Aaker and Erich Joachimsthaler, the authors build a case that "when a high level of perceived quality has been (or can be) created, raising the price not only provides margin dollars but also aids perceptions." Their basic premise is that "strong brands command a price premium."

Reasons to invest in brand identity

Make it easy for the customer to buy

Compelling brand identity presents any company, any size, anywhere with an immediately recognizable, distinctive professional image that positions it for success. An identity helps manage the perception of a company and differentiates it from its competitors. A smart system conveys respect for the customer and makes it easy to understand features and benefits. A new product design or a better environment can delight a customer and create loyalty. An effective identity encompasses such elements as a name that is easy to remember or a distinctive package design for a product.

Make it easy for the sales force to sell

Whether it is the CEO of a global conglomerate communicating a new vision to the board, a first-time entrepreneur pitching to venture capital firms, or a financial advisor creating a need for investment products, everyone is selling. Nonprofits, whether fundraising or soliciting new volunteers, are continually selling. Strategic brand identity works across diverse audiences and cultures to build an awareness and understanding of a company and its strengths. By making intelligence visible, effective identity seeks to clearly communicate a company's unique value proposition. The coherence of communications across various media sends a strong signal to the customer about the laserlike focus of a company.

Make it easy to build brand equity

The goal of all public companies is to increase shareholder value. A brand, or a company's reputation, is considered to be one of the most valuable company assets. Small companies and nonprofits also need to build brand equity. Their future success is dependent on building public awareness, preserving their reputations, and upholding their value. A strong brand identity will help build brand equity through increased recognition, awareness, and customer loyalty, which in turn helps make a company more successful. Managers who seize every opportunity to communicate their company's brand value and what the brand stands for sleep better at night. They are building a precious asset.

Branding imperatives

Acknowledge that we live in a branded world.

Seize every opportunity to position your company in your customers' minds.

Communicate a strong brand idea over and over again.

Go beyond declaring a competitive advantage. Demonstrate it!

Understand the customers. Build on their perceptions, preferences, dreams, values, and lifestyles.

Identify touchpoints—places in which customers interface with the product or service.

Use brand identity to create sensory magnets to attract and retain customers.

Brands are intangible assets and account for, on average 75% of the value of a company.

Blake Deutsch

Brand strategy

Effective brand strategy provides a central unifying idea around which all behavior, actions, and communications are aligned. It works across products and services, and is effective over time. The best brand strategies are so differentiated and powerful that they deflect the competition. They are easy to talk about, whether you are the CEO or an employee.

Brand strategy builds on a vision, is aligned with business strategy, emerges from a company's values and culture, and reflects an in-depth understanding of the customer's needs and perceptions. Brand strategy defines positioning, differentiation, the competitive advantage, and a unique value proposition.

Brand strategy needs to resonate with all stakeholders: external customers, the media, and internal customers (e.g., employees, the board, core suppliers). Brand strategy is a road map that guides marketing, makes it easier for the sales force to sell more, and provides clarity, context, and inspiration to employees.

The best brand strategy is developed as a creative partnership between the client, the strategist, and the designer.

Connie Birdsall, Creative Director
Lippincott

Alignment ········· vision ········· actions ········· expression ········· experience

Aligning an organization's vision with its customers' experience is the goal of brand strategy.

Who develops brand strategy?

It is usually a team of people; no one does it alone. It is a result of an extended dialogue among the CEO, marketing, sales, advertising, public relations, operations, and distribution. Global companies frequently bring in brand strategists: independent thinkers and authorities, strategic marketing firms, and brand consultants. It often takes someone from the outside who is an experienced strategic and creative thinker to help a company articulate what is already there.

Sometimes a brand strategy is born at the inception of a company by a visionary, such as Steve Jobs, Jeff Bezos, or Anita Roddick. Sometimes it takes a visionary leader, such as Lou Gerstner, former CEO of IBM, to redefine brand strategy. Companies frequently survive and prosper because they have a clear brand strategy. Companies falter because they do not have one.

The role of the consultant in developing brand strategy is to facilitate the process: asking the right questions, providing relevant input and ideas, getting key issues to surface, and achieving resolution.

Erich Sippel
President
Erich Sippel & Company

The importance of brand strategy and the cost of building brand identity should be understood at the highest levels of an organization and across functional areas—not just sales and marketing—but in legal, finance, operations, and human resources as well.

Sally Hudson
Marketing Consultant

Every senior leader in an organization must be focused and accountable for translating the brand strategy.

Betty Nelson
Group Director, Global Communications
IMS Health

©David Arky Photography

Wana is Morocco's new full-service global telecom company offering fixed line, mobile, and internet services. With the core idea of putting the customer in control, Wana revolutionized the telecom market in Morocco by delivering on this promise at every touchpoint from name through design and product experience and offering. The name Wana means close to you. The Wana symbol, a dynamic star, references the Moroccan flag and connects with the Moroccan spirit.

Wana: Lippincott

Positioning

Supporting every effective brand is a positioning strategy that drives planning, marketing, and sales. Positioning evolves to create openings in a market that is continually changing, a market in which consumers are saturated with products and messages. Positioning takes advantage of changes in demographics, technology, marketing cycles, consumer trends, and gaps in the market to find new ways of appealing to the public.

Positioning is a revolutionary branding concept developed by Al Ries and Jack Trout in 1981. They defined positioning as the scaffolding on which companies build their brands, strategize their planning, and extend their relationships with customers. Positioning takes into account the mix of price, product, promotion, and place—the four dimensions that affect sales.

Ries and Trout were convinced that each company must determine its position in the customer's mind, considering the needs of the customer, the strengths and weaknesses of that company, and the competitive landscape. This concept continues to be a fundamental precept in all marketing communications, branding, and advertising.

Henry Ford said customers could have any color they wanted as long as it was black. General Motors came along with five colors and stole the show.

Positioning breaks through barriers of oversaturated markets to create new opportunities.

Lissa Reidel
Marketing Consultant

Brand positioning
Developed by Brand Engine

If you can't say that you are the only, you need to fix **your** business, not your brand. Start with a solid platform to effectively articulate your brand's value.

Will Burke
CEO
Brand Engine.

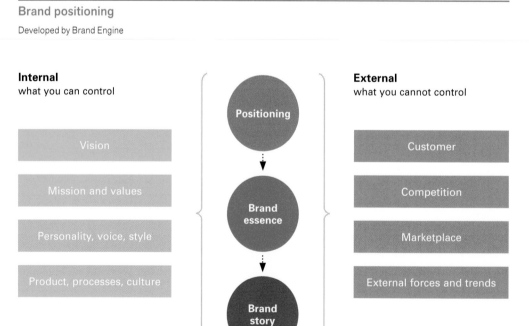

Internal
what you can control

Vision

Mission and values

Personality, voice, style

Product, processes, culture

Positioning

Brand essence

Brand story

External
what you cannot control

Customer

Competition

Marketplace

External forces and trends

Repositioning history

Sneakers

In the 1950s, everyone had one pair of white tennis sneakers. Then sneakers were redesigned and repositioned in consumers' minds. They became endowed with celebrity status and were transformed into symbols of empowerment in the mid-1970s, when Nike and Reebok picked up on the increased interest in health, changed the perception, and raised the price. Today, sneakers have brand status, and everyone needs more than one pair.

Water

Until the 1980s, tap water tasted good. If consumers thought about water at all, it was only that they should have eight glasses a day. Health trends coincided with the water supply becoming less than the dependable utility it had always been. The three-martini lunch was no longer hip, yet people still wanted something with cachet to drink. Presto: bottled water reassured people that they were drinking something healthy and ordering something trendy. And now, tap water has regained its sustainable cache. Plastic begone.

Big-box stores

Target created a new position for itself as a big-box store with products that were designed by some of the best designers in the world. Target's positioning is dramatically different from that of Walmart, the biggest store on earth. While Walmart is about the lowest price, Target's positioning is created around appeal (design), as well as necessity and price. Target has built recognition of its brand to the degree that some ad campaigns feature the Target logo in audacious applications, including fabric patterns and spots on a dog, without mentioning the company name.

The difference between sales and marketing

Sales and marketing use similar approaches. In a sales campaign, the focus is the product. A company that is market-driven focuses on consumers. The product is defined and finite, but in the minds of clients there are infinite possibilities. Marketing penetrates into the psyches of customers. The company that markets has its finger on the pulse of consumers.

The onliness statement
Developed by Marty Neumeier, *ZAG*

What: The only (category)

How: that (differentiation characteristic)

Who: for (customer)

Where: in (market geography)

Why: who (need state)

When: during (underlying trend).

Example: Harley Davidson is...

What: The only motorcycle manufacturer

How: that makes big, loud motorcycles

Who: for macho guys (and "macho wannabees")

Where: mostly in the United States

Why: who want to join a gang of cowboys

When: in an era of decreasing personal freedom.

Big idea

A big idea functions as an organizational totem pole around which strategy, behavior, actions, and communications are aligned. These simply worded statements are used internally as a beacon of a distinctive culture and externally as a competitive advantage that helps consumers make choices.

Big ideas are a springboard for responsible creative work (thinking, designing, naming) and a litmus test for measuring success.

The simplicity of the language is deceptive because the process of getting there is difficult. It requires extensive dialogue, patience, and the courage to say less. A skilled facilitator, experienced in building consensus, is usually needed to ask the right questions and to achieve closure. The result of this work is a critical component in the realization of a compelling brand strategy and a differentiated brand identity.

A brand becomes stronger when you narrow the focus.

Al Ries and Laura Ries
The 22 Immutable Laws of Branding

For GE, imagination at work is more than a slogan or a tagline. It is a reason for being.

Jeffrey R. Immelt, CEO
GE

Vision
Values
Mission
Value proposition
Culture
Target market
Segments
Stakeholder perceptions
Services
Products
Infrastructure

Understanding

Marketing strategy
Competition
Trends
Pricing
Distribution
Research
Environment
Economics
Sociopolitics
Strengths/weaknesses
Opportunities
Threats

Less is more

Apple	Harley Davidson	At the heart of the strategy is our commitment to delight our guests by consistently delivering the right combination of innovation, design, and value in our merchandising, in our marketing, and in our stores. This is the essence of our 'Expect more. Pay less.' brand promise.
Think different	Rider passion	
Target	Disney	Bob Ulrich
Expect more. Pay less.	Make people happy	Chairman and CEO
eBay	Virgin Mobile	Target
The world's online marketplace	Live without a plan	
Unilever	GE	
Adding vitality to life	Imagination at work	
Volvo	Method	
Safety	People against dirty	
FedEx	Coca-Cola	
The world on time	Happiness in a bottle	
	Mini Cooper	
	Let's motor.	

Core values
Brand attributes

Differentiation
Value proposition

Central idea
Unifying concept

Clarifying → **Positioning** → **Brand Essence**

Big idea

!

Competitive advantage
Brand strategy

Business category

Key messages
Voice and tone

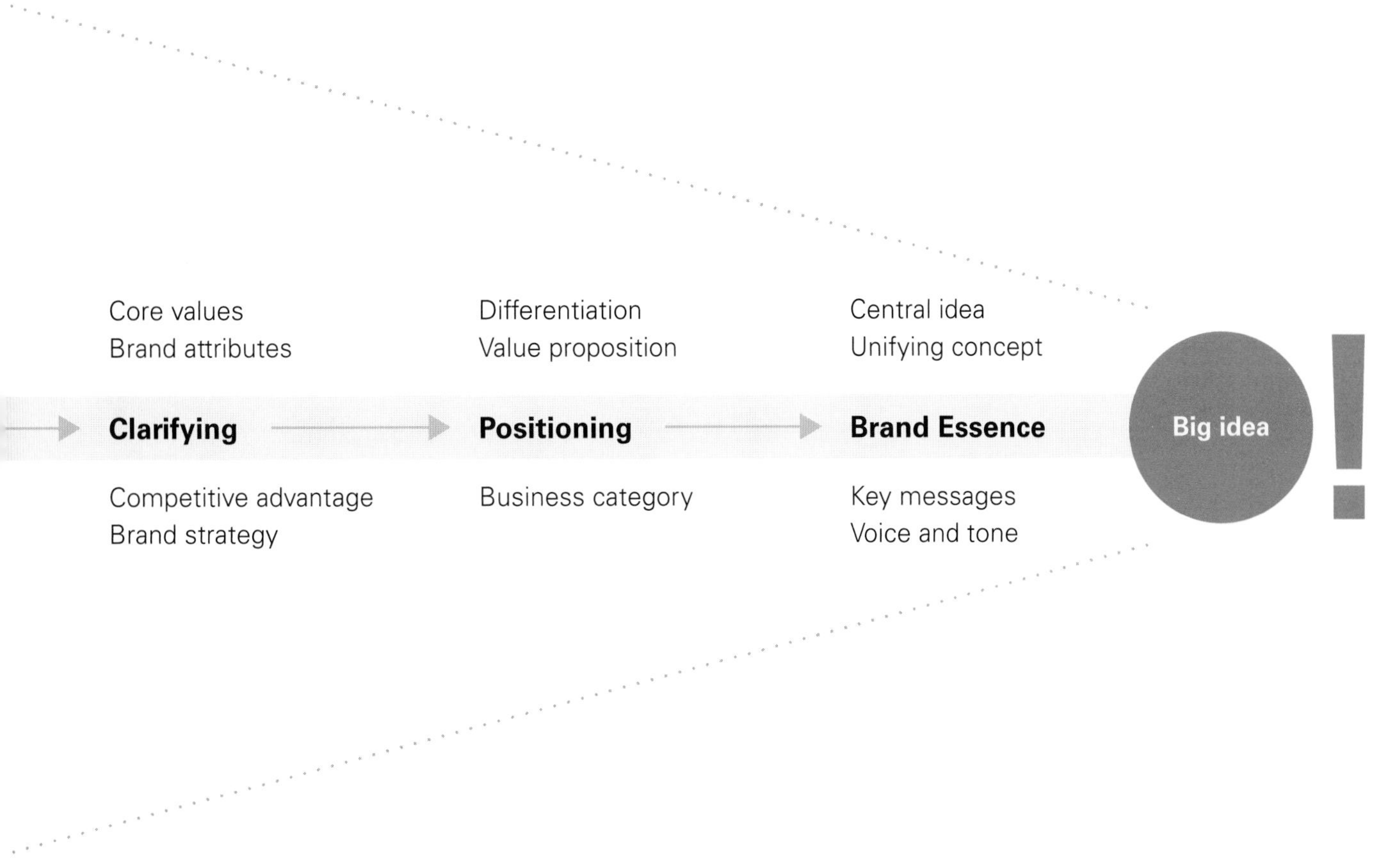

Customer experience

It is essential for the branding team to look up from the desktop and see the world through the eyes of the customer. Shopping has become a subset to being engaged and entertained. The next disciplinary seismic shift in branding is customer experience: building loyalty and lifelong relationships at each point of contact.

The vast amount of purchasing choices is inspiring companies to enhance the brand experience to lure and keep customers. Every customer contact provides an opportunity to enhance an emotional connection. A good experience generates positive buzz; a bad experience becomes a lost opportunity sabotaging the brand.

The customer goes to the Genius Bar at the Apple Store for education, the American Girl Place for afternoon tea, and the sushi bar at Whole Foods for a free taste of something new.

Even the most mundane transactions can be turned into memorable experiences.

B. Joseph Pine II and James H. Gilmore
The Experience Economy

Sip, surf, and save is the value proposition at ING Direct's hip wireless cafés. The coffee is good and the shopping for cool orange stuff is fun. Since 2000, the company has signed more than 3.2 million customers. Cafés are in key urban locations.

Our orange ING Direct cafés welcome the public to buy a cup of coffee, experience our brand, and learn about the great deals we offer to anyone who wants to save money, simply and easily.

Arkadi Kuhlmann
President and CEO
ING Direct

Donovan/Green identified moments of truth for a hotel guest that ranged from sighting the hotel from the highway, walking into the front lobby, and glimpsing into the room. The firm viewed each touchpoint as an opportunity to create a memorable and positive experience to support the brand culture.

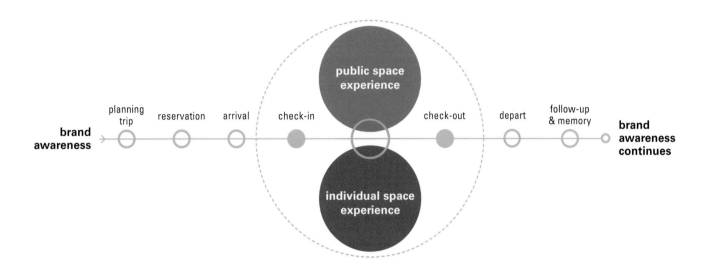

Those businesses that relegate themselves to the diminishing world of goods and services will be rendered irrelevant. To avoid this fate, you must learn to stage a rich, compelling experience.

B. Joseph Pine II and
James H. Gilmore

The Experience Economy

Shopping at Trader Joe's gives me a sense of discovery. There is always something new to try.

Blake Deutsch

The art of being a great retailer is to preserve the core while enhancing the experience. It is very hard to do and many people have lost their way. We need to push for reinvention and renewal and to extend things without diluting ourselves.

Howard Schultz
Founder and CEO
Starbucks

Names

The right name is timeless, tireless, easy to say and remember; it stands for something, and facilitates brand extensions. Its sound has rhythm. It looks great in the text of an email and in the logo. A well-chosen name is an essential brand asset, as well as a 24/7 workhorse.

A name is transmitted day in and day out, in conversations, emails, voicemails, websites, on the product, on business cards, and in presentations.

The wrong name for a company, product, or service can hinder marketing efforts, through miscommunication or because people cannot pronounce it or remember it. It can subject a company to unnecessary legal risks or alienate a market segment. Finding the right name that is legally available is a gargantuan challenge. Naming requires a creative, disciplined, strategic approach.

The right name captures the imagination and connects with the people you want to reach.

Danny Altman, Founder + Creative Director
A Hundred Monkeys

Naming myths

Naming a company is easy, like naming a baby.

Naming is a rigorous and exhaustive process. Frequently hundreds of names are reviewed prior to finding one that is legally available and works.

I will know it when I hear it.

People often indicate that they will be able to make a decision after hearing a name once. In fact, good names are strategies and need to be examined, tested, sold, and proven.

We will just do the search ourselves.

Various thoughtful techniques must be utilized to analyze the effectiveness of a name to ensure that its connotations are positive in the markets served.

We cannot afford to test the name.

Intellectual property lawyers need to conduct extensive searches to ensure that there are no conflicting names and to make record of similar names. It is too large a risk—names need to last over time.

Just by naming a process, a level of service, or a new service feature, you are creating a valuable asset that can add to the worth of your business.

Jim Bitetto
Partner
Keusey Tutunjian & Bitetto, PC

Companies miss a huge opportunity when they fail to communicate the meaning of a new name. Audiences will better remember a name if they understand its rationale.

Lori Kapner
Principal
Kapner Consulting

Qualities of an effective name

Meaningful

It communicates something about the essence of the brand. It supports the image that the company wants to convey.

Distinctive

It is unique, as well as easy to remember, pronounce, and spell. It is differentiated from the competition.

Future-oriented

It positions the company for growth, change, and success. It has sustainability and preserves possibilities. It has long legs.

Modular

It enables a company to build brand extensions with ease.

Protectable

It can be owned and trademarked. A domain is available.

Positive

It has positive connotations in the markets served. It has no strong negative connotations.

Visual

It lends itself well to graphic presentation in a logo, in text, and in brand architecture.

Types of names

Founder

Many companies are named after founders: Ben & Jerry's, Martha Stewart, Ralph Lauren, Mrs. Fields. It might be easier to protect. It satisfies an ego. The downside is that it is inextricably tied to a real human being.

Descriptive

These names convey the nature of the business, such as Toys "R" Us, Find Great People, or E*TRADE. The benefit of a descriptive name is that it clearly communicates the intent of the company. The potential disadvantage is that as a company grows and diversifies, the name may become limiting. Some descriptive names are difficult to protect since they are so generic.

Fabricated

A made-up name, like Kodak, Xerox, or TiVo, is distinctive and might be easier to copyright. However, a company must invest a significant amount of capital into educating its market as to the nature of the business, service, or product. Häagen-Dazs is a fabricated foreign name that has been extremely effective in the consumer market.

Metaphor

Things, places, people, animals, processes, mythological names, or foreign words are used in this type of name to allude to a quality of a company. Names like Nike and Patagonia are interesting to visualize and often can tell a good story.

Acronym

These names are difficult to remember and difficult to copyright. IBM and GE became well known only after the companies established themselves with the full spelling of their names. There are so many acronyms that new ones are increasingly more difficult to learn and require a substantial investment in advertising. Other examples: USAA, AARP, DKNY, and CNN.

Magic spell

Some names alter a word's spelling in order to create a distinctive, protectable name, like Cingular and Netflix.

Combinations of the above

Some of the best names combine name types. Some good examples are Cingular Wireless, Citibank, and Hope's Cookies. Customers and investors like names that they can understand.

Brand architecture

Brand architecture refers to the hierarchy of brands within a single company. It is the interrelationship of the parent company, subsidiary companies, products, and services, and should mirror the marketing strategy. It is important to bring consistency, visual and verbal order, thought, and intention to disparate elements to help a company grow and market more effectively.

As companies merge with others and acquire new companies and products, the branding, nomenclature, and marketing decisions become exceedingly complex. Decision makers examine marketing, cost, time, and legal implications.

The need for brand architecture is not limited to Fortune 100 companies or for-profit companies. Any company or institution that is growing needs to evaluate which brand architecture strategy will support future growth. Most large companies that sell products and services have a mixture of strategies.

Strategic questions

What are the benefits of leveraging the name of the parent company?

Does the positioning of our new entity require that we distance it from the parent?

Will co-branding confuse consumers?

Do we change the name or build on existing equity even though it was owned by a competitor?

Should we ensure that the parent company is always visible in a secondary position?

How do we brand this new acquisition?

Corporation

Express

Ground

Freight

Custom Critical

Trade Networks

FedEx is an example of monolithic brand architecture. The program, designed by Landor Associates, uses color to emphasize sub-brands.

Types of brand architecture

Various marketing strategists identified numerous brand architecture scenarios, however there is no universal agreement on brand architecture terms.

Monolithic brand architecture

Characterized by a strong, single master brand. Customers make choices based on brand loyalty. Features and benefits matter less to the consumer than the brand promise and persona. Brand extensions use the parent's identity, and generic descriptors.

Google + Google Maps
FedEx + FedEx Express
GE + GE Healthcare
Virgin + Virgin Mobile
Vanguard + Vanguard ETF

Endorsed brand architecture

Characterized by marketing synergy between the product or division, and the parent. The product or division has a clearly defined market presence, and benefits from the association, endorsement, and visibility of the parent.

iPod + Apple
Polo + Ralph Lauren
Oreo + Nabisco
Navy Seals + the U.S. Navy

Pluralistic brand architecture

Characterized by a series of well-known consumer brands. The name of the parent may be either invisible or inconsequential to the consumer, and known only to the investment community. Many parent companies develop a system for corporate endorsement that is tertiary.

Wharton (University of Pennsylvania)
Tang (Kraft Foods)
Godiva Chocolate (Campbell Soup)
The Ritz-Carlton (Marriott)
Hellmann's Mayonnaise (Unilever)

iPod
iPhone
iLife
iWork
iTunes
iPhoto
iMovie
iWeb
iDVD

Taglines

Taglines influence consumers' buying behavior by evoking an emotional response. A tagline is a short phrase that captures a company's brand essence, personality, and positioning, and distinguishes the company from its competitors.

A tagline's frequent and consistent exposure in the media and in popular culture reinforces its message. Traditionally used in advertising, taglines are also applied on marketing collateral as the centerpiece of a positioning strategy.

Taglines have a shorter life span than logos. Like advertising campaigns, they are susceptible to marketplace and lifestyle changes. Deceptively simple, taglines are not arbitrary. They grow out of an intensive strategic and creative process.

A tagline is a slogan, clarifier, mantra, company statement, or guiding principle that describes, synopsizes, or helps create an interest.

Debra Koontz Traverso
Outsmarting Goliath

The origin of the word "slogan" comes from the Gaelic *slaughgaiirm*, used by Scottish clans to mean "war cry."

Essential characteristics

Short

Differentiated from its competitors

Unique

Captures the brand essence and positioning

Easy to say and remember

No negative connotations

Displayed in a small font

Can be protected and trademarked

Evokes an emotional response

Difficult to create

**Taglines sum up the sell,
and the best of them evoke an
emotional response.**

Jerry Selber
LevLane

A cross-section of taglines

Imperative: Commands action and usually starts with a verb

YouTube	Broadcast yourself
Nike	Just do it
MINI Cooper	Let's motor
Hewlett-Packard	Invent
Apple	Think different
Toshiba	Don't copy. Lead.
Mutual of Omaha	Begin today
Virgin Mobile	Live without a plan
Outward Bound	Live bigger

Descriptive: Describes the service, product, or brand promise

Philips	Sense and sensibility
PNC	The thinking behind the money
Target	Expect more. Pay less.
Concentrics	People. Process. Results.
MSNBC	The whole picture
Ernst & Young	From thought to finish
Allstate	You're in good hands
GE	Imagination at work

Superlative: Positions the company as best in class

DeBeers	A diamond is forever
BMW	The ultimate driving machine
Lufthansa	There's no better way to fly
National Guard	Americans at their best
Hoechst	Future in life sciences

Provocative: Thought-provoking; frequently a question

Sears	Where else?
Microsoft	Where are you going today?
Mercedes-Benz	What makes a symbol endure?
Dairy Council	Got milk?

Specific: Reveals the business category

HSBC	The world's local bank
The New York Times	All the news that's fit to print
Olay	Love the skin you're in
Volkswagen	Drivers wanted
eBay	Happy hunting
Minolta	The essentials of imaging

Staying on message

Stay on message is the brand mantra. The best brands speak with one distinctive voice. On the web, in a tweet, in conversations with a salesperson, in a speech given by the president, the company needs to project the same unified message. It must be memorable, identifiable, and centered on the customer.

Voice and tone work harmoniously with clarity and personality to engage customers, whether they are listening, scanning, or reading. Each word offers an opportunity to inform, inspire, and fuel word of mouth.

Whether it is a call to action or a product description, language must be vital, straightforward, eloquent, and substantive. Be sure the meaning is accessible to all customers. When developing key messages and company descriptions, preserve the impact by cutting through hype and clutter. Brand messages work well if they distill the essence of the product or service. A memorable message grows with repetition, taking on a life of its own.

Language and communications are intrinsic to all brand expressions. Unified, consistent high-level messages demand buy-in at all levels: the commitment must be long-term. Integrated communications require that content and design work together to differentiate the brand.

Let's give them something to talk about.

Bonnie Raitt

Each word is an opportunity to be intentional

Nomenclature	Brand esssence	Communications	Information	Touchpoints
Company name formal	Mission statements	Voice	Content	Websites + blogs
Company name informal	Vision statements	Tone	Call to action	News releases
Taglines	Value propositions	Headline style	Phone numbers	FAQs
Descriptors	Key messages	Punctuation	URLs	Press kits
Product names	Guiding principles	Capitalization	Email signatures	Annual reports
Process names	Customer pledges	Emphasis	Voicemail messages	Brochures
Service names	Vocabulary	Accuracy	Abbreviations	Shareholder communications
Division names	History	Clarity	Titles	Call center scripts
	Boilerplate	Consistency	Addresses	Sales scripts
	Elevator speak		Directions	Presentations
				Announcements
				Blast emails
				Advertising campaigns
				Direct mail
				Product directions
				Signage

Fundamental principles of staying on message

Developed by Lissa Reidel, Marketing Consultant

Use language that resonates with meaning. Readers will complete the message with layers of their own experience.

Aim for clarity, brevity, and precision. A busy executive with only minutes to spare can glean what she needs to know.

Polish and cut as if you were a jeweler. Every sentence will reveal new, intriguing facets to the customer.

Cut through the clutter to produce soundbites that acquire a vibrant identity when they are heard again and again. Consistency is built on repetition.

Edit out modifying phrases, adverbs, and extraneous conversational text and what remains is the distillation, the essence. Eliminate distracting references and the text will have impact. Less is more.

Powers of three

In brand communications, the unified big idea is ideally supported by three key messages.

Originally developed by Dr. Vincent Covello as a risk communications strategy, message mapping was developed because people at risk can only comprehend three messages. This thinking is helpful in brand communications and press relations.

Twitter's 140 characters challenges us all to be more concise.

We had our client team take each word in the long scientific name, and put it into different parts of speech (verb, adjective, adverb, noun). It was a starting point to exploring meaning, understanding nuance, participating in discovery, and coming together as a team to discuss key messages.

Margaret Anderson
Managing Principal
Stellarvisions

Establishing our key messages for the holding company helps protect our assets and conveys to our operating companies that we value clarity and strategic communications.

Jessica Berwind
Managing Trustee
Berwind Corporation

Vigorous writing is concise. A sentence should contain no unnecessary words, a paragraph no unnecessary sentences, for the same reason that a drawing should have no unnecessary lines and a machine no unnecessary parts.

William Strunk, Jr. and E. B. White
The Elements of Style

Cross cultures

The web has made us all global companies. In cyberspace, on our desktops, and on our mobiles, geography has become irrelevant. While globalization has blurred the distinctions among cultures, the best brands pay attention to cultural differences.

Cultural insight is critical to anyone who is building a brand. Naming, logo design, image development, color, key messages, and retail spaces require the creative team to pay attention to connotation and the complexity of subtle cultural differences. The history of marketing is filled with too many stories about companies offending the very market that they were trying to impress. Assumptions and stereotypes stand in the way of building brands that understand customers and celebrate their uniqueness.

Cultures are intensely complex. Customs, attitudes, and preferences are often too subtle for the visitor to notice.

Ronnie Lipton
Designing Across Cultures

Photography: Ed Wheeler

Pay attention

Diversity

America is diverse. The twenty-first century is diverse. Names, symbols, and brand attributes need to have no strong negative connotations in ethnic and religious communities.

Market niche

The process should always begin with an understanding of the target market. For example, American Latino populations include people from many countries who speak Spanish differently, have different accents and slang, and have different physical characteristics.

Change and contradictions

A negative association in one culture might mean a positive association in another. Thoughtful analysis facilitates responsible creative solutions.

Color

Each culture has its own unique heritage. In China the color white was historically associated with mourning. In Korea the color yellow is associated with the center of life.

Naming

Certain names in English may have unintended connotations in different languages. For example, according to naming lore, Chevy named one of its models "Nova," discovering after it was launched that it means "won't go" in Spanish.

Symbols

Visual iconography has the ability to transcend language barriers. However, a symbol with positive or sacred connotations in one culture may have exactly the opposite connotation in another.

Fundamental principles
Inspired by Ronnie Lipton

Assume nothing. "Latino," "Asian," or "Chinese" is not "a" market.

Submerge your team in the culture(s) of your customers with native experts. Explore perceptions, values, behaviors, and trends.

Identify and eliminate stereotypes and assumptions.

Research everything. Test everything. Observe everything. Test it again.

Identify experts to trust. Subtle cultural differences and trends are often invisible to outsiders and understood by the native inhabitant.

Be sensitive to nuance.

Horchata Liqueur : Estudio Ray

Overview

Ideals are essential to a responsible creative process regardless of the size of a company or the nature of a business. These ideals hold true whether the brand identity engagement is launching an entrepreneurial venture, creating a new product or service, repositioning a brand, working on a merger, or creating a retail presence.

Functional criteria do not get to the heart of brand identity. There are over one million trademarks registered with the U.S. Patent and Trademark Office. The basic question is what makes one better than another and why?

What are the essential characteristics of the best identities? How do we define the best identities? These ideals are not about a certain aesthetic. Design excellence is a given.

The best identities advance a brand.

Functional criteria

Bold, memorable, and appropriate	Legally protectable
Immediately recognizable	Has enduring value
Provides a consistent image of the company	Works well across media and scale
Clearly communicates the company's persona	Works both in black and white and in color

Vision

A compelling vision by an effective, articulate, and passionate leader is the foundation and the inspiration for the best brands.

Meaning

The best brands stand for something—a big idea, a strategic position, a defined set of values, a voice that stands apart.

Authenticity

Authenticity is not possible without an organization having clarity about its market, positioning, value proposition, and competitive difference.

Differentiation

Brands always compete with each other within their business category, and at some level, compete with all brands that want our attention, our loyalty, and our money.

Durability

Durability is the ability to have longevity in a world in constant flux, characterized by future permutations that no one can predict.

Coherence

Whenever a customer experiences a brand, it must feel familiar and have the desired effect. Consistency does not need to be rigid or limiting in order to feel like one company.

Flexibility

An effective brand identity positions a company for change and growth in the future. It supports an evolving marketing strategy.

Commitment

Organizations need to actively manage their assets, including the brand name, the trademarks, the integrated sales and marketing systems, and the standards.

Value

Building awareness, increasing recognition, communicating uniqueness and quality, and expressing a competitive difference create measurable results.

Vision

Vision requires courage. Big ideas, enterprises, products, and services are sustained by individuals who have the ability to imagine what others cannot see and the tenacity to deliver what they believe is possible. Behind every successful brand is a passionate individual who inspires others to see the future in a new way.

Brand identity begins with a conversation about the future. Hearing the vision face to face is critical to the brand identity process. Leaders who take the time to share their most audacious dreams and challenges frequently understand the power of symbols and storytelling to build their culture and brands.

Strategic designers have the uncanny ability to listen deeply and synthesize vast amounts of business-critical information with an overarching vision. The role of design is to anticipate the future before it happens. Brand identity systems often prototype the possibilities and spark meaningful dialogue.

A business is rightly judged by its products and services, but it must also face scrutiny as to its humanity.

D. J. DePree
Founder
Herman Miller

Design advocates the future.

Bill Stumpf
Designer

Our business practice is focused on offering people avenues to express their idealism, passion, and commitment to causes larger than themselves at every point along our supply chain—from suppliers and partners to shareholders, customers, and our own staff.

Jeffrey Hollender
Chief Inspired Protagonist
Seventh Generation

Great leaders see the future, set a course, and pursue it relentlessly. They conquer the present despite criticism, ambiguity, adversity. They reflect on, learn from, and weave patterns from the past. Great leaders possess the humility, optimism, passion, and wisdom to inspire others and evoke their full commitment.

Dr. Karol Wasylyshyn
President
Leadership Development Forum

The desire to connect with others is the most basic human desire. Living a bit more publicly, and with more transparency, can have powerful, positive effects. You meet people, you're provided with new opportunities, you have the ability to express yourself, and to have an authentic open way to live your life.

Evan Williams
Co-founder, Twitter
Founder, Blogger

The client is the author. We are the interpreter. Bart Crosby, Crosby Associates

Being a sustainable business is intrinsic to Herman Miller's spirit, values-based leadership, and heritage, as is its leadership in design innovation. The company that designed the Aeron chair is also the company that helped form the US Green Building Council. Herman Miller believes in design as a way to solve significant problems. Over its history, collaborations with designers like George Nelson, Charles and Ray Eames, Bob Probst, Bill Stumpf, Studio 7.5, Ayse Birsel, and Yves Béhar have changed the course of residential furniture and the interior landscape of workplaces worldwide. As creative director, Steve Frykholm, ensures that design innovation extends to all brand touchpoints across media.

Meaning

The best brands stand for something: a big idea, a strategic position, a defined set of values, a voice that stands apart. Symbols are vessels for meaning. They become more powerful with frequent use and when people understand what they stand for. They are the fastest form of communication known to man. Meaning is rarely immediate and evolves over time.

Symbols engage intelligence, imagination, emotion, in a way that no other learning does.

Georgetown University Identity Standards Manual

Nike was named after the Greek goddess of victory. Nike's logo, an abstraction of a wing, designed by Carolyn Davidson in 1971, was meaningful to a company that marketed running shoes. In 1988, Nike's "Just do it" campaign became a battle cry for an entire generation of athletes. When consumers see the "swoosh," as it is called, they are inspired by the bigger idea to live the slogan.

Apple customers quickly become brand zealots. When they see the Apple logo, they think innovation and delight. The logo, designed by Rob Janoff in 1976, is an apple with a bite out of it–a friendly symbol of knowledge, and as lore has it, a symbol of anarchy from the PC world. The original logo was filled with rainbow stripes, but now it is a simple one-color icon.

When the Mercedes-Benz logo was originally created by Gottlieb Daimler in 1909, it consisted of a simple depiction of a three-pointed star that represented the company's "domination of the land, the sea, and the air." Now this brandmark stands first and foremost for luxury and for the fastest cars on the road. The symbol has been dramatically simplified over the last century and remains highly recognizable.

This symbol was designed for Barack Obama's U.S. presidential campaign in 2006. The O, created by Sol Sender and his firm, Sender LLC, symbolized the dawn of a new day. Obama's messages of hope and change charged the symbol with a deeper level of meaning that resonated with citizens the world over, and became part of the largest social media campaign in history.

The logo is the gateway to the brand.

Milton Glaser
Designer

Meaning drives creativity

Designers distill meaning into unique visual form and expression. It is critical that this meaning is explained so that it can be understood, communicated, and approved. All elements of the brand identity system should have framework of meaning and logic.

Meaning builds consensus

Meaning is like a campfire. It's a rallying point used to build consensus with a group of decision makers. Agreement on brand essence and attributes builds critical synergy and precedes any presentation of visual solutions, naming conventions, or key messages.

Meaning evolves over time

As companies grow, their businesses may change significantly. Similarly, the meaning assigned to a brandmark will probably evolve from its original intention. The logo is the most visible and frequent reminder of what the brand stands for.

Think flag.

A nation's flag begins as a design. Distinctive colors and shapes are chosen for their symbolic meaning. The flag is unique and dramatically different from other nations. Seeing the flag arouses feelings of pride, passion, or disdain. Logos are the same.

Mitsubishi stands for quality and reliability and embodies a 130-year-old commitment to earning the trust and confidence of people worldwide. Protecting the trademark, designed by Yataro Iwasaki, is a top corporate priority. Each diamond represents a core principle: corporate responsibility to society, integrity and fairness, and international understanding through trade.

The CBS eye has been the television network's symbol for over a half century. It has remained unchanged, and has retained its original powerful, all-seeing iconic quality. Originally inspired by the human eye paintings on the side of Shaker barns to ward off evil, it is a highly recognized symbol around the world. Designed by William Golden, it was one of the first symbols designed to function primarily on the screen.

The Leadership in Energy and Environmental Design (LEED) Green Building Rating System™ encourages and accelerates global adoption of sustainable green building through the implementation of universally understood and accepted tools and performance criteria. This emblem on a building engenders trust. It communicates that the building project is environmentally responsible, profitable, and a healthy place to live and work.

Authenticity

In psychology, authenticity refers to self-knowledge and making decisions that are congruent with that self-knowledge. Organizations who know who they are, and what they stand for, start the identity process from a position of strength. They create brands that are sustainable and genuine. Brand expression must be appropriate to the organization's unique mission, history, culture, values, and personality.

As reality is qualified, altered, and commercialized, consumers respond to what is engaging, personal, memorable and above all, what they perceive as authentic.

B. Joseph Pine II and James H. Gilmore
Authenticity

Know thyself.

Plato
First Alcibiades

Authenticity, for me, is doing what you promise, not "being who you are."

Seth Godin

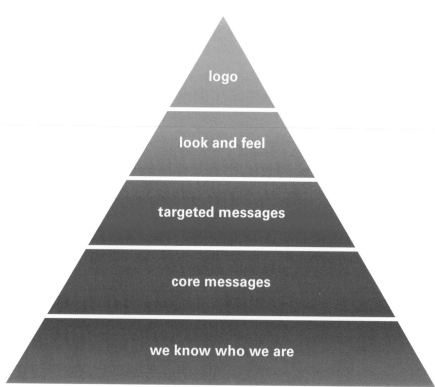

Each day, 1.2 billion people around the world have a Coca-Cola product. Turner Duckworth revitalized the iconic brand presence and created a visual celebration of the simple pleasure of having a Coke across everything from cups to trucks. Research revealed that there was a cultural longing for Coke to be great again. The branding process gave Coke the confidence to drive simplicity, and communicate more emotion and meaning through iconography, wit, and bold design.

Coca-Cola: Turner Duckworth

Differentiation

Bumper-to-bumper brands clamor for our attention. The world is a noisy place filled with a panoply of choice. Why should consumers choose one brand over others? It is not enough to be different. Brands need to demonstrate their difference and make it easy for customers to understand that difference.

If your brand suddenly didn't exist, would anyone miss it? A really good brand leaves a big gap.

Juan Pablo Ramírez
Brand Strategist
Saffron Brand Consultants

When everybody zigs, zag.

Marty Neumeier
ZAG

In order to be irreplaceable one must always be different.

Coco Chanel
House of Chanel

Durability

Brands are messengers of trust. We are all moving at blinding speed and our institutions, technology, science, lifestyles, and vocabulary are in a state of continuous flux. Consumers are reassured by trademarks that are recognizable and familiar. Durability is achieved through a commitment to the equity of a central idea over time, and the capacity to transcend change.

Trademarks, by definition, must last well beyond the fashion of the moment.

Chermayeff + Geismar

Three years after the car was born (1896), Bibendum, the name of the Michelin Man, became the company's unique symbol. Redrawn numerous times, the "tire man" is immediately recognizable around the world.

Trademarks and their date of origination

Löwenbräu	1383	Greyhound	1926	Exxon	1966
Guinness	1862	London Underground	1933	Metropolitan Life	1967
Olympics	1865	Volkswagen	1938	L'Eggs	1971
Mitsubishi	1870	IKEA	1943	Eastman Kodak	1971
Nestlé	1875	CBS	1951	Nike	1971
Bass Ale	1875	NBC	1956	Quaker Oats	1972
John Deere	1876	Chase Manhattan	1960	Atari	1973
Johnson & Johnson	1886	International Paper	1960	Merrill Lynch	1973
Coca-Cola	1887	Motorola	1960	United Way	1974
General Electric	1892	Westinghouse	1960	Dunkin' Donuts	1974
Prudential	1896	UPS	1961	I Love NY	1975
Michelin	1896	Weyerhaeuser	1961	Citicorp	1976
Shell	1900	McDonald's	1962	PBS	1976
Nabisco	1900	General Foods	1962	United	1976
Ford	1903	Wool Bureau	1964	Apple	1977
Rolls-Royce	1905	Rohm & Haas	1964	Transamerica	1979
Mercedes-Benz	1911	Mobil	1965	AT&T	1984
IBM	1924	Diners Club	1966	Google	1998

Since John Deere's founding, the leaping deer has been the core identity element.

1878

1912

1936

1937

1950

1956

1968

2000

Coherence

Whether a customer is using a product, talking to a service representative, or making a purchase on their iPhone, the brand should feel familiar and the experience should have the desired effect. Coherence is the quality that ensures that all the pieces hold together in a way that feels seamless to the customer. It doesn't need to be rigid and limiting—rather, it is a baseline that is designed to build trust, foster loyalty, and delight the customer.

The goal in creating a brand identity is not just surface consistency but inner coherence.

Aubrey Balkind

How is coherence achieved?

Unified voice, a dynamic central idea

The company is clear about its positioning and how it wants to be perceived. Every communication uses a consistent voice and evolves from a central dynamic idea.

One company strategy

As companies diversify into new areas of business, consistency jumpstarts awareness and acceptance of new initiatives.

Every touchpoint

Coherence emerges from understanding the needs and preferences of the target customer and designing a brand experience that produces a desired perception. Every touchpoint is considered a brand experience.

Look and feel

A brand identity system is unified visually and structurally. It builds on cohesive brand architecture and utilizes specially designed colors, typeface families, and formats. The identity system advances immediate recognition of the company and supports brand attributes across various media.

Uniform quality

A high and uniform level of quality imparts a degree of care that is given to each of the company's products and services. Anything less than superior quality reduces the value of the asset on both a conscious and unconscious level.

Clarity and simplicity

Using clear language consistently to communicate about products and services helps the customer navigate choices. Naming that is logical and consistent within the brand architecture also makes it easier for the customer.

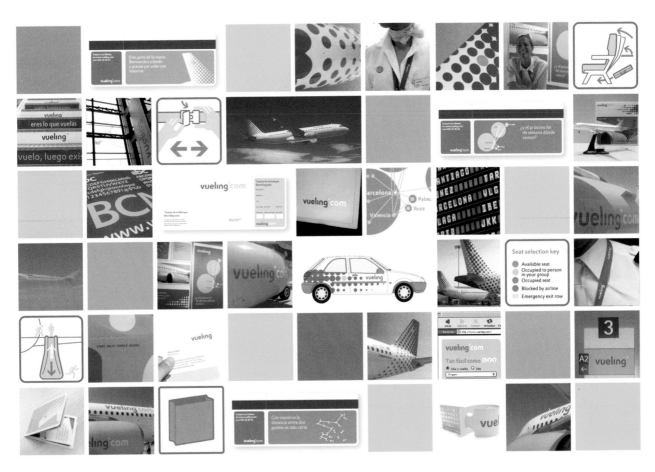

Vueling: Saffron Brand Consultants

vueling

All brand expressions for this high-style, low-cost airline embody *espíritu* Vueling, doing things 'the Vueling way' from staff-customer contact to online interface to music and menu planning. Straightforward and fast forward, *espíritu* Vueling inspires all customer touchpoints to feel fresh, cosmopolitan, and cool. All brand communications speak informally by using *tu*, not the formal *usted*. Vueling partnered with Saffron Brand Consultants.

Flexibility

Innovation requires brands to be flexible. No one can say with certainty which new products or services a company might offer in five years. Or for that matter, what devices we will all be using to communicate with one another and how we will be purchasing our worldly goods. Brands that are open to change need to have flexible brand identity systems in place to quickly seize new opportunities in the marketplace.

> The best thing about the future is that it comes one day at a time.

Abraham Lincoln

Get ready for the future

Marketing flexibility

An effective identity positions a company for change and growth in the future. It needs to be a workhorse in a wide range of customer touchpoints from the website to an invoice to a vehicle or retail environment. A good system embraces the evolution of marketing strategies and methods.

Fresh, relevant, and recognizable

The brand identity toolbox encourages creativity within parameters that always keep the brand immediately recognizable. A carefully designed balance between control and creativity makes it possible to adhere to the identity standards while achieving specific marketing objectives.

Brand architecture

Brand identity systems should have long legs, which means that the marketing of any new product or service is facilitated by a durable and flexible brand architecture and an overarching logic to anticipate the future.

Unilever

Unilever leads its brands through a single idea: 'adding vitality to life.' The vitality theme is used to invent new products and projects that deliver vitality, as well as in the recruitment process to train employees how to pass on stories that underlie this idea. Unilever's U brandmark is composed of twenty-five individual marks that express the vitality theme in many different ways. The visual identity exists on all Unilever products and is deconstructed imaginatively on a range of applications. Unilever partnered with Wolff Olins on this initiative.

Unilever: Wolff Olins

Commitment

A brand is an asset that needs to be protected, preserved, and nurtured. Actively managing the asset requires a top down mandate and a bottom up understanding of why it's important. The best companies provide their employees with tools that make it easy to be a brand champion. Building, protecting, and enhancing the brand requires desire and a disciplined approach to insure its integrity and relevance.

Our goal is to share GE's brand strategy and to create an engaged community of brand advocates.

Ivan Cayabyab, Global Brand and Digital Manager
GE

Manage the asset

Perhaps the most important characteristic of a sustainable identity is taking responsibility for actively managing the asset, which includes the brand name, trademarks, system, and standards. A common mistake is assuming that once a company has a new brand identity, the hardest work has been accomplished. In reality the whole process is just beginning, and the hard work is ahead.

Build the brand

Managing a brand identity system is not exclusive to large global corporations. Small companies and nonprofits also need an individual who has the responsibility of overseeing the brand assets and who reports directly to the president. The mantra is to keep moving—with ongoing management, dynamic adherence to the central idea, monitoring of standards that help preserve the asset, and tools the organization needs to build its brand.

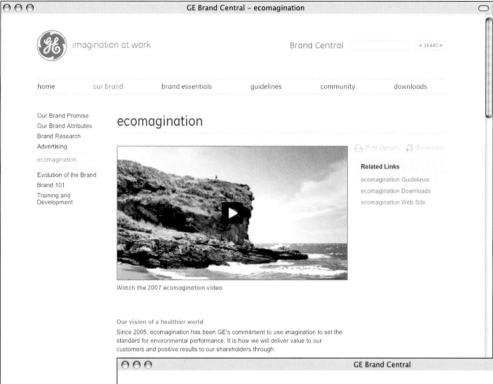

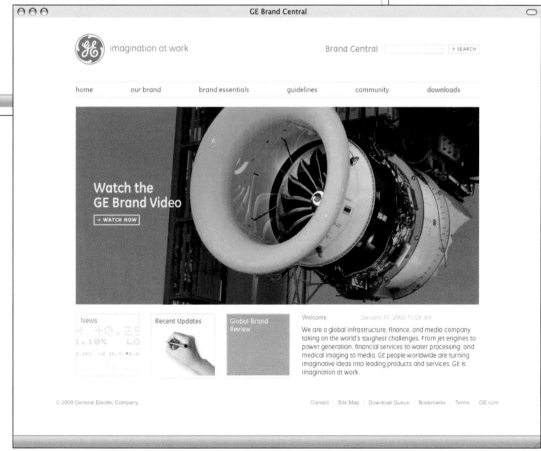

GE has a commitment to protecting its brand assets. In 2008, GE shifted the focus of the GE Brand Center from guideline compliance to brand engagement. New features include a more robust brand strategy section, enhanced guidelines and policies, best practice library, project management tools, and a system to facilitate site updates by GE Brand Management team members and agencies. GE partnered with Monigle Associates.

GE: Monigle Associates

Value

Creating value is the indisputable goal of most organizations. The quest for sustainability has expanded the value conversation with consumers. Being socially responsible, environmentally conscious, and profitable is the new business model for all brands. A brand is an intangible asset—brand identity, which includes all tangible expression from packaging to websites, upholds that value.

A strong brand commands a premium.

David A. Aaker and Erich Joachimsthaler
Brand Leadership

Brand identity is an asset

The brand identity is viewed as a strategic business tool and an asset that seizes every opportunity to build awareness, increase recognition, communicate uniqueness and quality, and express a competitive difference. Adherence to brand identity uniform standards and the relentless pursuit of quality are business priorities.

Value is preserved through legal protection

Trademarks and trade dress are protected in the range of markets that are served, both local and global. Employees and vendors are educated about compliance issues.

Truvia™, a breakthrough product, required a breakthrough design strategy. Most American food packaging underestimates the intelligence of the consumer. We applaud Cargill for the courage to lead.

Paula Scher
Partner
Pentagram

truvía

Truvia™ natural sweetener represents a genuine innovation in its category: it comes from the leaves of the stevia plant, and not a lab. Unlike its competition, it can be used in cooking and tastes good. Its refreshingly simple and beautiful carton is designed to be reusable and visible, like a sugar canister. Pentagram, worked with Cargill and The Coca-Cola Company, to develop core brand attributes before beginning the design process. Partner Paula Scher and Lenny Naar's identity design feels pure and authentic. Partner Daniel Weil designed the innovative packaging structure, which features a hinged lid.

Truvia: Pentagram

Brandmarks

Designed with an almost infinite variety of shapes and personalities, brandmarks can be assigned to a number of general categories. From literal through symbolic, from word-driven to image-driven, the world of brandmarks expands each day.

The boundaries among these categories are pliant, and many marks may combine elements of more than one category.

Is there a compelling practical reason to categorize them? Although there are no hard-and-fast rules to determine the best type of visual identifier for a particular type of company, the designer's process is to examine a range of solutions based on both aspirational and functional criteria. The designer will determine a design approach that best serves the needs of the client and create a rationale for each distinct approach.

The designer is the medium between the client and the audience. A mark should embody and imply the client's business goals and positioning, and address the end user's needs and wants.

Joel Katz
Joel Katz Design Associates

Signature

A signature is the structured relationship between a logotype, brandmark, and tagline. Some programs accommodate split signatures that allow the mark and the logotype to be separated. Other variations may include a vertical or horizontal signature that allows choices based on application need.

Spectrum Health: Crosby Associates

Topology of marks

There are no hard and fast rules about which approach works best. Each particular type of identity has benefits and shortcomings that are dependent on numerous factors. At the end of the day, it's important that the design solution responds to the problem that needs to be solved.

Synonyms

Brandmark
Trademark
Symbol
Mark
Logo
Identity

Wordmarks

A freestanding acronym, company name, or product name that has been designed to convey a brand attribute or positioning

examples: IKEA, ebay, Google, Tate, Nokia, MoMA

Letterforms

A unique design using one or more letterforms that act as a mnemonic device for a company name

examples: Univision, IBM, OLIN, Unilever, Tory Burch, HP, GE, UPS, B Corporation

Emblems

A mark in which the company name is inextricably connected to a pictorial element

examples: TiVo, OXO, LEED, Elmer's Glue-All

Pictorial marks

An immediately recognizable literal image that has been simplified and stylized

examples: Apple, NBC, CBS, Polo, Lacoste, Greyhound, Twitter

Abstract/symbolic marks

A symbol that conveys a big idea, and often embodies strategic ambiguity

examples: Target, Sprint, Nike, HSBC, Merck, Herman Miller

Sequence of cognition

Brand awareness and recognition are facilitated by a visual identity that is easy to remember and immediately recognizable. Visual identity triggers perceptions and unlocks associations of the brand. Sight, more than any other sense, provides information about the world.

Through repeated exposure, symbols become so recognizable that companies such as Target, Apple, and Nike have actually dropped the logotype from their corporate signatures in national advertising. Color becomes a mnemonic device—when you see a brown truck out of the corner of your eye, you know it is a UPS truck.

Identity designers are in the business of managing perception through the integration of meaning and distinctive visual form. Understanding the sequence of visual perception and cognition provides valuable insight into what will work best.

Think about how IBM triggers an immediate response with its horizontal banded television ads. Before the ad even runs, you know it's IBM, and you know it's going to be intelligent and engaging.

Marjorie Gorman
Marketing Consultant

The sequence of cognition

The science of perception examines how individuals recognize and interpret sensory stimuli. The brain acknowledges and remembers shapes first. Visual images can be remembered and recognized directly, while words must be decoded into meaning.

Shape

Reading is not necessary to identify shapes, but identifying shapes is necessary to read. The brain acknowledges distinctive shapes that make a faster imprint on memory.

Color

Color is second in the sequence. Color can trigger an emotion and evoke a brand association. Distinctive colors need to be chosen carefully, not only to build brand awareness but to express differentiation. Companies, such as Kodak and Tiffany, have trademarked their core brand colors.

Form

The brain takes more time to process language, so content is third in the sequence behind shape and color.

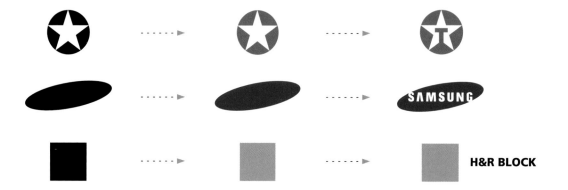

Heidi Cody © 2000

Wordmarks

A wordmark is a freestanding word or words. It may be a company name or an acronym.
The best wordmarks imbue a legible word(s) with distinctive font characteristics, and
may integrate abstract elements or pictorial elements. The distinctive tilted "E" in "Dell"
activates and strengthens the one-syllable name. The IBM acronym has transcended
enormous technological change in its industry.

Late July: Louise Fili Ltd.

Alvin Ailey: Chermayeff + Geismar

Late July:
Louise Fili Ltd.

Dell:
Siegel + Gale

Braun:
Wolfgang Schmittel redesign

IBM: Paul Rand

Oslo Airport:
Mollerup Design Lab

DesignPhiladelphia:
Polite Design

truth:
Crispin Porter + Bogusky

Kubota:
Pentagram

Letterform marks

The single letter is frequently used by designers as a distinctive graphic focal point for a brandmark. The letter is always a unique and proprietary design that is infused with significant personality and meaning. The letterform acts as a mnemonic device, e.g., the "M" for Motorola, the "Q" for Quest Diagnostics. The Westinghouse mark by Paul Rand represents the ideal marriage of letterform and symbolism.

Letterforms A to Z
Opposite page:

Arvin Industries: Bart Crosby

Brokers Insurance: Rev Group

Champion International: Crosby Associates

Dominion: Lizette Gecel

Energy Department Store:
Joel Katz Design Associates

Fine Line Features: Woody Pirtle

Goertz Fashion House:
Allemann Almquist + Jones

Herman Miller: George Nelson

Irwin Financial Corporation:
Chermayeff + Geismar

JoongAng Ilbo: Infinite

Joel Katz: Joel Katz Design Associates

LifeMark Partners: Rev Group

Motorola: Morton Goldsholl

NEPTCO: Malcolm Grear Designers

Dallas Opera: Woody Pirtle

Preferred: Jon Bjornson

Quest Diagnostics: Q Cassetti

Rogers Ford: Summerford Design

Seatrain Lines:
Chermayeff + Geismar

Telemundo:
Chermayeff + Geismar

Univision: Chermayeff + Geismar

Vanderbilt University:
Malcolm Grear Designers

Westinghouse: Paul Rand

X31: Matchstic

Yahoo: unknown

Zeek's Pizzeria:
Nick Glenn Design

Vanderbilt University:
Malcolm Grear Designers

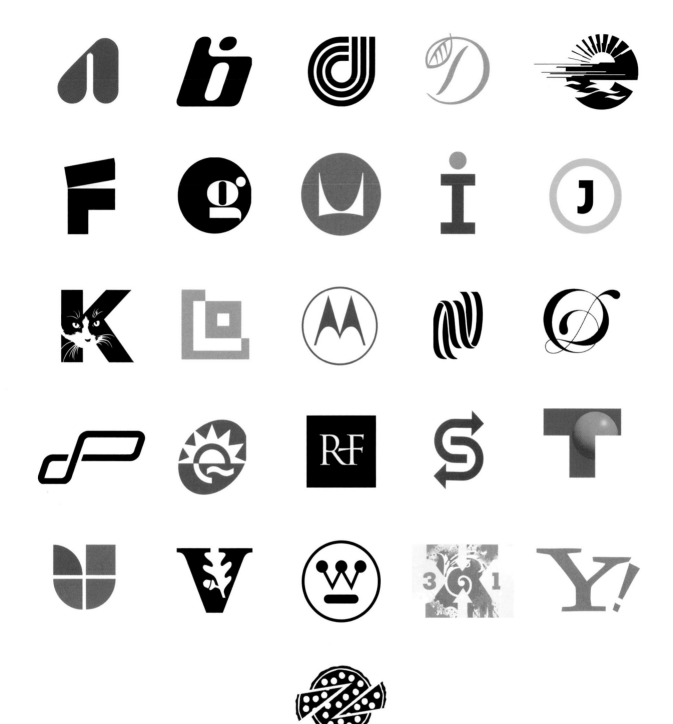

Pictorial marks

A pictorial mark uses a literal and recognizable image. The image itself may allude to the name of the company or its mission, or it may be symbolic of a brand attribute. The eagle of the U.S. Postal Service is both a symbol of America and a symbol of speed and dependability.

My Apple MacBook Pro

Abstract marks

An abstract mark uses visual form to convey a big idea or a brand attribute. These marks, by their nature, can provide strategic ambiguity, and work effectively for large companies with numerous and unrelated divisions. Marks, such as Chase's, have survived a series of mergers easily. Abstract marks are especially effective for service-based and technology companies; however, they are extremely difficult to design well.

Dosirak: KBR and Associates

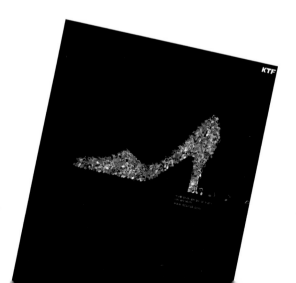

Dosirak's mark can become an amorphous texture filling everyday objects in a range of applications.

Abstract marks

From left to right

Hyatt:
Lippincott

Merck:
Chermayeff + Geismar

Darien Library:
C & G Partners

EUE Screen Gems:
Chermayeff + Geismar

BP:
Landor Associates

Penn's Landing:
Joel Katz

Sprint:
Lippincott

Time Warner:
Chermayeff + Geismar

Alina Wheeler:
Rev Group

Sacred Heart Hospital:
Infinite

Franklin Institute:
Allemann Almquist + Jones

Brinker Capital:
Rev Group

Emblems

Emblems are trademarks featuring a shape inextricably connected to the name of the organization. The elements are never isolated. Emblems look terrific on a package, as a sign, or as an embroidered patch on a uniform. As mobile devices continue to shrink and multi-branding ads with one-sixth-inch logos increase, the emblem presents the biggest legibility challenge when miniaturized.

The sea nymph that dwells inside the green and black Starbucks Coffee trademark will never swim away from her green circular band.

Bayn is a pre-pay service designed to give control back to the Moroccan consumer. The mark's flexibility to lead with the Arabic or roman namestyle for the Bayn name allowed the brand to adapt to its national and regional audiences.

Bayn: Lippincott

Rusk Renovations:
Louise Fili Ltd.

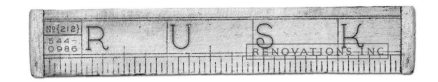

Bruegger's Bagels:
Milton Glaser

Tazo:
Sandstrom Design

City Church Eastside:
Matchstic

Zao Noodle Bar:
Cronan

Bayn: Lippincott

John Templeton Foundation:
Rev Group

TiVo:
Cronan

333 Belrose Bar & Grill:
Anne Pagliarulo

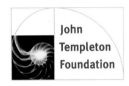  

Studio 360:
Opto Design

Brooklyn Brewery:
Milton Glaser

92:
Louise Fili Ltd.

Characters

It's alive! A character trademark embodies brand attributes or values. Characters quickly become central to advertising campaigns, and the best ones become cultural icons cherished by children and customers alike. Along with their distinctive appearance and personality, many characters have recognizable voices and jingles, enabling them to leap off the silent shelf space onto your desktop.

While the ideas that drive the personification may be timeless and universal, characters rarely age well and usually need to be redrawn and dragged into contemporary culture. The Michelin Man, well over 100 years old, has been modified numerous times. As moms became working women, Betty Crocker was caught between generations. The Columbia Pictures goddess received a major facelift, but she has never looked happy and satisfied holding that torch. Each Olympics creates a mascot that will be animated and deanimated in thousands of stuffed animals. Who knew a gecko could sell car insurance?

Elsie the Cow was created in 1939 by Stuart Peabody, Director of Advertising for Borden Dairy Products.

In 1948, on the eve of the presidential election, 88% of the American public knew who Elsie was, compared to 84% for the Republican candidate, Thomas Dewey.

In 1957, in Borden's centennial year, Elsie had twins. A name-the-calves contest drew 3 million entries via mail.

Reddy Kilowatt

Eveready Energizer Bunny

Historic characters

Character	Company	Year created
Uncle Sam	Government war bonds	1838
Aunt Jemima	Pancake mix and syrup	1893
Michelin Man	Michelin tires	1898
Mr. Peanut	Planters	1916
Betty Crocker	Food products	1921
Reddy Kilowatt	Electric company	1926
Jolly Green Giant	Green Giant vegetables	1928
Leo the Lion	MGM Pictures	1928
Mickey Mouse	Walt Disney Co.	1928
Windy	Zippo lighter	1937
Elsie the Cow	Borden dairy products	1939
Rosie the Riveter	Illustration for working woman, WWII	1943
Smokey the Bear	U.S. Forest Service	1944
Elmer the Bull	Elmer's Glue-All	1947
Tony the Tiger	Kellogg's Frosted Flakes	1951
Trix the Bunny	General Mills cereal	1960
Charlie the Tuna	Starkist tuna	1960
Columbia Goddess	Columbia Pictures Corporation	1961
Ronald McDonald	McDonald's restaurants	1963
Exxon Tiger	Exxon Oil Company	1964
Pillsbury Doughboy	Assorted Pillsbury foods	1969
Ernie Keebler & the elves	Kellogg's crackers	1969
Nesquik Bunny	Nesquik	1970s
Energizer Bunny	Eveready Energizer batteries	1989
Jeeves	Ask Jeeves	1996
AFLAC duck	AFLAC Insurance	2000
Gecko	Geico	2002

Elmer the Bull was originally created to be Elsie's husband. Since 1947 Elmer has been the mascot of America's best-known consumer adhesive brand, Elmer's Glue-All, and has appeared on hundreds of products.

Look and feel

Look and feel is the visual language that makes a system proprietary and immediately recognizable. It also expresses a point of view. This support system of color, imagery, typography, and composition is what makes an entire program cohesive and differentiated.

In the best programs, designers create an overall look that resonates in the mind of the customer and rises above the clutter of a visual environment. All elements of a visual language should be intentionally designed to advance the brand strategy, each doing its part and working together as a whole to unify and distinguish.

Look is defined by color, scale, proportion, typography, and motion. Feel is experiential and emotional.

Abbott Miller
Partner, Pentagram

You should be able to cover up the logo and still identify the company because the look and feel is so distinctive.

Michael Bierut
Partner, Pentagram

Look and feel basics

Design

Design is intelligence made visible. The marriage of design and content is the only marriage that lasts.

Color palettes

Systems may have two color palettes: primary and secondary. Business lines or products may have their own colors. A color palette may have a pastel range and a primary range.

Imagery

Within the category of content, style, focus, and color, all need to be considered whether the imagery is photography, illustration, or iconography.

Typography

Systems incorporate typeface families, one or sometimes two. It is not unusual for a special typeface to be designed for a high visibility brand.

Sensory

There are also material qualities (how something feels in your hand—texture and weight), interactive qualities (how something opens or moves), and auditory and olfactory qualities (how something sounds and smells, respectively).

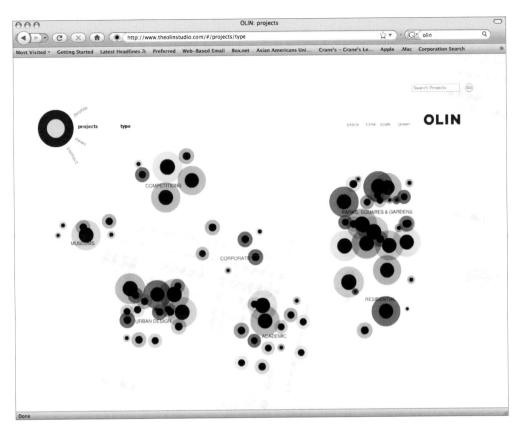

OLIN is an internationally recognized landscape architecture, urban design, and planning firm, whose spaces promote social interaction and sustainability. Whether Olin's design is a large public garden or a square, there are social spaces and a clear sense of order. The firm, based in Philadelphia, was previously known as Olin Partnership. The new identity and website were designed by Pentagram partner, Abbott Miller, with Kristen Spilman. The website is a fluid and highly interactive experience that uses the visual language of landscape architecture. Fastspot managed the website development.

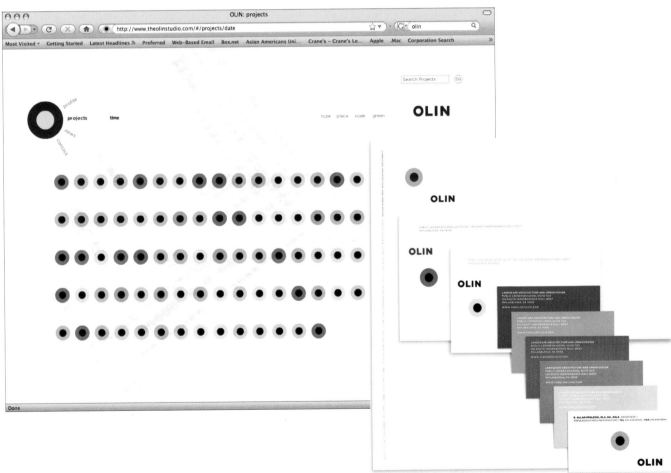

OLIN: Pentagram

Brand dynamics

What's the next big thing? Does it matter? Does it have long legs or is it a fad? What begins as an idea on the outer fringes may quickly snowball and become mainstream, or it may fizzle. Brands are about relevance and permanence. Seismic shift in the culture, in the capital markets, and technology provide brand makers food for thought.

Change almost never fails because it's too early. It almost always fails because it's too late.

Seth Godin
Tribes

All truth passes through three stages. First, it is ridiculed. Second, it is violently opposed. Third, it is accepted as being self-evident.

Arthur Schopenhauer

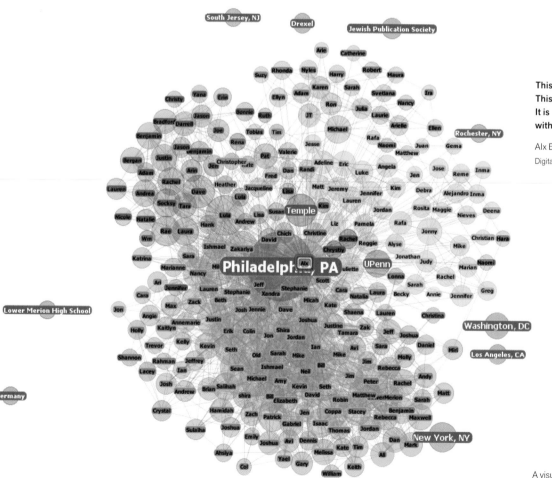

This is me.
This is my network.
It is me interacting
with the world.

Alx Block
Digital Brand Manager, JPS

A visual display of relational data by TouchGraph.

Moving into the mainstream

Sustainability

James O'Toole and Warren Bennis, *Harvard Business Review*, June 2009

Moving forward, it appears that the new metric of corporate leadership will be closer to this: the extent to which executives create organizations that are economically, ethically, and socially sustainable.

Social media

Lee Aase, Manager, Social Media, Mayo Clinic

Social media combines the potential worldwide reach of news media stories with the personal touch of a friend's recommendation.

Transparency

James O'Toole and Warren Bennis, *Harvard Business Review*, June 2009

Because no organization can be honest with the public if it's not honest with itself, we define transparency broadly, as the degree to which information flows freely within an organization, among managers and employees, and outward to stakeholders.

Design thinking

Marty Neumeier, *The Designful Company*

Design drives innovation; innovation powers brand; brand builds loyalty; and loyalty sustains profits. If you want long-term profits, start with design.

Personal branding

Tom Peters

Regardless of age, regardless of position, regardless of the business we happen to be in, all of us need to understand the importance of branding. We are CEOs of our own companies: Me Inc. To be in business today, our most important job is to be head marketer for the brand called You.

With some effort, you may come to view Twitter as I do: the best new marketing tool of this century. Tweet long and prosper.

Guy Kawasaki

It doesn't matter whether you're shipping paper clips, pork bellies, or videos of Britney in a bikini, blogs are a phenomenon that you cannot ignore, postpone, or delegate. Given the changes barreling down upon us, blogs are not a business elective. They're a prerequisite.

Stephen Baker and
Heather Green
BusinessWeek, February 2009

Our digital devices have become our lifelines, our portable toolkits, and objects of desire. We're a nanosecond way from having mobile implants.

Blake Deutsch

Sustainability

Making a difference has become essential to building a brand. Consumers are shopping their values, and businesses are rethinking their value proposition. The triple bottom line—people, planet, profit—is a new business model that represents a fundamental shift in how businesses measure success.

Historically, the purpose of business has been to create shareholder value. The new imperative integrates economic prosperity with protecting the environment, and demonstrating care for communities and employees. For many, sustainability will require radical innovation:

retooling what they make, how they make it, and how it is distributed. A new generation of companies envisions sustainability as the core purpose of their brand promise. Authenticity is critical. Social networks quickly broadcast brands that don't stand true to their promise.

Doing good is good business.

Sustainability touchpoints: where businesses can make a difference

Questions worth asking

Chris Hacker
SVP of Design, Johnson & Johnson

Do we really need it?

Is it designed to minimize waste?

Can it be smaller or lighter or made of fewer materials?

Is it designed to be durable or multifunctional?

Does it use renewable resources?

Is reuse practical and encouraged?

Are the product and packaging refillable, recyclable or repairable?

Is it made with post-consumer recycled or reclaimed materials? If so, how much?

Are the materials available in a less toxic form?

Does it come from a socially and environmentally responsible company?

Is it made locally?

Patagonia

The Footprint Chronicles is an interactive mini-site that allows you to track the impact of Patagonia products from design through delivery.

Seventh Generation

The leading brand of green cleaners offers people avenues to express their idealism, passion, and commitment to causes larger than themselves at every point along its supply chain— from suppliers and partners to shareholders, customers, and its own staff.

Herman Miller

Embody is 95% recyclable, has 42% recycled content, and contains no PVCs. Adheres to the McDonough Braungart Design Chemistry (MBDC) Cradle-to-Cradle protocol.

Certified B Corporation
bcorporation.net

B Corporation

A new type of corporation that uses the power of business to solve social and environmental problems. They are unlike traditional responsible businesses because they meet comprehensive and transparent social and environmental performance standards.

ShoreBank

ShoreBank is a pioneer in demonstrating that a regulated bank can be instrumental in revitalizing underserved communities and encouraging sustainable economic development.

TOMS Shoes

TOMS was founded on a simple premise: With every pair you purchase, TOMS will give a pair of new shoes to a child in need. One for One.

71

Social media

The consumer is no longer a faceless statistic in a report; she has become an active participant in the brand building process. Share, tag, and comment are her new mantras. Charity and commerce coagulate, as do ideas and agendas for change. Imagine a global cafe where everyone is a player, producer, director and distributor.

Formal hierarchies don't exist; there's no barrier to entry and transparency is valued. Social media tools enable individuals to instantly communicate with the universe using a simple keystroke.

Word of mouth has become word of mouse.

Lula Jones

Social media is word of mouth on steroids.

Blake Deutsch

The blog is the next business card.

Alx Block

Communications media		Social media
Space defined by media owner	➤	Space defined by consumer
Brand in control	➤	Consumer in control
One way—delivering a message	➤	Two way—being a part of a conversation
Repeating the message	➤	Adapting the message/beta
Focused on the brand	➤	Focused on the consumer/Adding value
Entertaining	➤	Influencing, involving
Company-created content	➤	User-created content/Co-creation

Slide 10 from "What's Next In Media?" by Neil Perkin

Social media categories

Communication

Blogs
Micro blogs
Internet forum
Social network
List serve

Collaboration

Wikis
Social bookmarks
Social news
Reviews

Entertainment

Photo sharing
Video sharing
Live casting
Audio and music sharing
Virtual worlds
Games

No more one-way brand conversations

Before social media

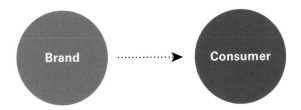

Anyone interested in building a brand—businesses, organizations, and individuals—needs to tap into the raw enthusiasm of web users in order to be successful.

After social media

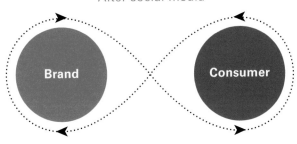

We call it participatory media.

Jinal Shah

Average Customer Review
★★★★☆ (1,908 customer reviews)

Share your thoughts with other customers

Create your own review

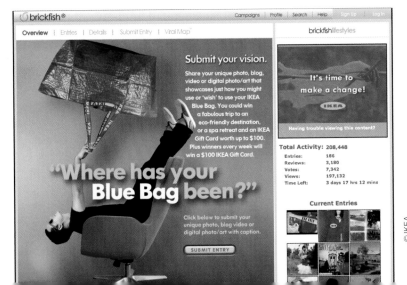

IKEA's "Where has your Blue Bag been?" campaign has been a creative way to underscore our work and commitment to sustainability, while building our good company brand.

Mona Astra Liss
US Corporate PR Director
IKEA

IKEA:
Marcolina Design

© IKEA

Brand licensing

Licensing is big business for established brand owners who generate revenue from royalties on sales of products bearing their brand's logo, name, slogan, or other legally protected asset. It's an opportunity to attract new customers, and to delight existing brand champions.

The world of brand owners seeking new distribution channels for their intellectual property assets is expanding beyond consumer and entertainment brands to include nonprofits, branded destinations, and cultural venues.

Whether a property is a consumer brand, a media personality, a comic character, an artist or designer (dead or alive), the business imperative is the same: protecting and preserving the brand asset, being clear about what the brand stands for, and ensuring that each licensing opportunity is strategic. Brand owners (licensors) want experienced licensing agents to find and negotiate deals with licensees, who develop, manufacture, market, and sell approved products to approved retailers.

Consumers find comfort in brands they're familiar with—and have a greater propensity to purchase new products from those brands.

David Milch
President
Perpetual Licensing

Strategic licensing builds brands, protects trademarks, and generates revenues.

David Milch, President
Perpetual Licensing

Being a Philips brand licensee means a pledge to continually drive and deliver on our brand promise.

www.philips.com

We didn't start with a logo and a widget and set out to create an emotional tie. We started with a purely personal relationship between a unique individual and the public.

Jack Soden
CEO
Elvis Presley Enterprises

We are very judicious about how we approach the licensing business. It's about the history and the heritage of the brand.

Ruth Crowley
Former VP, General Merchandise
Harley-Davidson

Benefits of brand licensing
Developed by Perpetual Licensing

Licensors or Brand Owners

Enhances the brand image

Grows the value of the brand

Increases awareness of the brand

Reinforces brand positioning and brand message

Attracts new consumers to the brand

Builds competitive advantage

Builds stronger relationships with customers

Gains entry into new distribution channels

Lets consumers exhibit their love of the brand

Protects the brand via trademark registration and policing of marketplace

Provides consumers genuine alternatives for illegal and unauthorized products

Generates incremental revenues through:
Increased sales of core product
Royalties from the sale of licensed product

Licensees or Manufacturers

Increases market share

Opens new retail channels

Gains shelf space at retail

Increases awareness of their product

Attracts new customers to their product

Builds competitive advantage

Increases sales through a wider assortment of products

Lends credibility to their products

Generates incremental revenues through the sale of licensed product

Top 5 licensors
Disney
Iconix
Warner Brothers
Marvel
Nickelodeon

Brand roles
Developed by Perpetual Licensing

Licensor

Set licensing goals and establish objectives

Approve annual strategic licensing plan

Approve prospective licensees

Approve licensed products, packaging, marketing and collateral materials

Provide access to licensable assets and/or develop style guide

Register trademarks in appropriate categories

Pursue trademark infringers

Execute license agreements

Licensee

Set licensing goals and establish objectives

Approve annual strategic licensing plan (brand acquisition)

Approve prospective licensors

Develop, manufacture, and market approved products

Monitor marketplace for trademark infringers

Deliver quarterly royalty reports and payments

Agent

Develop strategic licensing program for presentation and approval

Create sales materials to solicit interest from licensees or licensors

Prospect qualified licensees or licensors

Negotiate terms of license agreement

Guide contract management process

Lead the acquisition and/or development of licensable assets, or the creation of a style guide

Manage product, packaging, and collateral material approval process

Administer royalties

Police marketplace for trademark infringement

Handle daily program needs

Private labeling

For many retailers, private labeling has become a powerful marketing strategy to build brand equity and a differentiator that gives consumers more reasons to shop at their store. The perceptual shift has begun from low quality to value-added, accelerated by more upscale and better designed packaging, combined with insights about consumers' unmet needs.

The days when you could recognize a private label brand immediately because it looked generic, cheap, and low quality are over. Initially, private labeling was a business strategy aimed at higher profit margins per product and increased revenues. A private label product line is created and branded by a store, usually a large retail chain. The products themselves are produced by a third-party supplier, which usually makes other name brand products for established national brands. Companies like IKEA use the master brand on all of their products, while companies like Safeway and Aldi create multiple brands.

We are trying to build brand propositions that are exclusive or proprietary...and unique in solving critical consumer need states.

James White, SVP, Corporate Brands
Safeway

We upped the quality, upped the price, and we're selling more units. Because it's the best tuna you could buy.

Richard Galanti
Chief Financial Officer
Costco

The new design has a better brand billboard and much more appetizing food photography. And we are not just dressing up the outside. We have worked hard on what we are putting on the inside.

Andrea Thomas
SVP, Private Brands
Walmart

Private Label Brand Architecture Strategy

Tesco in the UK offers petrol; President's Choice from Canadian retailer Loblaw offers everything from cookies to financial services; and Costco's private label, Kirkland Signature, offers tires alongside fresh food and alcoholic beverages.

Robin Rusch
Private Labels: Does Branding Matter
Brandchannel

Multiple brands
Pluralistic brand architecture

A&P

Greenway

Hartford Reserve

America's Choice

Aldi

Fit & Active

Clarissa

Shique

Casa Mamita

Grandessa

Rain Fresh

Kwik n' Fresh

Costco

Kirkland Signature

Food Lion

Nature's Place

Smart Options

Blue Stream

Giant Eagle

Smart Option

Taste of Inspiration

Nature's Place

On the Go Bistro

Home 360

Loblaw

President's Choice

Safeway

O Organics

Eating Right

Waterfront Bistro

Supervalue

Urban Fresh

Target

Archer Farms

Market Pantry

Sutton & Dodge

Tesco

Fresh & Easy

Smart & Final

Walmart

Great Value

Sam's Choice

Ol' Roy

Marketside

Wegmans

Italian Classics

Discover the Orient

Whole Foods

365 Organic

Wild Oats

Single master brand
Monolithic brand architecture

IKEA

Trader Joe's

Carrefour

Best Buy

CVS

Tesco

Saks Fifth Avenue

O Organics, Safeway's private label brand, has over 200 SKUs.

O Organics: Philippe Becker Design

Waterfront Bistro:
Philippe Becker Design

Certification

As the proliferation of choices grows exponentially, consumers are looking for ways to facilitate their decisions and align their values with their purchases. Which products and companies should they trust? Which brands are environmentally and socially responsible? Which products are safe? Is their privacy protected?

To qualify for certification, products must undergo a series of rigorous tests by government bodies or professional associations. As the world continues to shrink and the number of certification symbols continues to grow, it will be essential to develop clear and trustworthy symbols that communicate across cultures.

B Corporations earn certification by meeting higher standards of social and environmental performance, accountability, and transparency. B Corps earn a minimum score on the B Impact Ratings System which measures their impact on their employees, suppliers, community, consumers, and environment, legally expanding their corporate responsibilities to include consideration of stakeholder interests.

Jay Coen Gilbert
Co-founder
B Corporation

Certification matters because we all want to be able to tell the difference between 'good companies' and just good marketing.

Jay Coen Gilbert, Co-founder
B Corporation

Green building	Green products		Sustainabile Business

Efficiency

Social justice		No animal testing

HTTPS Https is "Hypertext Transfer Protocol" with an added "s", or Secure Socket Layer, another protocol developed with secure, safe internet transactions in mind.

ISO Certification Because "International Organization for Standardization" would have different acronyms in different languages ("IOS" in English, "OIN" in French for Organisation internationale de normalisation), its founders decided to also give it a short, all-purpose name. They chose "ISO", derived from the Greek isos, meaning "equal". Whatever the country, whatever the language, the short form of the organization's name is always ISO.

Data and privacy

Product safety

Food

Heart-healthy

Responsible forestry

Recycling

Environmental responsibility

Personal branding

We used to count the business cards in our Rolodex. Now we count the colleagues on LinkedIn, the number of friends on Facebook, and sleep with our digital devices under our pillows. Social media and digital devices have accelerated the blur between business and life, work and leisure, and public and private.

Every time a person sends an email, it's personal branding. Colleagues used to exchange business cards; now, blogs are becoming mainstream for anyone in business. Being authentic is critical because the web never forgets.

Personal branding (think Sun King, Napoleon Bonaparte, and Cleopatra) used to be for indulgent monarchs. Now it's *de riguer* for being in business whether you are a corporate exec, a design guru, an aspiring entrepreneur, or a sales associate. We are all rock stars now. Social media have made the world our stage. And the competition is fierce.

Why has personal branding become so important? Jobs no longer last forever. The number of self-employed individuals has increased dramatically over the last decade. A third of our workforce is now self-employed. And we are all connected 24/7.

Be who you are wherever you are.
Be in the energy of the space. Belong to the moment.

Carol Moog, Ph.D., Practicing psychologist, Theatre improvisor
Author, *Are they selling her lips?*, Harmonica player, Tattar Tucker & Moog
Clinical Director, Social Learning Disorders Program, University of Pennsylvania

In a world that is bewildering in terms of competitive clamour, in which rational choice has become almost impossible, brands represent clarity, reassurance, consistency, status, membership—everything that enables human beings to help define themselves. Brands represent identity.

Wally Olins
On Brand

Six career secrets

1. There is no plan.

2. Think strengths, not weaknesses.

3. It's not about you.

4. Persistence trumps talent.

5. Make excellent mistakes.

6. Leave an imprint.

Daniel H. Pink
The Adventures of Johnny Bunko

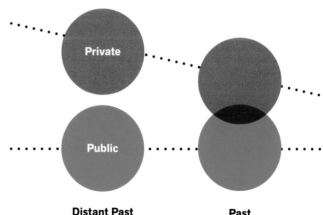

Distant Past   **Past**

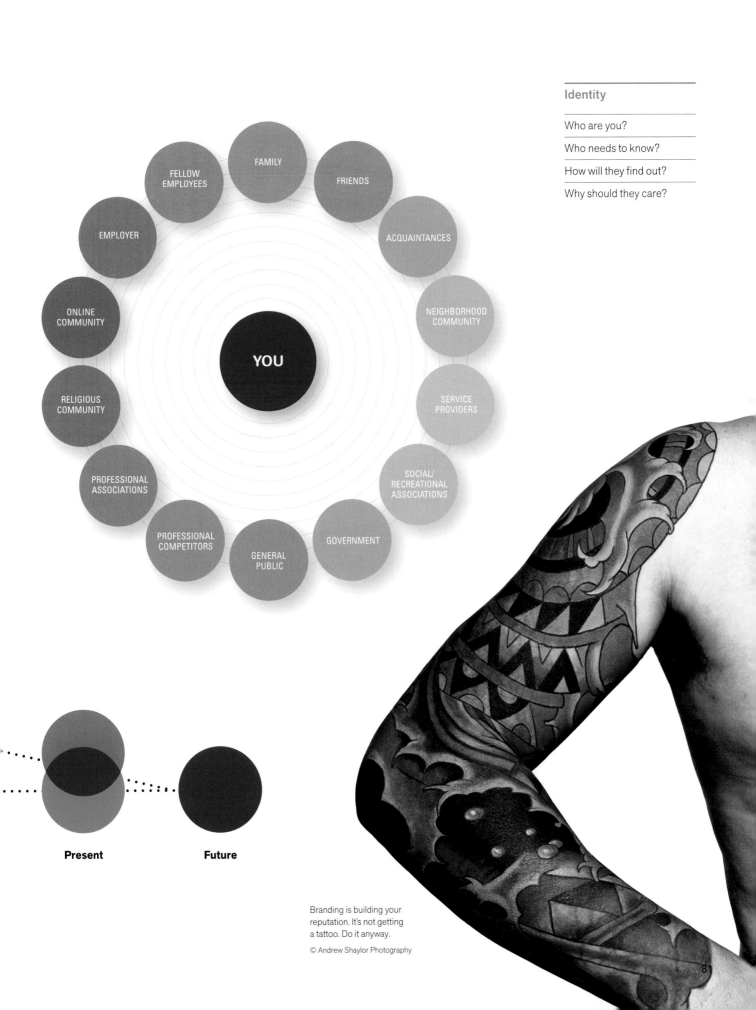

Identity

Who are you?

Who needs to know?

How will they find out?

Why should they care?

FAMILY

FELLOW EMPLOYEES

FRIENDS

EMPLOYER

ACQUAINTANCES

ONLINE COMMUNITY

NEIGHBORHOOD COMMUNITY

YOU

RELIGIOUS COMMUNITY

SERVICE PROVIDERS

PROFESSIONAL ASSOCIATIONS

SOCIAL/ RECREATIONAL ASSOCIATIONS

PROFESSIONAL COMPETITORS

GOVERNMENT

GENERAL PUBLIC

Present   **Future**

Branding is building your reputation. It's not getting a tattoo. Do it anyway.

© Andrew Shaylor Photography

81

As organizations grow, their purpose becomes more lucid, their positioning is refined, and the stakes may shift as new markets open. The creative team is challenged by three crucial questions: What is the business imperative for the change? What elements need to be maintained to preserve brand equity? Should the change be evolutionary or revolutionary? Most brand identity initiatives involve redesign.

Personality is the unique, authentic, and talkable soul of your brand that people can get passionate about.

Rohit Bhargava
Personality not Included

Merger

Before	After

To signal a fresh, new era we developed an evolution of the classic (AT +T) Saul Bass logo to visually communicate the new brand positioning.

Interbrand

Cingular: VSA Partners

The new BNY Mellon symbol conveys two parts becoming one, moving forward in a common direction.

Alex de Jánosi
Partner
Lippincott

New name

Before	After	
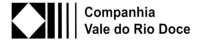		The new name is short, easy to pronounce and spell, and has positive meanings in all major languages. James Bell Senior Partner Lippincott
		To ignite a movement, we created a new name that is a succinct statement of the goal—one everyone essentially understands. Michael Cronan CRONAN
		When Chicago GSB, the University of Chicago Graduate School of Business, was renamed The University of Chicago Booth School of Business, continuity was maintained in the logotype. Bart Crosby Crosby Associates
		The FedEx Office name better describes the wide range of services available at its retail centers and takes full advantage of the FedEx brand. www.fedex.com FedEx: Landor Associates
		A symbolic gesture of an apple expressed The Colorado Health Foundation's two core brand attributes: Health and Education. Matt Coffman President Anabliss Design + Brand Strategy

The logo is the gateway
to the brand.

Milton Glaser
Designer

Redesign

Before	After

We tried to signal
continuous change, the
essence of fashion.

Michael Bierut
Partner
Pentagram

Brooklyn Botanic Garden
was redesigned to embody
the new tagline "Where
plants come to life."

Carbone Smolan Agency

We wanted to help the
ACLU look like the guardians
of freedom.

Sylvia Harris
Design strategist

Walmart's approachable
typeface and spark of
innovation suggests smart
ideas and living better.

Su Mathews
Senior Partner
Lippincott

Before	After	
Thomas Jefferson's **Poplar Forest**	THOMAS JEFFERSON'S 	Jefferson's handwriting is a counterbalance to a symbol of his octagonal retreat where he sojourned in his retirement. Anna Bentson Director, Public Relations + Marketing Thomas Jefferson's Poplar Forest
		Unilever's new brand identity expressed a core brand idea aligned with the mission "Adding Vitality to Life." Wolff Olins
		The iconic Hot Wheels logo, was evolved to better fit on the Hot Wheels cars. riCardo Crespo WW Group Creative Director Hot Wheels™
		Columbus Salame was repositioned to appeal to more sophisticated, upscale customers. Pentagram
		Preferred's new identity embodies the company's entrepreneurial, forward-thinking culture of "unlimited possibility." Jon Bjornson

Packaging

Before

After

Simplifying the Lean Cuisine identity allowed us to recapture the brand's equities, drive shelf impact, and by color coding, helped enhance shopability.

Amanda Bach

Design Director
Nestlé

Lean Cuisine: Wallace Church

Dropps' redesign captures its positioning as an innovative laundry product with a playful, friendly spirit.

Remy Wildrick

Brand Manager
Dropps

Dropps: Amy Grove Bigham

HP's new packaging increases appeal to a younger audience while staying true to HP's world-class leadership position.

Will Burke

CEO
Brand Engine

The redesign of Wildwood elevates the brand image, making it more competitive and relevant to today's consumer.

Eric Read

Co-Founder + Creative Director
Brand Engine

Before   **After**

We revolutionized Sesmark's identity to tell a compelling health from the heartland story to capture the brand's authentic, all-natural positioning.

Rob Wallace
Managing Partner
Wallace Church

Renuzit's new design seeks to engage consumers on many levels to expand the brand's perception beyond just an air freshener to total air care.

Rob Wallace
Managing Partner
Wallace Church

A new logo featuring a wood engraving, and botanical illustrations on the labels, brought new life to this family business.

Louise Fili
Louise Fili Ltd.

A makeover for Irving Farm Coffee was inspired by 19th century engravings and typography.

Louise Fili
Louise Fili Ltd.

Work with talented people to create something
that will be of compelling benefit to the customer.

Susan Avarde, Managing Director, Global Branding
Citigroup Consumer Businesses

2 Process

Part 2 presents a universal brand identity process that underlies all successful brand identity initiatives, regardless of the project's complexity. This section answers the question "Why does it take so long?" and addresses collaboration and decision making.

A process for success

The brand identity process demands a combination of investigation, strategic thinking, design excellence, and project management skills. It requires an extraordinary amount of patience, an obsession with getting it right, and an ability to synthesize vast amounts of information.

Regardless of the nature of the client and the complexity of the engagement, the process remains the same. What changes is the depth with which each phase is conducted, the length of time and the number of resources allocated, and the size of the team, on both the identity firm and client sides.

The process is defined by distinct phases with logical beginnings and endpoints, which facilitate decision making at the appropriate intervals. Eliminating steps or reorganizing the process might present an appealing way to cut costs and time, but doing so can pose substantial risks and impede long-term benefits. The process, when done right, can produce remarkable results.

The process is the process, but then you need a spark of genius.

Brian P. Tierney, Esq., Founder
Tierney Communications

Process: ···········

1 : conducting research

Clarify vision, strategies, goals, and values.

Research stakeholders' needs and perceptions.

Conduct marketing, competitive, technology, legal, and language audits.

Interview key management.

Evaluate existing brands and brand architecture.

Present audit readout.

2 : clarifying strategy

Synthesize learnings.

Clarify brand strategy.

Develop a positioning platform.

Co-create brand attributes.

Write a brand brief.

Achieve agreement.

Create a naming strategy.

Develop key messages.

Write a creative brief.

Process is a competitive advantage

Assures that a proven method is being used to achieve business results

Accelerates understanding of the investment of necessary time and resources

Engenders trust and confidence in the identity team

Positions project management as smart, efficient, and cost-effective

Builds credibility and strengthens identity solutions

Sets expectations for the complexity of the process

Navigating through the political process—building trust—building relationships—it's everything.

Paula Scher
Partner
Pentagram

Most processes leave out the stuff that no one wants to talk about: magic, intuition, and leaps of faith.

Michael Bierut
Partner
Pentagram

3 : designing identity

4 : creating touchpoints

5 : managing assets

Visualize the future.
Brainstorm big idea.
Design brand identity.
Explore applications.
Finalize brand architecture.
Present visual strategy.
Achieve agreement.

Finalize identity design.
Develop look and feel.
Initiate trademark protection.
Prioritize and design applications.
Design program.
Apply brand architecture.

Build synergy around the new brand.
Develop launch strategy and plan.
Launch internally first.
Launch externally.
Develop standards and guidelines.
Nurture brand champions.

Managing the process

Astute project management is critical to achieving the long-term goals of a brand identity project. Responsible project management is the foundation for mutual respect, confidence, and long-term success. The identity process demands a range of skills on both the client side and the identity firm side. It demands leadership and creativity working hand in hand with planning, coordinating, analyzing, understanding, and managing time, resources, and money. In addition to organization and discipline, the process requires patience, enthusiasm, and a laserlike focus on achieving the end goal.

Time factors

The length of a brand identity project is affected by the following factors:

Size of organization

Complexity of business

Number of markets served

Type of market: global, national, regional, local

Nature of problem

Research required

Legal requirements (merger or public offering)

Decision-making process

Number of decision makers

Number of applications

How long will it take?

All clients have a sense of urgency, regardless of the size and nature of the company. There are no shortcuts to the process, and eliminating steps may be detrimental to achieving long-term goals. Developing an effective and sustainable identity takes time. There are no instant answers, and a commitment to a responsible process is imperative.

Pay as much attention to the process as to the content.

Michael Hirshhorn
Organizational dynamics expert

Your goal is to identify the most appropriate talent for your business, your brands, your organization, and your culture. You need the right skills, for the right challenges, at the right time, for the right value.

John Gleason
President
A Better View Strategic Consulting

PROCESS: PROJECT MANAGEMENT

> **Team protocol**

Identify client project manager and team.

Identify firm contact and team.

Clearly define team goals.

Establish roles and responsibilities.

Understand policies and procedures.

Circulate pertinent contact data.

> **Team commitment**

Team must commit to:

Robust debate

Open communications

Confidentiality

Dedication to brand

Mutual respect

> **Benchmarks and schedule**

Identify deliverables.

Identify key dates.

Develop project schedule.

Update schedules as necessary.

Develop task matrix.

> **Decision-making protocol**

Establish process.

Determine decision makers.

Clarify benefits and disadvantages.

Put all decisions in writing.

> **Communications protocol**

Establish document flow.

Decide who gets copied how.

Put everything in writing.

Create agendas.

Circulate meeting notes.

Develop internet project site if appropriate to scale of project.

Who manages the project?

Client side

For a small business, the founder or owner is invariably the project leader, the key decision maker, and the visionary. In a larger company, the project manager is whomever the CEO designates: the director of marketing and communications, the brand manager, or maybe the CFO.

The project manager must be someone with authority who can make things happen, given the enormous amount of coordination, scheduling, and information gathering. He or she must also have direct access to the CEO and other decision makers. In a large company, the CEO usually forms a brand team, which may include representatives from different divisions or business lines. Although this team may not be the ultimate decision-making group, they must have access to the key decision makers.

Identity firm side

In a large brand consultancy, a dedicated project manager is the key client contact. Various tasks are handled by specialists, from market researchers and business analysts, to naming specialists and designers. In a small to midsize firm, the principal may be the main client contact, senior creative director, and senior designer. A firm may bring on specialists as needed, from market research firms, to naming experts, to create a virtual team that meets the unique needs of the client.

Project management best practices

Developed by Dr. Ginny Vanderslice, Praxis Consulting Group

Focus: ability to see and maintain the big picture while also breaking it down into smaller, ordered pieces; ability to keep moving despite challenges and constraints

Discipline: ability to plan, track numerous tasks, and balance time and cost factors

Strong communication skills: ability to communicate clearly and respectfully, and to keep team members informed in a timely manner

Empathy: ability to understand and respond to the needs, viewpoints, and perspectives of all players in the project

Effective management skills: ability to define needs, priorities, and tasks; ability to make decisions; ability to flag problems; ability to hold people accountable

Flexibility (adaptability): ability to stay focused and in control when things go wrong or change in midstream

Creative problem-solving ability: willingness to see problems as challenges to address rather than as obstacles

Insight: understanding policies, procedures, corporate culture, key people, and politics

> **Documentation**	> **Information gathering**	> **Legal protocol**	> **Presentation protocol**
Date all documents.	Determine responsibilities.	Identify intellectual property resource.	Circulate goals in advance.
Date each sketch process.	Determine dates.	Understand compliance issues.	Hand out agenda at meeting.
Assign version numbers to key documents.	Identify proprietary information.	Gather confidentiality statements.	Determine presentation medium.
	Develop task matrix.		Develop uniform presentation system.
	Develop audit.		Obtain approvals and sign-offs.
	Determine how you will collect audit materials.		Identify next steps.

Measuring success

Brand identity systems are a long-term investment of time, human resources, and capital. Each positive experience with a brand helps build its brand equity and increases the likelihood of repeat purchasing and lifelong customer relationships. A return on investment is achieved, in part, through making it easier and more appealing for the customer to buy, making it easier for the sales force to sell, and being vigilant about the customer experience. Clarity about the brand, a clear process, and smart tools for employees, fuel success.

Decision makers frequently ask, "Why should we make this investment? Can you prove to me that it has a return?" It's difficult to isolate the impact of a new logo, a better brand architecture, or an integrated marketing communications system. It is critical that companies develop their own measures of success. Those who don't expect instant results, and think in the cumulative long term, understand the value of incremental change and focus.

Pride

Wow factor

I get it

Confidence

Your boss is happy

The CEO gets it

You get what you measure.

Blake Deutsch

Human capital

Once they understood our vision, our employees accepted responsibility enthusiastically, which sparked numerous simultaneous and energetic developments in the company.

Jan Carlzon
Former CEO
Scandinavian Airlines Group
Moments of Truth

Brand is about real value — value in human terms, which doesn't mean only numbers. It's what people do, usually together, to fulfill an implied promise.

Ken Roberts
Chairman and CEO
Lippincott

Engagement happens when employees hear the message, believe the message, and then live or act upon it.

Enterprise IG

Sustainability

What makes a successful business and how it is measured has fundamentally changed in the 21st century.

Adam Lowry
Co-Founder
Method

Eco-friendly packaging

Reducing e-waste and trash

Reducing hazardous materials in product design

Saving energy

Reducing carbon footprint

Commitment to an environmental policy

Metrics for brand management Source: Prophet

Perception metrics		Performance metrics		Financial metrics
Awareness	**Familiarity + consideration**	**Purchase decision**	**Loyalty**	**Value creation**
Are customers *aware* of your brand?	What do customers *think* and *feel* about the brand?	How do customers *act*?	How do customers *behave over time*?	How does customer behavior *create tangible economic value*?
Saliency	Differentiation	Customer leads	Customer satisfaction	Market share
Brand recognition	Relevance	Customer acquisition	Retention	Revenue
	Credibility	Trial	Revenue per customer	Operating cash flow
	Likability	Repeat	Share of wallet	Market cap
	Perceived quality	Preference	Customer lifetime value (LTV)	Analyst ratings
	Purchase intent	Price premium	Referrals	Brand valuation
			ROI	
			Cost savings	

Metrics for isolated touchpoints

Advertising	Websites	Direct mail	Packaging	Online branding tools
Awareness	Number of visitors	Response rate	Market share vis-à-vis competition	Visits to site
Conversion	Returning visitors		Sales change after new packaging	Amount of time on site
Revenues	Length of time spent on site	**Trade shows**	Compare sales change to overall project cost	Reduction in production time
	Clickstreams (where prospect has been)	Number of leads generated	Money saved because of engineering and materials	Increased adherence to guidelines
Electronic banners	Cost per visitor (CPV)	Number of sales	Eye-tracking studies, to track what they see first (shelf impact)	Less decision making time
Clickstreams	Sales per visitor	Number of inquiries	More shelf space	More efficient ordering
	Leads or inquiries per visitor		Home usage/observation consumer/field test	Number of transactions
Public relations	Site traffic	**Licensing**	Entrée to a new retailer	More compliance
Buzz	Usage patterns	Revenues	Press coverage; buzz	
Awareness	Page views (impressions)	Protecting assets	Number of line extensions	**Standards + guidelines**
	Fewer calls to customer service		Product placement	More consistent marketing and communications
Intellectual property	Usability studies	**Product placement**	Sales cycle time	Customer receives "one company"
Protecting assets		Reach	Consumer feedback	More efficient use of time
Preventing litigation	**Social media**	Impressions	Influence on purchasing decision	Less decision making
Adhering to compliance	Penetrating viral networks	Awareness		Fewer corrections
	Blog posts			Reduction in legal costs
	Embeds			

Metrics rethought

Design

The Design Council study of share prices of UK quoted companies over the last decade found that a group of companies, recognized as effective users of design, outperformed key FTSE indices by 200%.

Steady investment in, and commitment to, design is rewarded by lasting competitiveness rather than isolated successes.

The Design Council

Evidence-based design

Research has demonstrated that more thoughtfully designed health care environments have a positive effect on an individual's health and wellness.

Mergers

In the UK, over 70% of what was paid in the acquisition of companies was for the goodwill from intangibles including corporate brand value.

Turnbridge Consulting

Everyone wants to know in the beginning of an engagement that there is a clear measurement program, even though at the end of the project they never do it.

Anonymous

Collaboration

Great outcomes require vision, commitment, and collaboration. Collaboration is not consensus or compromise. It evolves from a thoughtful and genuine focus on problem solving, generating an interdependent, connected approach. It also acknowledges the tension between different viewpoints and different disciplines.

Most brand identity projects involve individuals from various departments with different agendas. Even small organizations have silos that stand in the way of achievement. Collaboration requires the ability to suspend judgment, listen carefully, and transcend politics.

You may have the greatest bunch of individual stars in the world, but if they don't play together, the club won't be worth a dime.

Babe Ruth

It was an amazing collaborative experience. There is so much complexity in making something so simple. Each one of us had a piece of soul in this Centennial Olympic project.

Malcolm Grear
CEO
Malcolm Grear Designers

Let go of stereotypes. Intellectual property lawyers do have creative thoughts, investment bankers can feel compassion, and designers can do math.

Blake Deutsch

When I work with a writer, we shed our own passionate and personal viewpoints, listen deeply, and allow a third person to emerge with a new vision.

Ed Williamson
Art Director

Principles of collaboration
Developed by Linda Wingate, Wingate Consulting

Leadership must believe in collaboration and its organizational benefits.

Listen to all perspectives; share your viewpoint honestly; put all issues on the table.

Promote participation.

Everyone's contribution is important.

Develop strong professional relationships, building high levels of trust and rapport; suspend titles and organizational roles.

Engage in dialogue; find a common purpose and language for learning and communicating; construct guiding principles for decision making.

Provide equal access to information; create a common work process; examine assumptions and data objectively.

Create team protocols.

Guarantee cooperation, engagement, and ownership; recognize that rewards are earned for the group, not for individuals; shed any competitive "win–lose" mentality.

Like King Arthur's Round Table, effective teams acknowledge and respect diverse expertise, share power, actively debate, unite around a common purpose, and use their collective intelligence to achieve ambitious goals.

Moira Cullen
Senior Director, Global Design
The Hershey Company

To be on a team, you have to let go of your ego, and strive for the endpoint.

Cathy Feierstein
Vice President, Organizational Learning
Assurant

The meta team is the best way to manage large-scale creativity. Hire best-of-breed specialists and get them to work together as a single team.

Marty Neumeier
The Designful Company

Decision making

Decision making can be designed to be an intelligent, engaging process that builds trust and helps organizations make the right choices to build their brand. Most people can recall a scenario in which the wrong decision was made because of either politics or too many decision makers. Experts in the social sciences believe that decisions made by large groups tend to be more conservative and less inspired than decisions made by small groups. Yet organizational development experts may tell you that decision by consensus has the potential to result in higher-quality decisions because the organization uses the resources of its members.

The path to reconciling these seemingly conflicting points of view leads to a brand champion or CEO with strong leadership skills—someone who can elicit ideas and opinions from a wider group without succumbing to group-think. In an ideal situation, the final decision makers, regardless of the size of the organization, should be kept to a very small group led by the CEO. The group makes informed choices that are aligned with the vision of the organization, and is involved throughout the process at key decision points, e.g., agreement on goals, brand strategy, names, taglines, and brandmarks.

Smart organizations often use the branding process to refocus stakeholders in the vision and mission of the organization. When it is done well, people throughout the organization feel valued and begin to "own" the new brand.

Decision making requires trusting yourself, your process and your team.

Dr. Barbara Riley, Managing Partner
Chambers Group LLC

If you have gone through a process with people you respect, a decision is not a leap of faith. It's planning.

Dr. Barbara Riley

Critcal success factors

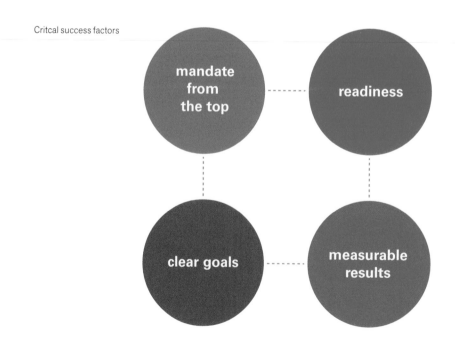

mandate from the top

readiness

clear goals

measurable results

Essential characteristics

The CEO leads a small group that includes marketing brand champions.

The entire process is clearly communicated to key stakeholders.

Decisions are aligned with vision and goals.

All members are trusted and respected.

Agreement on goals and positioning strategy precedes creative strategy.

All relevant information and concerns are voiced and tracked.

Pros and cons are always fully discussed.

A commitment is made to communicate about the brand through all levels of the organization.

Focus groups are used as a tool, not as a thought leader.

Decisions are communicated internally first.

Confidentiality is honored.

Challenging scenarios

When the CEO is not involved.

When new decision makers get involved in the middle of the process.

When team members' opinions are not respected.

When critical steps in the process are eliminated to save money and time.

When personal aesthetics get confused with functional criteria.

Mergers and acquisitions

Financial stakes are high.

Difficult to gather input when confidentiality is critical.

Time frame is compressed and atmosphere is tense.

Names and marks used in a symbolic chess match.

Everyone needs attention of leadership.

Critical to maintain focus on customer benefit.

Critical success factors

The CEO supports this initiative.

The company is ready to invest time, resources, and brainpower.

There is an endpoint that everyone understands and agrees on.

Everyone agrees on how success will be measured. There is value to the outcome.

Decide how you are going to decide and stick to it.

A lot of decisions are made in quiet conference rooms where new work can look radical or intimidating. But the work—the branded experience—needs to work OUT THERE. It's a noisy and busy world. You can spend a lot of money and discover that the customer doesn't know the difference. When you build things by consensus, you can lose your distinctiveness.

Susan Avarde
Managing Director, Global Branding
Citigroup Consumer Businesses

Insight

Designing an identity is a dance between the intuitive and intentional. The greatest challenge of the brand identity process is to realize that you cannot control anything other than your focus and attention. Trusting the process and keeping the ball in the air will always deliver extraordinary outcomes.

Just breathe.

Although research is the business discipline for gathering and interpreting data, insight comes from a more personal and intuitive place. Observing the world and listening nonjudgmentally to the ideas of others opens up possibilities. The work itself becomes the hero.

One-on-one interviews
Focus groups
SWOTs
Visioning

Insight leads to compelling new customer experiences.

Michael Dunn, CEO
Prophet

Market sizing
Awareness
Attitudes
Recognition
Reputation
Statistics
Demographics

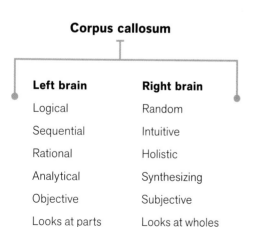

Corpus callosum

Left brain	**Right brain**
Logical	Random
Sequential	Intuitive
Rational	Holistic
Analytical	Synthesizing
Objective	Subjective
Looks at parts	Looks at wholes

design

Imagine
Realize
Celebrate
Simplify

Analytics are important, providing the data that allows marketers to stay focused and pragmatic, while also serving to set boundaries and provide the underlying rationale for marketing decisions. But analytics shouldn't be allowed to overwhelm the intuition that characterizes great marketers. It's the insights that the data leads to that result in breakthrough products and compelling new customer experiences.

Michael Dunn
CEO
Prophet

The future belongs to a very different kind of person with a very different kind of mind—creators and empathizers, pattern recognizers and meaning makers. These people (are) artists, inventors, designers, storytellers, caregivers, consolers, big picture thinkers. We are moving from an economy and a society built on the logical, linear, computer-like capabilities of the Information Age to an economy and a society built on the inventive, empathic, big picture capabilities of what's rising in its place, the Conceptual Age.

Dan Pink
A Whole New Mind

Insights appear when we stop thinking and let go. Answers to an intractable problem can come on a walk, in a dream, or in the shower. When we least expect it, fragmented thinking falls away and the whole appears, with the solution in bold type.

Lissa Reidel
Marketing Consultant

observing

Customer experience
Ethnography
Digital ethnography
Usability studies
Mystery shopping
Eye tracking

weaving

History and future
Competitive analysis
Trend analysis
Benchmarking
Perceptual mapping
Audit readout

dreaming

Visioning
Mood board

focusing

Goals
Segmentation
Mind map
Positioning

Hold that thought!

Timing is everything. "Parking lots" are documents that capture insights as they happen. At various points in the process, revisit them. Powerful and creative thoughts are preserved through the swirl of deadlines and politics.

risk-taking

Conducting research: overview

Brand identity requires business acumen and design thinking. The first priority is to understand the organization: its mission, vision, target markets, corporate culture, competitive advantage, strengths and weaknesses, marketing strategies, and challenges for the future.

Answering questions is relatively easy.
Asking the right question is more difficult.

Michael Cronan
Cronan

Learning must be focused and accelerated. Clients hire firms with the intellectual capacity to understand the business as a way of ensuring that the solutions are linked to business goals and strategies.

Understanding comes from various sources— from reading strategic documents and business plans to interviewing key stakeholders. Requesting the appropriate information from a client is the first step; it should precede interviewing of any key management or stake- holders. Listening to the organization's vision and strategies for the future forms the nucleus of the creative process for a new identity.

Interviewing key people face-to-face provides invaluable insight into the voice, cadence, and personality of an organization. Frequently, ideas and strategies that may never have been recorded before emerge during an interview.

Understanding may also be achieved by experi- encing the organization from a customer's perspective, gaining insight from navigating the website, and seeing how easy it is to understand the product offerings, receive a sales pitch, or use the products. The goals are to uncover the essence of this company and to understand how the organization fits into the larger competitive environment.

Baseline information to request

Request these business background materials to learn more about the organization prior to any interviews. If it is a public company, examine what financial analysts say about the company's performance and future prospects.

Mission		Existing marketing research
Vision		Cultural assessments
Values statement		Employee surveys
Value proposition		CEO speeches
Organization chart		Press releases
Strategic planning documents		News clippings
Business plans		History
Marketing plans		Domains
Annual reports		Intranet access

Interviewing key stakeholders

Interviewing key management is best done face-to-face. Recording the interview facilitates eye contact and a better interview. If necessary, interviewing can be done over the telephone. Building trust is another agenda. The quality of the questions and the rapport established in the interview set the tone for an important relationship. Encourage individuals to be brief and succinct. Do not provide questions in advance, if possible, since spontaneous answers may be more insightful. It is absolutely critical for you to read through the baseline information about the company before conducting any interview.

It is important to convey that you have already examined the documents provided. The list of who should be interviewed is co-created with a client. It is best to keep interviews under 45 minutes in length. The following questions should be customized before the interview.

Core interview questions

What business are you in?

What is your mission? What are your three most important goals?

Why was this company created?

Describe your products or services.

Who is your target market?

Prioritize your stakeholders in order of importance. How do you want to be perceived by each audience?

What is your competitive advantage? Why do your customers choose your product or service? What do you do better than anyone else?

Who is your competition? Is there a competitor that you admire most? If so, why?

How do you market your product and services?

What are the trends and changes that affect your industry?

Where will you be in five years? In ten years?

How do you measure success?

What values and beliefs unify your employees and drive their performance?

What are the potential barriers to the success of your product or service?

What keeps you up at night?

Place yourself in the future. If your company could do anything or be anything, what would it be?

If you could communicate a single message about your company, what would it be?

Market research

Smart research can be a catalyst for change; misguided research can stand in the way of innovation. Market research is the gathering, evaluation, and interpretation of data affecting customer preferences for products, services, and brands. Understanding and revealing new insights about attitudes, awareness, and behavior of prospects and customers often indicate opportunities for future growth.

According to Christine Ecklund, President, Christine Ecklund & Associates, "The market research departments of more and more companies are renaming themselves 'Consumer Insights' departments as the value added is recognized to be the insight gained from the data, not just the execution of the research."

Research must be appropriately designed and correctly analyzed to ensure findings are accurate and not misleading. Although anyone can access secondary research on the web, research itself does not provide answers. Interpreting data is a skill in itself. There are many proprietary research tools and client intelligence competencies to help global corporations develop brand strategy. Smaller branding firms may partner with market research firms and, in many cases, are provided with existing research reports about customer preferences or marketing segments.

Types of research

Primary research

Collection of new information designed to fit specific needs.

Secondary research

Interpretation and application of existing statistical, demographic, or qualitative data.

> Not everything that counts can be counted, and not everything that can be counted counts.
>
> Albert Einstein

Qualitative research

Qualitative research reveals customers' perceptions, beliefs, feelings, and motives. Findings are often rich in context and may offer new insights and perspectives about the brand.

Ethnography

Observes customer behavior in everyday life either in a work or home environment. Typically used by designers to gain insight and inspiration. There's a school of thought that claims that traditional ethnography can only be conducted by professionals who have studied the social sciences.

One-on-one interviews

Individual in-depth interviews with senior management, customers, and thought leaders are ideally conducted face-to-face, but may be conducted on the phone. Information and anecdotes yielded by this method are rich and particularly valuable to the branding process.

Focus groups

A fast-paced group discussion about predetermined topics led by a moderator with carefully selected participants who share common characteristics. Focus groups are best used to uncover attitudes, perceptions, needs, prejudices, and ways of using products.

Mystery shopping

Trained mystery shoppers anonymously visit stores, branch banks, and other locations where they pose as customers. They evaluate the shopping experience, salesmanship, professionalism, closing skills, follow-up, and overall satisfaction. Mystery shoppers follow a list of predefined steps, make mental notes, observe conditions and performance, and produce audit reports that provide objective feedback.

> **Focus groups were originally invented to FOCUS the research, not BE the research. They rarely deliver the consensus-building clarity needed to innovate.**
>
> Marty Neumeier
> *The Designful Company*

Quantitative research

How the research is designed and executed is critical; however, it is the consumer insight gained from research that ultimately drives the brand.

Christine Ecklund
President
Christine Ecklund & Associates

Quantitative research creates statistically valid market information. The aim is to provide enough data from enough different people to enable companies to predict—with an acceptable range of confidence—what might happen. A large group of people is asked exactly the same questions in precisely the same way. The sample is a microcosm that has the same characteristics of the overall target market. Researchers attempt to project the opinions of a relatively small number of people (the sample) to model the opinions of the entire population.

Online surveys

One of several ways to gather primary research data. This approach uses the internet to gather information from respondents as they sit at their own computers. Typically, potential respondents receive an email inviting them to take a survey, with a link to the survey itself.

Usability testing

Designers and human-factor engineers observe through a two-way mirror in a formal laboratory testing environment. Users are selected carefully, and results are analyzed in depth.

Product testing

Products can be tested "in home" to replicate real life or at a "central location" to get a point-in-time user experience. Whether it is preparing and eating a food product or driving a new vehicle, product testing is critical to the long-term success of a brand.

Competitive intelligence

Many business information database services on the web provide data and information about industries, private and public companies, and their stock activity and management. Some of this information is free and easy to access, while a good deal of it is through subscription. Brokers are also a good source of industry and stock reports, as are press archives.

Eye tracking

Eye movement recorders examine how an individual views packaging, advertisements, signs, shelf displays, or computer screens by tracking eye movements. These devices show when the subject starts to view a picture, the order in which the elements of the image were examined and reexamined, and the amount of viewing time given each element.

Segmentation

Divides consumers and businesses into clustered groups, each with its own special interests, lifestyles, and affinity for particular goods and services. Consumer segments are usually defined by demographic and psychographic information. Demographics are vital statistics, such as age, sex, marital status, ethnicity, family size and composition, education, income, occupation, and housing. Psychographics refer to psychological attributes that describe an individual's lifestyle or attitudes.

Equity tracking

Monitors ongoing brand health and advertising effectiveness. Most large brands conduct continual in-market equity tracking that includes key brand ratings, brand and advertising awareness, and brand usage trended over time.

Syndicated data

Standardized data that is regularly recorded and sold by suppliers such as Nielsen, IRI, and NET.

Market structure

Defines how a category is structured and how its brands interact. Provides a hierarchy for attributes such as size, form, or flavor. Identifies "white space" or market opportunities where no brands are currently competing.

Researchers use information to quantify, qualify, define, benchmark, and cast a critical eye on a company and its brand, the markets they serve, and the opportunities they seek.

Dennis Dunn, Ph.D.
Principal
B2BPulse

Phase 1

Usability

Usability testing is a research tool used by designers, engineers, and marketing teams to develop and refine new and existing products. This method can be extended to any part of the customer experience, purchasing, delivery, and customer service. Unlike other research methods, usability testing relies on "live" customer experiences with a product. Through the careful observation of a handful of typical users, product development teams can acquire immediate feedback on the product's strengths and weaknesses. By documenting the actual experiences of people using the product, the development team can isolate and remedy any design flaws before releasing it to the market.

The benefit of this approach is that it makes the end user's needs central to the product development process, rather than an afterthought.

Focus group results are what site visitors think they might do. Usability testing shows what visitors actually do.

Kelly Goto & Emily Cotler
Web ReDesign 2.0: Workflow that Works

The point of testing is not to prove or disprove something. It's to inform your judgment.

Steve Krug
Don't Make Me Think: A Common Sense Approach to Web Usability

PROCESS: USABILITY TESTING*

> **Develop test plan**

Review testing goals.

Communicate research questions.

Summarize participant characteristics.

Describe the method.

List the tasks.

Describe the test environment, equipment, and logistics.

Explain moderator role.

List the data you will collect.

Describe how the results will be reported.

> **Set up environment**

Decide on location and space.

Gather and check equipment, artifacts, and tools.

Identify co-researchers, assistants, and observers.

Determine documentation techniques.

> **Find + select participants**

Define the behavior and motivation selection criteria for each user group.

Characterize users.

Define the criteria for each user group.

Determine the number of participants to test.

Screen and select participants.

Schedule and confirm participants.

> **Prepare test materials**

Develop a script for moderator.

Develop task scenarios for participants to perform.

Develop background questionnaire to collect demographic data.

Develop pretest questionnaires and interviews.

Develop post-test questionnaire about experience.

* From *Handbook of Usability Testing,* Second Edition, by Jeffrey Rubin and Dana Chisnell

Benefits of usability testing

Informs design solutions

Creates satisfying (and even delightful) products.

Eliminates design problems and frustrations.

Creates a historical record of usability benchmarks
for future releases.

Development teams using usability methods are
quicker to market.

Puts customer at center of the process

Increases customer satisfaction.

Creates products that are useful and easy to use.

Features are more likely to be those that users
will use.

Improves profitability

Reduces development costs over the life of a
product.

Minimizes the cost of service and support calls.

Increases sales and the probability of repeat sales.

Minimizes risk and complaints.

Characteristics of a good test moderator

Understands basics of user-experience design

Quick learner

Instant rapport with participants

Excellent memory

Good listener

Comfortable with ambiguity

Flexible

Long attention span

Empathetic people person

Big picture thinker

Good communicator

Good organizer and coordinator

> ### Conduct test sessions

Moderate the session impartially.

Probe and interact with the
participant as appropriate.

Don't "rescue" participants when
they struggle.

Have participants fill out pretest
questionnaires.

Have participants fill out
post-test questionnaires.

Debrief participants.

Debrief observers.

> ### Analyze data + observations

Summarize performance data.

Summarize preference data.

Summarize scores by group
or version.

Identify what causes errors and
frustrations.

Conduct a source of error analysis.

Prioritize problems.

> ### Report findings + recommendations

Focus on solutions that will have
the widest impact.

Provide short- and long-term
recommendations.

Take business and technology
constraints into account.

Indicate areas where further
research is required.

Create a highlights video.

Present findings.

Marketing audit

Repositioning an organization, revitalizing and redesigning an existing identity system, or developing a new identity for a merger requires an examination of the communications and marketing tools an organization has used in the past. Identifying what has worked and what has been successful or even dysfunctional provides valuable learning in the creation of a new identity. Mergers present the most challenging audit scenarios because two companies that were competitors are now becoming aligned.

Marketing audits are used to methodically examine and analyze all marketing, communications, and identity systems, both existing

systems and those out of circulation. The process takes a magnifying glass to the brand and its multiple expressions over time. To develop a vision for an organization's brand in the future, you must have a sense of its history.

Inevitably, something of worth has been tossed out over time—a tagline, a symbol, a phrase, a point of view—for what seemed to be a good reason at the time. There might be something from the past that should be resuscitated or repurposed. Perhaps a color or a tagline has been in place since the founding of the company. Consider whether this equity should be moved forward.

Examine customer experience first and move to the intersection of strategy, content, and design.

Carla Hall, Creative Director
Carla Hall Design Group

PROCESS: MARKETING AUDIT

> Understand the big picture	> Request materials	> Create a system	> Solicit information	> Examine materials
Markets served	Existing and archival	Organization	Contextual/historical background	Business papers
Sales and distribution	Identity standards	Retrieval	Marketing management	Electronic communications
Marketing management	Business papers	Documentation	Communications functions	Sales and marketing
Communications functions	Sales and marketing	Review	Attitudes toward brand	Internal communications
Internal technology	Electronic communications		Attitudes toward identity	Environments
Challenges	Internal communications			Packaging
	Signage			
	Packaging			

Request materials

The following is the broad range of materials to request. It is important to create an effective organization and retrieval system since in all probability you will be amassing a large collection. It is important to have a person provide background about what has worked and what has not worked.

Organizing audits: create a war room

Create a war room, and put everything on the walls. Buy file boxes and create hanging files for categories. Devise a standard system to capture findings. Take a "before" picture.

Brand identity

All versions of all identities ever used

All signatures, marks, logotypes

Company names

Division names

Product names

All taglines

All trademarks owned

Standards and guidelines

Business papers

Letterhead, envelopes, labels, business cards

Fax forms

Invoices, statements

Proposal covers

Folders

Forms

Sales and marketing

Sales and product literature

Newsletters

Advertising campaigns

Investor relations materials

Annual reports

Seminar literature

PowerPoint presentations

Electronic communications

Website

Intranet

Extranet

Video

Banners

Blogs

Internal communications

Employee communications

Ephemera (T-shirts, baseball caps, pens, etc.)

Holiday greetings

Environmental applications

External signage

Internal signage

Store interiors

Banners

Trade show booths

Retail

Packaging

Promotions

Shopping bags

Menus

Merchandise

Displays

> **Examine identity**

Marks
Logotypes
Color
Imagery
Typography
Look and feel

> **Examine how things happen**

Process
Decision making
Communications responsibility
In-house and webmaster
Production
Advertising agency

> **Document learnings**

Equity
Brand architecture
Positioning
Key messages
Visual language

Competitive audit

A competitive audit is a dynamic, data-gathering process. Simply put, this audit examines the competition's brands, key messages, and identity in the marketplace, from brandmarks and taglines to ads and websites. More than ever, it is easy to gather information on the internet; however, a company should not stop there. Finding ways to experience the competition as a customer often provides valuable insights.

The greater the insight into the competition, the greater the competitive edge. Positioning the company in relationship to the competition is both a marketing and a design imperative. "Why should the customer choose our products or services over those of others?" is the marketing challenge. "We need to look and feel different" is the design imperative.

The breadth and depth of this audit can vary widely depending on the nature of the company and the scope of the project. Frequently, a company has its own competitive intelligence. Qualitative or quantitative research that can be a source of critical data need to be reviewed.

An audit is an opportunity to build a complete understanding of the business and establish a context for the branding solution.

David Kendall, Principal
Kendall Ross

PROCESS: COMPETITIVE AUDIT

> **Identify competitors**

Who are leading competitors?

Who most closely resembles the client, and in what ways?

Which companies compete indirectly?

> **Gather information/research**

List information needed.

Examine existing research and materials.

Determine if additional research is required.

Consider interviews, focus groups, online surveys.

> **Determine positioning**

Examine competitive positioning.

Identify features/benefits.

Identity strengths/weaknesses.

Examine brand personality.

> **Identify key messages**

Mission

Tagline

Descriptors

Themes from advertising and collaterals

> **Examine visual identity**

Symbols

Meaning

Shape

Color

Typography

Understanding the competition

Who are they?

What do their brands stand for?

What markets/audiences do they serve?

What advantages (strengths) do they have?

What disadvantages (weaknesses) do they have?

What are their modes of selling and cultivating customers/clients?

How do they position themselves?

How do they characterize their customers/clients?

What are their key messages?

What is their financial condition?

How much market share do they hold?

How do they use brand identity to leverage success?

What do they look and feel like?

Using the competitive audit

Present audit at the end of the research phase.

Use learning to develop new brand and positioning strategy.

Use audit to inform the design process.

Consider meaning, shape, color, form, and content that the competition does not use.

Use audit when presenting new brand identity strategies to demonstrate differentiation.

> **Document identity**

Identity signatures

Marketing collateral materials and website

Sales and promotional tools

Brand architecture

Signage

> **Examine naming strategy**

Core brand name

Naming system for products and services

Descriptors and domains

> **Examine brand hierarchy**

What type of brand architecture?

How integrated or independent is the core brand in relation to subsidiaries or subbrands?

How are the products and services organized?

> **Experience the competition**

Navigate websites.

Visit shops and offices.

Purchase and use products.

Use services.

Listen to a sales pitch.

Call customer service.

> **Synthesize learnings**

Make conclusions.

Start seeing opportunities.

Organize presentation.

Language audit

A language audit has many names. Voice audit, message audit, and content audit are among the most popular. Regardless of the moniker, it is the Mount Everest of audits. Every organization aspires to conduct one, but very few accomplish it or go beyond base camp one. Although language is an intrinsic part of the marketing audit, many companies do not tackle "voice" until after they have designed a new brand identity program.

The courageous look at content and design at the same time, revealing the entire spectrum of how language is used. Analyzing the intersection of customer experience, design, and content is an intensive and rigorous endeavor that demands the left brain and right brain to work in tandem.

Vigorous writing is concise.

William Strunk, Jr. and E. B. White
The Elements of Style

PROCESS: EXAMINING LANGUAGE

Criteria for evaluating communications

Developed by Siegel + Gale

Adherence to brand values

Is the tone and look of the information consistent with your brand attributes?

Customization

Is content based on what you already know about the customer?

Structure and navigational ease

Is the purpose of the document readily apparent, and is the document easy to use?

Educational value

Did you take the opportunity to anticipate unfamiliar concepts or terminology?

Visual appeal

Does the document look inviting and in keeping with a company's positioning?

Marketing potential

Does the communication seize the opportunity to cross-sell products in a meaningful, informed way?

Loyalty support

Does the communication thank customers for their business or in some way reward them for extending their relationship with you?

Utility

Is the document well suited to its function?

Call to action   Phone numbers   URLs   Email signatures   Voicemail messages   Titles   Addresses   Diagrams   Forms   Directions

Navigation

News releases   FAQs   Press kits   Annual reports   Brochures   Shareholder communications   Call center scripts   Customer service scripts   Sales scripts   Presentations   Announcements   Web content   Blog content   Blast emails   Advertising campaigns   Direct mail

Information

Audit readout

An audit readout signals the end of the research and analysis phase. It is a formal presentation made to the key decision makers that synthesizes key learnings from the interviews, research, and audits. The biggest challenge is organizing a vast amount of information into a succinct and strategic presentation. The audit readout is a valuable assessment tool for senior management, and a critical tool for the creative team to do responsible, differentiated work. It is a tool used as a reference throughout the entire process.

It is rare that an audit readout does not engender epiphanies. Although marketing and communications may not be top of mind for some management teams, seeing a lack of consistency across media, or seeing how much more discipline the competition uses in its marketing systems, is a real eye-opener. The objective of the audit is to open up the possibilities that a more strategic, focused brand identity system can bring.

I can't believe we are using the same stock images as our biggest competitors.
Anonymous

Holy smokes! What do you mean we haven't trademarked our product name?
Anonymous

We see the opportunity. Others see how far the brand voice has strayed.

Joe Duffy, Chairman
Duffy & Partners

PROCESS: SYNTHESIZE LEARNINGS

> Interviews	> Brand	> Marketing research	> Marketing audit	> Language audit
Stakeholder categories	Strategy	Brand recognition	Logos and signatures	Voice and tone
Key learnings	Positioning	Survey results	Brand architecture	Clarity
Customer insights	Essence	Focus group findings	Across marketing channels, media, product lines	Naming
Excerpts		Perceptual mapping	Look and feel	Taglines
		SWOTs	Imagery	Key messages
		Gap analysis	Color	Navigation
		Benchmarking	Typography	Hierarchy
				Descriptors

Essential characteristics

Analysis requires an ability
to listen, read between
the lines, observe what
others don't see, make
connections, see patterns,
and identify opportunities.

Blake Deutsch

Focuses leaders on the possibilities

Jumpstarts robust conversations

Identifies gaps between positioning and expression

Uncovers inconsistencies

Reveals need for more differentiation

Adds value and sense of urgency to the process

Informs the creative team

Unearths brilliant and forgotten ideas, images,
and words

Builds commitment to doing things right
in the future

We presented ACLU's visual
history at the national and
affiliate level: identity,
imagery, printed donor
materials, and the identities
of other advocacy groups.
We summarized our
interview findings, other
research, and our analysis.
We ended the presentation
with the new design
directives.

Sylvia Harris
Design Strategist

ACLU audit readout presentation

> **Competitive
audit**

Positioning

Logos

Brand architecture

Taglines

Key messages

Look and feel

Imagery

Color

Typography

> **Intellectual
property audit**

Trademarks

Compliance issues

> **Process
audit**

Existing guidelines

Technology

Collaboration

Clarifying strategy: overview

Phase 2 involves both methodical examination and strategic imagination. It is about analysis, discovery, synthesis, simplicity, and clarity. This combination of rational thinking and creative intelligence characterizes the best strategies, which go where others have not.

Look into a microscope with one eye and
a telescope with the other.

Blake Deutsch

In Phase 2, all of the learnings from the research and audits are distilled into a unifying idea and a positioning strategy. Agreement is solidified about target markets, competitive advantage, brand core values, brand attributes, and project goals. More often than not, the definitions of the problem and its challenges have evolved. Although many companies have their values and attributes in place, they may not have taken the time to articulate and refine them, or to share them beyond an off-site management retreat. The role of the consultant here is to identify, articulate, illuminate, weave, and play back the possibilities.

Phase 2 can lead to a number of possible outcomes. In a merger, a new brand strategy for the combined enterprise is necessary. Other scenarios require a unifying idea that will be effective across business lines in a new brand identity program. A brand brief is created, and a discussion about findings and epiphanies follows. When there is openness and candor between the client and the consultant, true collaboration can produce exceptional results. Key success factors during this phase are trust and mutual respect.

Different scenarios determine the scope of services during the second phase.

A clearly defined brand strategy

When Turner Duckworth worked with Amazon.com and Jeff Bezos, brand strategy was already clearly defined and articulated. What Amazon needed was a world-class brand identity. When Sandstrom Design was brought in by Steve Sandoz, a creative director at Weiden Kennedy, to work on Tazo tea, a vision that was articulated as "Marco Polo meets Merlin" was already in place. What the Tazo team needed was a firm that knew how to design the product offering and render it "otherworldly." When Bernhardt Fudyma worked with Nabisco to evaluate its familiar red triangle trademark design, the firm conducted an in-depth evaluation process, which did not require strategy development.

A need to redefine brand strategy

When Harley-Davidson set out to turn its business around and reinvent itself, senior leadership decided to build a brand strategy based on existing rider passion. Over the years they worked collaboratively with David Aaker, a preeminent brand strategist, as well as their agencies, VSA Partners and Carmichael Lynch, to evolve and express their strategy. When the Tate in the United Kingdom wanted to enhance its appeal and attract more visitors to its four museums, Sir Nicholas Serota, the Tate's director, and his communications staff worked closely with Wolff Olins to develop a central brand idea that would unify the different museums. "Look again, think again" was an invitation to visitors to reconsider their experience of art.

A need to create brand strategy

Aside from new business creation, mergers are by far the most challenging scenarios that require new brand strategy. Determining a unified strategy and a new name for two companies that may have been competitors and working with a transition team in a compressed timeframe takes extraordinary skill and diplomacy. VSA Partners created a brand strategy and a new name, Cingular, for the joint venture of Bell South Mobility and SBC Wireless in six weeks. The new name would represent eleven former brands and more than 21 million customers. The brand strategy positioned Cingular as the embodiment of human expression since VSA viewed the wireless space evolving from a features-and-functions buying decision to a lifestyle choice.

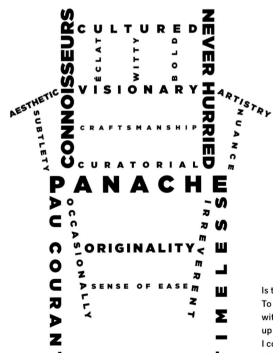

Is this chair comfortable? To spark a conversation with the founders of a start-up about their strategy, I composed their brand attributes in an image of their product category.

Jon Bjornson
Brand Strategist

Narrowing the focus

It is never enough to examine a company's current business strategy, core values, target markets, competitors, distribution channels, technology, and competitive advantage. It is crucial to stand back and look at the big picture—what are the economic, sociopolitical, global, or social trends that will affect the brand in the future? What are the drivers that have made the company successful in the past?

Interviews with senior management, employees, customers, and industry experts will provide an intimate glance into the uniqueness of a company. Often, the CEO has a clear picture of an ideal future and all its possibilities. A good consultant will hold up a mirror and say, "This is what you have told me and I heard it again from your customers and your sales force. And this is why it is powerful." It is important to look for the gold. Sometimes old ideas that are framed in a new way do not resonate immediately.

A brand becomes stronger when you narrow the focus.

Al Ries and Laura Ries
The 22 Immutable Laws of Branding

If you want to build a brand, you must focus your branding efforts on owning a word in the prospect's mind. A word that no one else owns. What prestige is to Mercedes, safety is to Volvo.

Al Ries and Laura Ries
The 22 Immutable Laws of Branding

As the mass and volume of information increases, people search for a clear signal—one that gives pattern, shape, direction to the voice.

Bruce Mau
Designer

Vision
Values
Mission
Value proposition
Culture
Target market
Segments
Stakeholder perceptions
Services
Products
Infrastructure

Understanding

Marketing strategy
Competition
Trends
Pricing
Distribution
Research
Environment
Economics
Sociopolitics
Strengths/weaknesses
Opportunities
Threats

Engage in meaningful dialogue

Companies frequently do not take the time to revisit who they are and what they are about. The beauty of this process is that it gives senior managers an explicit reason to go off-site and spin a dream. It is a worthwhile exercise. Superb consultants know how to facilitate a dialogue between core leaders in which various brand scenarios are explored and brand attributes surface.

Uncover brand essence (or simple truth)

What does a company do that is best in world? Why do its customers choose it over its competition? What business are they in? How are they really different than their most successful competitor? What are three adjectives that summarize how this company wants to be perceived? What are its strengths and weaknesses? The clarity of these answers is an important driver in this phase.

Develop a positioning platform

Subsequent to information gathering and analysis are the development and refinement of a positioning strategy. Perceptual mapping is frequently a technique used to brainstorm a positioning strategy. On which dimension can a company compete? What can it own?

Create the big idea

The big idea can always be expressed in one sentence, although the rationale could usually fill a book. Sometimes the big idea becomes the tagline or the battle cry. The big idea must be simple and transportable. It must carry enough ambiguity to allow for future developments that cannot be predicted. It must create an emotional connection, and it must be easy to talk about, whether you are the CEO or an employee.

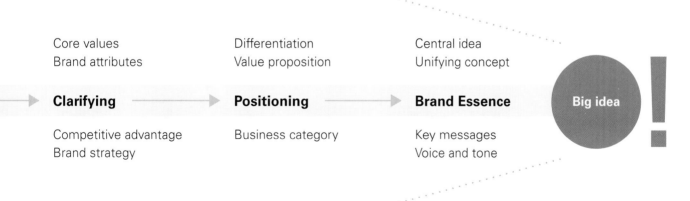

Core values	Differentiation	Central idea	
Brand attributes	Value proposition	Unifying concept	
Clarifying →	**Positioning** →	**Brand Essence**	Big idea !
Competitive advantage	Business category	Key messages	
Brand strategy		Voice and tone	

Brand brief

Documenting fundamental precepts of the brand is the most important task of Phase 2. What seems to most like a blinding flash of the obvious is frequently not. Robust discussions are facilitated by a simple, clear one-page diagram, as opposed to a twenty-page treatise that no one has read or remembers. Getting key decision makers to agree begins the creative process on a solid shared understanding of the brand.

The second objective is to write the creative brief, which is a road map for the creative team. Never write it until the brand brief is approved.

The best briefs are succinct and strategic, and approved by the most senior levels in an organization early in the process. If these briefs are approved, the balance of the project is more likely to be on track and successful.

The briefs are a result of a collaborative process—that is, a result of the best thinking and an ability to agree on brand attributes and positioning first, and the desired endpoint and criteria of the process second.

The brevity of the brand brief helps decision makers stick to the fundamental precepts of the brand.

Jon Bjornson

Diagramming our vision, core beliefs, and methods helped our trustees focus on brand decisions.

Pamela Thompson
Vice President Communications
John Templeton Foundation

Create a succinct and strategic diagram

Many entrepreneurial companies have visionaries who walk around with this information in their heads; getting it on paper helps anyone who has the responsibility to execute the vision. This is a hard task but well worth the time invested because a sustainable tool is created.

Writing the brief invariably includes meetings, numerous emails, and versions. The actual document is most effective when it can be captured as a diagram on one 11" x 17" page. When the final version is a word processing document, the temptation is to keep changing it.

Brand brief components

Vision

Mission

Big idea or brand essence

Brand attributes

Value proposition

Guiding principles/key beliefs

Target audience

Key markets

Key competitors

Competitive advantage

Stakeholders

Driving force

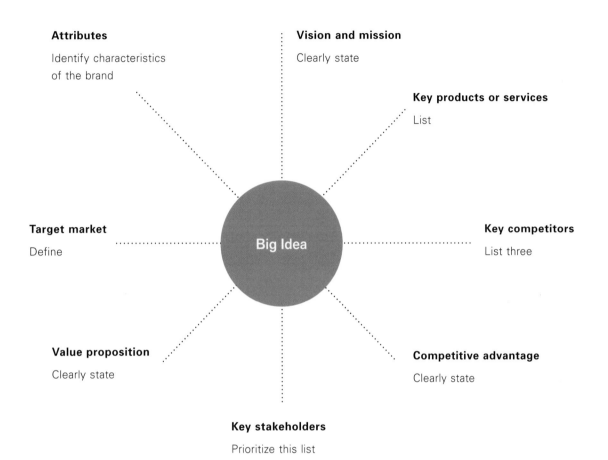

Attributes

Identify characteristics
of the brand

Vision and mission

Clearly state

Key products or services

List

Target market

Define

Big Idea

Key competitors

List three

Value proposition

Clearly state

Competitive advantage

Clearly state

Key stakeholders

Prioritize this list

Brief variations

Large companies will create positioning briefs
for marketing segments or business lines. Large
research studies are also synthesized in briefs
that highlight key learnings.

Version control

Writing a brief is an iterative process and it is
important to have version control. Each version
should be saved and have a version number
and a date on it.

Naming

Naming is not for the faint of heart. It is a complex, creative, and iterative process requiring experience in linguistics, marketing, research, and trademark law. Even for the experts, finding a name for today's company, product, or service that can be legally protected presents a formidable challenge.

Various brainstorming techniques are used to generate hundreds, if not thousands, of options. Culling the large list takes skill and patience.

Names need to be judged against positioning goals, performance criteria, and availability within a sector. It is natural to want to fall in love with a name, but the bottom line is that meaning and associations are built over time. Agreement is not easy to achieve, especially when choices seem limited. Contextual testing is smart, and helps decision making.

Naming is 20% creative and 80% political.

Danny Altman, Founder and Creative Director
A Hundred Monkeys

Don't pick a name that makes you one of the trees in the forest, and then spend the rest of your marketing budget trying to stand out.

Danny Altman
Founder + Creative Director
A Hundred Monkeys

The ability to foster consensus among decision makers is as critical as creativity in the naming process.

Lori Kapner
President
Kapner Consulting

PROCESS: NAMING

> **Revisit positioning**

Examine brand goals and target market needs.

Evaluate existing names.

Examine competitor names.

> **Get organized**

Develop timeline.

Determine team.

Identify brainstorming techniques.

Determine search mechanisms.

Develop decision-making process.

Organize reference resources.

> **Create naming criteria**

Performance criteria

Positioning criteria

Legal criteria

Regulatory criteria, if any

> **Brainstorm solutions**

Create numerous names.

Organize in categories and themes.

Look at hybrids and mimetics.

Be prolific.

Explore variations/iterations on a theme.

Inspiration

Language
Meaning
Personality
Dictionaries
Googling
Thesauruses
Latin
Greek
Foreign languages
Mass culture
Poetry
Television
Music
History
Art
Commerce
Colors
Symbols
Metaphors
Analogies
Sounds
Science
Technology
Astronomy
Myths
Stories
Values
Dreams

Remember

Names may be registered
in different classes of goods
and services.

Naming basics

Brand names are valuable assets.

When you are brainstorming, there are no stupid ideas.

Always examine a name in context.

Consider sound, cadence, and ease of pronunciation.

Be methodical in tracking name selections.

Determine smartest searching techniques.

Review all the criteria before you reject a name.

Meaning and association are built over time.

Voice of the stakeholders exercise

Create one page for each name candidate

Develop 5-10 statements using the name in context.
Example: New Name is the product I trust.

Attribute each statement to a key stakeholder.
Example: New Name is the product I trust. Tessa Wheeler, customer

Each decision-maker reads one statement out loud

Discuss what you like about this name first

Discuss what challenges the name presents next

> **Conduct initial screening**

Positioning
Linguistic
Legal
Common-law databases
Online search engines
Online phone directories
Domain registration
Creating a short list

> **Conduct contextual testing**

Say the name.
Leave a voicemail.
Email the name.
Put it on a business card.
Put it in an ad headline.
Put it into the voice of the stakeholders.

> **Testing**

Determine methods to trust.
Check for red flags.
Unearth trademark conflicts.
Check language connotations.
Check cultural connotations.
Do linguistic analysis.

> **Final legal screen**

Domestic
International
Domain
Regulatory
Registration

Designing identity: overview

Investigation and analysis are complete; the brand brief has been agreed upon, and the creative design process begins in Phase 3. Design is an iterative process that seeks to integrate meaning with form. The best designers work at the intersection of strategic imagination, intuition, design excellence, and experience.

We never know what the process will reveal.

Hans-U. Allemann
Allemann, Almquist + Jones

Reducing a complex idea to its visual essence requires skill, focus, patience, and unending discipline. A designer may examine hundreds of ideas before focusing on a final choice. Even after a final idea emerges, testing its viability begins yet another round of exploration. It is an enormous responsibility to design something that in all probability will be reproduced hundreds of thousands, if not millions, of times and has a lifetime of twenty years or more.

Creativity takes many roads. In some offices numerous designers work on the same idea, whereas in other offices each designer might develop a different idea or positioning strategy. Routinely hundreds of sketches are put up on the wall for a group discussion. Each preliminary approach can be a catalyst to a new approach. It is difficult to create a simple form that is bold, memorable, and appropriate because we live in

an oversaturated visual environment, making it critical to ensure that the solution is unique and differentiated. In addition an identity will need to be a workhorse across various media and applications.

In projects that involve redesign the designer must also carefully examine the equity of the existing form and understand what it has meant to a company's culture. Paul Rand's logos for UPS, Westinghouse, and Cummins were all redesigns. In each case Rand's genius was finding a way to maintain elements from the original identity and to transform them into bigger ideas and stronger, more sustainable visual forms. His strategy was always to present one idea. His brilliant design sensibility was matched by his strategic presentations, in which he traced the evolution of his recommendation.

Examine

Meaning
Attributes
Acronyms
Inspiration
History
Form
Counterform
Abstract
Pictorial
Letterform
Wordmark
Combination
Time
Space
Light
Still
Motion
Transition
Perspective
Reality
Fantasy
Straight
Curve
Angle
Intersection
Patterns

A designer's perspective

Paul Rand

as excerpted from *Paul Rand* by Steven Heller

Rand designed logos for endurance. 'I think permanence is something you find out,' he once said. 'It isn't something you design for. You design for durability, for function, for usefulness, for rightness, for beauty. But permanence is up to God and time.'

Per Mollerup

as excerpted from *Marks of Excellence*

The study of trademarks has its roots in fields as diverse as anthropology, history, heraldry, psychology, marketing, semiotics, communication theory, and of course, graphic design.

Identification, description, and the creation of value are just some of the possible functions of a trademark.

Steff Geissbuhler

We have run out of abstract, geometric marks and symbols, where an artificially adopted notion of growth, global business and aggressive, forward-moving technology becomes meaningless and overused, because it's everybody's strategy, mission, and positioning.

We have found that our audiences react much more directly and emotionally to recognizable symbols and cultural icons with clear connotations, characteristics, and qualities.

The trademark, although a most important key element, can never tell the whole story. At best it conveys one or two notions or aspects of the business. The identity has to be supported by a visual language and a vocabulary.

Paula Scher

My best idea is always my first idea.

Hans-U. Allemann

We usually begin with very predictable and obvious ideas, but the beauty of the identity design process is that it is totally unpredictable. We never know what the process will reveal. I have been designing marks for 40 years, and the process still astonishes me.

The best identity designers have a strong understanding of how to communicate effectively through the use of signs and symbols, a keen sense of form and letterforms, and an understanding of the history of design.

Malcolm Grear

Form and counterform. Light and tension. Expanded meaning that is not exhausted at first glance. These are the things that fascinate me.

You need to know the enterprise inside and out.

Beyond mere legibility, we aspire to convey our client's essential nature through imagery that is strong, profound, and elegant.

Meejoo Kwon

The design process is a triangle created from public perception, client insight, and designer's intuition.

In 1946, the Herman Miller logo was designed by the George Nelson office. Irving Harper, the designer, had stylized the "M" in Miller to create this mark. Over the years it has evolved. The Nelson office reworked it in 1960 and John Massey reworked it in 1968. In 1998, the Herman Miller creative team designed the one currently in use.

Steve Frykholm
Vice President, Creative Director
Herman Miller

Logotype + signature

A logotype is a word (or words) in a determined font, which may be standard, modified, or entirely redrawn. Frequently, a logotype is juxtaposed with a symbol in a formal relationship called the signature. Logotypes need to be not only distinctive, but durable and sustainable. Legibility at various scales and in a range of media is imperative, whether a logotype is silk-screened on the side of a ballpoint pen or illuminated in an external sign twenty stories off the ground.

The best logotypes are a result of careful typographic exploration. Designers consider the attributes of each letterform, as well as the relationships between letterforms. In the best logotypes, letterforms may be redrawn, modified, and manipulated in order to express the appropriate personality and positioning of the company.

The designer begins his or her process by examining hundreds of typographic variations. Beginning with the basics—for example, whether the name should be set in all caps or caps and lowercase—the designer proceeds to look at classic and modern typefaces, roman and italic variations, and various weights, scales, and combinations. The designer then proceeds to manipulate and customize the logotype. Each decision is driven by visual and performance considerations, as well as by what the typography itself communicates.

A signature is the specific and nonnegotiable designed combination of the brandmark and the logotype. The best signatures have specific isolation zones to protect their presence. A company may have numerous signatures, for various business lines or with and without a tagline.

Thomas Jefferson's Poplar Forest:
Rev Group

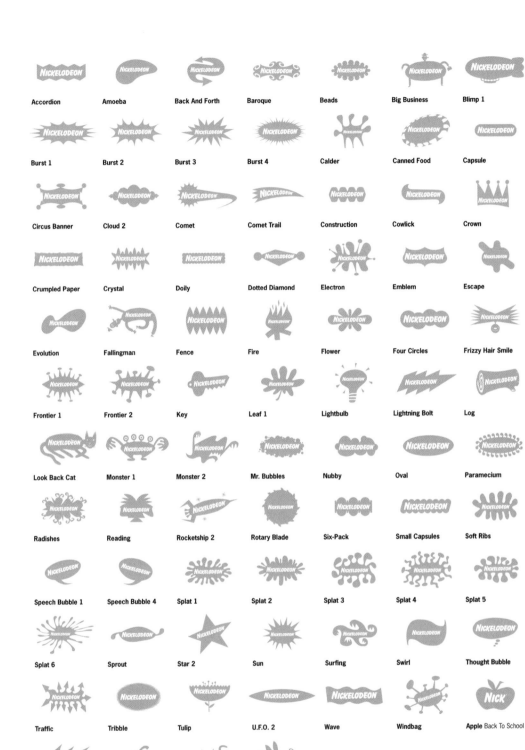

Accordion	Amoeba	Back And Forth	Baroque	Beads	Big Business	Blimp 1
Burst 1	Burst 2	Burst 3	Burst 4	Calder	Canned Food	Capsule
Circus Banner	Cloud 2	Comet	Comet Trail	Construction	Cowlick	Crown
Crumpled Paper	Crystal	Doily	Dotted Diamond	Electron	Emblem	Escape
Evolution	Fallingman	Fence	Fire	Flower	Four Circles	Frizzy Hair Smile
Frontier 1	Frontier 2	Key	Leaf 1	Lightbulb	Lightning Bolt	Log
Look Back Cat	Monster 1	Monster 2	Mr. Bubbles	Nubby	Oval	Paramecium
Radishes	Reading	Rocketship 2	Rotary Blade	Six-Pack	Small Capsules	Soft Ribs
Speech Bubble 1	Speech Bubble 4	Splat 1	Splat 2	Splat 3	Splat 4	Splat 5
Splat 6	Sprout	Star 2	Sun	Surfing	Swirl	Thought Bubble
Traffic	Tribble	Tulip	U.F.O. 2	Wave	Windbag	Apple Back To School
Leaf Fall	Pumpkin Thanksgiving	Scary Cat Halloween	Turkey Thanksgiving			

We wanted to simplify Nickelodeon's toolkit, and focus internal creative on the core messages of the brand, with a system that was flexible and encouraged creative thinking and execution.

Sean Adams
Partner
AdamsMorioka

Life is short.
Laughter is important.
Please take a look at
MakeMyLogoBiggerCream
video by Agency Fusion.

Blake Deutsch

Color

Color is used to evoke emotion and express personality. It stimulates brand association and accelerates differentiation. As consumers we depend on the familiarity of Coca-Cola red. We don't need to read the type on a Tiffany gift box in order to know where the gift was purchased. We see the color and a set of impressions comes to us.

In the sequence of visual perception, the brain reads color after it registers a shape and before it reads content. Choosing a color for a new identity requires a core understanding of color theory, a clear vision of how the brand needs to be perceived and differentiated, and an ability to master consistency and meaning over a broad range of media.

While some colors are used to unify an identity, other colors may be used functionally to clarify brand architecture, through differentiating products or business lines. Traditionally the primary brand color is assigned to the symbol, and the secondary color is assigned to the logotype, business descriptor, or tagline. Families of color are developed to support a broad range of communications needs. Ensuring optimum reproduction of the brand color is an integral element of standards, and part of the challenge of unifying colors across packaging, printing, signage, and electronic media.

Color creates emotion, triggers memory, and gives sensation.

Gael Towey, Creative Director
Martha Stewart Living Omnimedia

Color brand identity basics

Use color to facilitate recognition and build brand equity.

Colors have different connotations in different cultures. Research.

Color is affected by various reproduction methods. Test.

The designer is the ultimate arbiter for setting color consistency across platforms. It's hard.

Ensuring consistency across applications is frequently is a challenge.

Remember, most of the world uses a PC. Test.

Sixty percent of the decision to buy a product is based on color.

You can never know enough about color. Depend on your basic color theory knowledge: warm, cool; values, hues; tints, shades; complementary colors, contrasting colors.

Quality insures that the brand identity asset is protected.

Test your brand for proprietary strength. When you cover up your identity is your brand still present?

Heidi Caldwell
VP Marketing
Brand Engine

essn.

A true measure of brand strategy success is when employees can articulate and act on the vision, and the customer experience reflects it.

Johanna Pino
Brand Strategist
Brand Engine

Essn is a sparkling beverage targeted at discerning twenty-somethings. The name "essn" is shorthand for the fruit essence of the drink. Focusing on the target customer's lifestyle, Brand Engine defines a brand voice that speaks to a group bored with the same old choices. The brand's personality is young, fresh, and stylish. Successful at launch, essn has developed a cult-like following on the party circuit, appearing in a *New York Times* article on popular alternative beverages.

More color

Testing the effectiveness of a color strategy

Is the color distinctive?

Is the color differentiated from that of competitors?

Is the color appropriate to the type of business?

Is the color aligned with brand strategy?

What do you want the color to communicate?

Will the color have sustainability?

What meaning have you assigned to the color?

Does the color have positive connotations in the target markets?

Does the color have positive or negative connotations in foreign markets?

Is the color reminiscent of any other product or service?

Will the color facilitate recognition and recall?

Did you consider a specially formulated color?

Can the color be legally protected?

Does the color work on white?

Can you reverse the mark out of black and still maintain the original intention?

What background colors are possible?

What background values are necessary?

How does scale affect the color?

When you have a one-color application, such as a fax or newspaper, how will you adjust the color so that it reads?

Are there technical challenges to getting the color right?

Can you achieve consistency across media?

Have you tested the color on a range of monitors, PC and Mac?

Have you looked at ink draws on coated and uncoated stock?

Have you considered that the PMS color may look dramatically different on coated and uncoated stock?

Will this color work in signage?

What are the color equivalents on the web?

Is there a vinyl binder color that is compatible?

Have you tested the color in the environment in which it will be used?

Have you created the appropriate color electronic files?

Wana: Lippincott

Color systems

Will the color system be flexible enough to allow for a range of dynamic applications?

Does the color system support a consistent experience of the brand?

Does the color system support the brand architecture?

Is the color system differentiated from that of the competition?

Have you examined the benefits and disadvantages of:

using color to differentiate products?

using color to identify business lines?

using color to help users navigate decisions?

using color to categorize information?

Do you need both a bold palette and a pastel palette?

Can you reproduce these colors?

Have you developed both a web palette and a print palette?

Have you named your colors?

Have you created identity standards that make it easy to use the color system?

Mergers, acquisitions, redesign

Have you examined the historical use of color?

Is there equity that should be preserved?

Is the color aligned with the new brand strategy?

Is there a symbolic color that communicates the positive outcome of the merged entities?

Will developing a new color for the company send a new and immediate signal about the future?

Will retiring an existing color confuse existing customers?

Color trivia

Kodak was the first company to trademark a signature color.

Bianchi created a special color green for its bicycles.

When British Petroleum and Amoco merged to form BP, British Petroleum's distinctive green and yellow colors were kept.

BP: Landor Associates

Our primary brand color is CIGNA teal. It is a specially formulated color that is unique to our industry. We want CIGNA to be strongly associated with CIGNA teal. Therefore, all businesses are encouraged to use this color broadly across their communications.

CIGNA Brand Identity Guidelines

Typography

Typography is a core building block of an effective identity program. Companies like Apple, Mercedes-Benz, and Citi are immediately recognizable in great part due to the distinctive and consistent typographical style that is used with intelligence and purpose throughout thousands of applications over time. A unified and coherent company image is not possible without typography that has a unique personality and an inherent legibility. Typography must support the positioning strategy and information hierarchy. Identity program typography needs to be sustainable and not on the curve of a fad.

Thousands of fonts have been created by renowned typographers, designers, and type foundries over the centuries, and new typefaces are being created each day. Some identity firms routinely design a proprietary font for a client. Choosing the right font requires a basic knowledge of the breadth of options and a core understanding of how effective typography functions. Issues of functionality differ dramatically on a form, a pharmaceutical package, a magazine ad, and a website. The typeface needs to be flexible and easy to use, and it must provide a wide range of expression. Clarity and legibility are the drivers.

Type is magical.
It not only communicates a word's information,
but it conveys a subliminal message.

Erik Spiekermann
Stop Stealing Sheep

Kontrapunkt designed a modern and highly legible typeface, Pharma, for the Association of Danish Pharmacies. Pharma is a contemporary interpretation of the hand-painted typography on 19th-century apothecary jars.

Typeface family basics

Typefaces are chosen for their legibility, their unique character, and their range of weights and widths.

Intelligent typography supports information hierarchy.

Typeface families must be chosen to complement the signature, not necessarily to replicate the signature.

The best standards identify a range of fonts but give the users flexibility to choose the appropriate font, weight, and size for the message conveyed.

Limiting the number of fonts that a company uses is cost-effective since licensing fonts is legally required.

The number of typeface families in a system is a matter of choice. Many companies choose serif and sans serif faces; some companies choose one font for everything.

Basic standards sometimes allow special display faces for unique situations.

A company website may require its own set of typefaces and typography standards.

The best typographers examine a level of detail that includes numerals and bullets.

Many companies identify separate typefaces for internally produced word-processed documents and electronic presentations.

Certain industries have compliance requirements regarding type size for certain consumer products and communications.

Type considerations

Serif
Sans serif
Size
Weight
Curves
Rhythm
Descenders
Ascenders
Capitalization
Headlines
Subheads
Text
Titles
Callouts
Captions
Bulleted lists
Leading
Line length
Letter spacing
Numerals
Symbols
Quotation marks

Examine typefaces that:

Convey feeling and reflect positioning

Cover the range of application needs

Work in a range of sizes

Work in black and white and color

Differ from the competition's

Are compatible with the signature

Are legible

Have personality

Are sustainable

Reflect culture

Type trivia

The Obama political campaign used Gotham, designed by Tobias Frere-Jones.

Frutiger was designed for an airport.

Matthew Carter designed Bell Gothic to increase legibility in the phone book.

Meta was designed by Meta Design for the German post office but never used.

Wolff Olins designed Tate for Tate Modern in London.

The character of a typeface changes dramatically with different letter spacing, word spacing, and leading.

Matthew Barthlomew
Designer/typographer/teacher

Sound

As bandwidth increases, sound is quickly becoming the next frontier for brand identity. Many of our appliances and devices talk to us, voice-activated prompts let us schedule a FedEx pickup without human interface, and the elegant voice of James Earl Jones is the gateway to Verizon Nationwide 411.

The ringtone revolution is upon us. Individuals program their cell phones so that distinctive rings signal a certain someone, and a huge industry has been born in 30-second slices of sound. Quicktime videos populate websites and emails. The sound of silence is a has-been.

Whether you are at the Buddha Bar in Paris or the shoe department at Nordstrom, sound puts you in the mood. Sound also sends a signal: "Hail to the Chief" announces the president's arrival, and Looney Tunes cartoons always ends with a "Tha-a-a-t's all folks." A foreign accent adds cachet to almost any brand. Being put on hold might mean a little Bach cantata, a humorous sound sales pitch, or a radio station (don't you hate that?).

Designing and integrating the right sound enhances the experience of a brand.

Kenny Kahn
Vice President of Marketing
Muzak

What is audio architecture?

Audio architecture is the integration of music, voice, and sound to create experiences between companies and customers.

Muzak

I love those Hallmark cards that play music. I can't get enough.

Branding sound

Motors

Harley-Davidson motorcycles tried to trademark its distinctive purr. When Miata designed the first hot sports car in the moderate price category, the sound of the motor was reminiscent of a classic upscale sportscar.

Retail environments

From cafés, to supermarkets, to fashion boutiques, music is used to appeal to a particular customer and put him or her in the mood to shop or revel in the experience.

Jingles

Catchy messages set to music will stick in the mind of the consumer.

Signals

The Intel chip has its own musical bleeps, and AOL's "You've got mail" ditty became so much a part of the culture that it became the name of a movie love story with Meg Ryan and Tom Hanks.

Websites and games

Sound is being used increasingly to aid navigation, as well as to delight the user. Sound effects on computer games heighten the adventure, and avatars can be customized by the user.

Talking products

Technology is making the way for pill dispensers that gently remind you to take a pill, and cars that remind you to fill the tank, get service, or turn left. A Mercedes will definitely sound different than a Volkswagen.

Multimedia presentations

Interactivity and new media require the integration of sound. Testimonials are given by real customers. Video clips of company visionaries are shown to employees.

Spokespersons

Famous people have been used throughout advertising history to endorse a product. Also, a receptionist with a great voice and a friendly personality can become the spokesperson of a small firm.

Recorded messages

Great museums are paying attention to the voices they choose for audio tours. Companies specialize in targeted messages while you're on hold.

Characters

While the AFLAC duck has a memorable quack, many characters, like Elmer of Elmer's Glue, are still silent.

Websites without sound are starting to sound naked.

Blake Deutsch

Fundamentals of sonic branding
Excerpted from "Sonic Branding Finds Its Voice" by Kim Barnet, on Interbrand's Brand Channel

Sound needs to complement the existing brand

Sound can intensify the experience of a brand

Music can trigger an emotional response

Sound, especially music, heightens the brain's speed of recall

Music can transcend cultures and language

Aural and visual branding are becoming increasingly complementary

Many businesses compose original music

Many audio effects are subliminal

No one who saw *2001: A Space Odyssey* will ever forget the voice that said, "Open the pod bay doors, Hal."

Motion

Bringing brands to life is facilitated by a world in which bandwidth no longer constricts creativity and communication. Although the tools and skills to animate trademarks are available, very few creative professionals have taken full advantage of the medium to communicate a competitive difference. Ideally, the animated version of an identity is part of the initial conceptualization, rather than an afterthought. Motion must support the essence and meaning of an identity, not trivialize it.

Avatar: a brand icon designed to move, morph, or otherwise operate freely across various media.

Dictionary of Brand

Rand did not foresee the animated potential of the Westinghouse logo when he first designed it, but the possibilities for bringing it to life soon became perfectly clear.

Steven Heller
Paul Rand

People think in motion. There's no better way to build a brand, tell stories, and bring a brand to life or bring new life to a brand.

Dan Marcolina, Creative Director
Marcolina Design

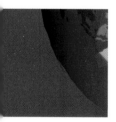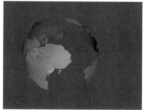

Motion principles

Developed by Sagi Haviv, Principal, Chermayeff + Geismar Studio

Essential

There must be a reason behind every decision made in the process of creating motion graphics, just like any other facet of design. Any nonessential element must be removed to ensure excellence.

Strategic

Animation should support brand essence, strive to communicate the brand's personality, and elaborate on the agenda expressed in the static mark. By ensuring the expression is appropriate to the brand positioning, the animation will protect brand equity.

Harmonious

Animation should evolve from the visual language of the brand identity. Often when looking at the static mark, an expert can identify what the mark "wants to do," namely what motion is innate in its graphic characteristics.

Communicative

Animation should tell a story—progression and drama, build-up, climax, and payoff are essential to captivate the audience and deliver the message.

Resonant

In this medium, movement is the expression and special care should be given to rhythm, speed, and transitions that define the mood and the emotional appeal of the piece.

The motion designer's control of time and timing supports surprise and enhances storytelling.

Chris Pullman
Vice President of Design
WGBH

Animation is an effective method to sell an idea. An animation created for Radio Free Europe/Radio Liberty introduced the new identity to the global Board of Governors. The animation was expanded for use in broadcast in various countries.

Steff Geissbuhler
Partner
C & G Partners

Radio Free Europe/Radio Liberty: Chermayeff + Geismar

Trial applications

It's important to choose a group of real applications to test the viability of concepts to work within a system. No mark should ever be shown on a blank piece of paper. Decision makers need to see the identity the way that a customer would see it. They need to see how it will take them into the future. Designers need to conduct rigorous testing before any concepts are shown and to demonstrate flexibility and durability.

A typical list for a small engagement might include a business card, a home page, an advertisement, a brochure cover, a letterhead, and something fun, like a baseball cap. On larger projects, the designer needs to demonstrate the effectiveness of brand extensions and the ability of the identity to work across business lines and markets served.

Dwell in possibilities.
Emily Dickinson

When we presented our vision for Studio 360's identity, it was important to explore a range of applications and engage the decision makers to imagine the possibilities for the radio show.

John Klotnia
Opto Design

Studio 360: Opto Design

Testing the concept

Choose the most visible applications.

Choose the most challenging applications.

Examine the flexibility of the identity.

Examine how to express coherence and consistency.

Does the signature work?

Is it differentiated enough from the competition's?

Is it scalable?

Does it maintain impact?

Does it stay legible at a small scale?

Will it work in different media?

Will it work on the internet?

Can it move?

Will it work both in color and in black and white?

Will it be conducive to brand extensions?

It works with the parent; will it work with the divisions?

Can it accommodate a tagline in the signature?

Will it work in other cultures?

Identity design testing basics

Use real scenarios and real text for application testing.

Continue asking the big questions in regard to appropriate meaning, sustainability, and flexibility.

Start thinking about the implications for the entire system of color and typeface families.

Always examine best-case and worst-case scenarios.

Remember, this is an iterative process.

If something does not work, deal with it immediately. Go back to the beginning if necessary to examine the core concept. The signature might need to be reworked.

Date and assign a version number to the entire sketch process; be obsessive about organization of this phase.

Think ahead to production: How will this look on a screen? Test it on a PC.

Solicit feedback from trusted colleagues—designers and nondesigners—to reveal any connotations that may not be apparent.

Anticipate what you will need to present the design strategy; start envisioning the presentation.

Continue to actively think about the future: five or ten years out is sooner than you think.

Presentation

The first major design presentation is the decisive moment. A design team has worked hard to get to this point, and it is the culmination of months of work. The expectations and stakes are high. Clients are usually impatient during the planning and analysis phase since they are so focused on the end goal, which is their new brand identity. There is usually a sense of urgency around scheduling this meeting. Everyone is ready to hit the ground running, even though the implementation phase of the work is not imminent.

Careful planning is essential to ensure the successful outcome of the meeting. The smartest, most appropriate, and most creative solutions can get annihilated in a mismanaged presentation. The larger the group of decision makers, the more difficult the meeting and the decision are to manage. Even presenting to one decision maker alone demands planning in advance.

Delivering a good presentation is something that a professional learns through experience and observation. The best presentations stay focused on the agenda, keep the meeting moving within the scheduled time, set out clear and reasonable expectations, and are based on a decision-making process that has been predetermined. The best presenters are well prepared and have practiced in advance. They are prepared to deal with any objections and can discuss the design solutions strategically, aligning them with the overall brand goals of the company. Larger projects routinely involve more than one presentation and numerous levels of building consensus.

Don't expect the work to speak for itself.
Even the most ingenious solutions must be sold.

Suzanne Young
Communications Strategist

Showing your concepts in a field of super brands helps decision makers make better decisions.

Pentagram used this slide when they were designing Citi's identity.

Citi: Pentagram

Presentation basics

PowerPoint is dead.

Blake Deutsch

Agree in advance about the agenda and the decision-making process.

Clarify who will attend the meeting and the role they will play. Individuals who have not participated in the early part of the process may derail the process.

Circulate the agenda in advance. Be sure to include the overall goals of the meeting.

Create an in-depth outline of your presentation and practice in advance. Create a handout if appropriate.

Look at the room's physical layout in advance to decide where you want to present from and where you want others to sit.

Arrive well in advance to set up the room and be there to greet all the attendees.

If the company is going to provide any equipment for the meeting, test it in advance. Familiarize yourself with the lighting and temperature controls in the room.

Web 2.0 applications have revolutionized the way we present our ideas and work collaboratively with our clients. Creating, sharing, rebranding and building brand consistency is facilitated by real-time online presentations.

Dan Marcolina
Creative Director
Marcolina Design

Presentation strategies

Begin the meeting with a review of the decisions made to date, including overall brand identity goals, definition of target audience, and positioning statement.

Present each approach as a strategy with a unique positioning concept. Talk about meaning, not aesthetics. Each strategy should be presented within several actual contexts (ad, home page, business card, etc.), as well as juxtaposed with the competition.

Always have a point of view. When presenting numerous solutions (never more than three), be ready to explain which one you would choose and why.

Be prepared to deal with objections: steer the conversation away from aesthetic criticism and toward functional and marketing criteria.

Never present anything that you do not believe in.

Never allow voting.

Be prepared to present next steps, including design development, trademarking, and application design.

Follow up the presentation with a memo outlining all decisions that were made.

Creating touchpoints: overview

Phase 4 is about design refinement and design development. The brand identity design concept has been approved, and a sense of urgency generates a fusillade of questions: "When we will get business cards?", followed by "How soon can we get our standards online?"

Design is intelligence made visible.

Lou Danziger
Designer and Educator

Now that the major decisions have been made, most companies want to hit the ground running. The challenge to the identity firm is to keep the momentum going while ensuring that critical details are finalized.

In Phase 3, hypothetical applications were designed in order to test the ideas, and to help sell the core concepts. The highest priority now is to refine and finalize the elements of the identity and to create signatures. This work requires an obsessive attention to detail; the files created are permanent. Final testing of the signature(s) in a variety of sizes and media is critical. Decisions about typeface families, color palettes, and secondary visual elements are finalized during this phase.

While the design team is fine-tuning, the company is organizing the final list of applications that need to be designed and produced. Core applications are prioritized, and content is either provided or developed. The intellectual property firm begins the trademark process, confirming what needs to be registered and in which industry classes. The lawyers confirm that there are no conflicting marks.

A brand identity program encompasses a unique visual language that will express itself across all applications. Regardless of the medium, the applications need to work in harmony. The challenge is to design the right balance between flexibility of expression and consistency in communications.

Creative brief

The creative brief cannot be written until the audit readout is complete and the brand brief is approved. Each member of the creative team must have a copy of both briefs, as well as a copy of the audit readout.

The creative brief synthesizes what the creative team needs to know in order to do responsible work aligned with the overall objectives of the project. This brief must be signed off by key decision makers before any conceptual or creative work is done. The best briefs are a result of collaboration between the client and the consulting team. Creative work includes the range of brand identity from naming, logo redesign, key message development, brand architecture, and packaging design, to integrated system design.

Creative brief contents

Team goals

Communications goals of all brand identity elements

Critical application list

Functional and performance criteria

Mind map or SWOTs

Positioning

Protocols

Confidentiality statement

Documentation system

Benchmarks and presentation dates

Application design essentials

Convey the brand personality.

Align with positioning strategy.

Create a point of view and a look and feel.

Make the design system work across all media.

Demonstrate understanding of the target customer.

Differentiate. Differentiate. Differentiate.

Design development basics

Design is an iterative process between the big picture and minutiae.

Designing real applications and the identity system are simultaneous.

Ensure that all assumptions are achievable.

Be open to additional discovery as it gets more real.

Application design imperatives

Seize every opportunity to manage perception.

Create a unified visual language.

Start thinking about launch strategy.

Create balance between consistency and flexibility.

Produce real applications before finalizing standards.

Work on the highest-visibility applications first.

Know when to identify outside experts for collaboration.

Use spreadsheets to keep track of numerous applications.

Never show any application without showing alignment with brand strategy.

Be obsessive about quality.

Gather notes during this phase for standards and guidelines.

Trademark process

A brand identity that is distinctive and differentiated from its competitors will always help a client legally protect this valuable and critical asset. Almost anything that serves to distinguish products or services from those of a competitor can serve as a trademark. Names, symbols, logotypes, taglines, slogans, packaging and product design, color, and sound are all brand identity assets that can be registered with the federal government and protected from future litigation.

Federal registration is in place to ensure that the consumer is not confused or misled by trademarks that are too similar. The government agency responsible is called the U.S. Patent and Trademark Office (USPTO). Trademarks are

always registered within industry classes, of which there are forty-five, and may be registered in more than one class. Intellectual property is the name of the legal discipline that specializes in providing the broadest scope of protection for brand identity assets. Intellectual property assets also include copyrights and patents.

There are different points in the brand identity process when research is conducted to determine whether there are any conflicting marks, names, or taglines. The various types of searches include common-law, federal, and state. Experienced legal counsel is needed to assess the risk of trademark infringement.

A distinctive identity is worth nothing unless you can protect it.

Roberta Jacobs-Meadway
Eckert Seamans

PROCESS: TRADEMARK SEARCH AND REGISTRATION

> Establish legal needs	> Establish legal resources	> Decide on type of search	> Conduct preliminary research
Determine what needs to be protected: name, symbol, logotype, product design.	Identify client legal counsel.	Common-law (anyone can conduct)	Determine quickly other ownership.
Determine type of registration: federal, state, country.	Identify intellectual property lawyer.	Short screening (level 1)	Search domain registration sites, newspapers, search engines, telephone directories.
Identify key dates.	Review other proprietary assets.	Comprehensive	Create short list for comprehensive search.
Identify any regulatory constraints.	Research search services.	Visual (for symbols, package, products)	
Determine industry class(es).			
Assign search responsibilities.			
Set up documentation system.			

Myths

Once you register a trademark, you own it forever and for everything.

Registering a domain name offers legal protection.

We can save money if we conduct the search ourselves.

By the end of 2001, the USPTO had 1,063,164 active registrations for trademarks.

The more differentiated an identity is from those of its competitors, the easier it is to protect from a legal perspective.

Registering a mark gives clients extra rights and the broadest scope of protection. Although trademark rights may be established by actual use, federal registration ultimately secures more benefits in trademark infringement.

Registration is done at the federal and state levels. State registrations are usually less expensive than federal registrations but are more subject to challenge.

Protection for marks in other countries must be sought country by country since legal protection differs from country to country.

An individual, a corporation, a joint venture, or a partnership can own a trademark. A trademark cannot have two independent owners.

In the case of litigation, defendants' failure to do a competent search may be evidence of bad faith.

Intellectual property is a specialty, and identifying a lawyer who has experience in this is critical. Anyone can search the USPTO or other databases on the web for federal registrations, but lawyers are trained to assess the risk of a brand identity strategy.

Certain industries, such as the financial industry, require state registrations with designated commissioners for product names that are sold nationally. What works in one state will not necessarily work in another.

Mergers usually have their own set of requirements that affect information sharing. Parties may request to restrict access to certain documents.

® denotes a registered trademark, and may only be used when marks have been federally registered.

TM

^{TM} is used to alert the public and does not require filing federal applications. It means trademark, which is a claim of ownership for goods and packaging.

SM

^{SM} means service mark and refers to a unique service. This appears on any form of advertising and promotional literature. It does not require filing federal registration.

> **Conduct comprehensive research**

Identify comprehensive database resources for naming, symbols, taglines, trade dress (package design), product design, color, sound.

Conduct and review searches.

Determine availability.

Choose what to eliminate or contest.

> **Conduct registration**

Finalize list of registrations.

Create documents as required.

Federal

State

Country

> **Monitor and educate**

Develop plan to monitor intellectual property assets.

Conduct annual intellectual property audits.

Educate employees and vendors.

Publish standards that clarify proper usage.

Make it easy to adhere to legal usage.

Letterhead

The art of correspondence and the letterhead have lasted from the quill pen to the typewriter and the computer. Although voicemails and emails have become the most widely used form of communication, the letterhead is not yet obsolete in the twenty-first century. The letter still comes to us in the same way that it has been coming to us since Ben Franklin became the first U.S. postmaster—unless, of course, it comes via FedEx, or as an attachment.

The letterhead, offset-printed on fine paper, remains a core application in the brand identity system even with electronic letterheads. The letterhead with an original signature is still an important conduit for doing business. It is regarded as a credible proof of being in business, and it frequently carries an important message or contractual agreement. It is still regarded as the most formal type of business communication and has an implicit dignity. For many years banks required businesses to write a letter on their letterhead in order to open an account.

Most of the world uses letterhead and envelopes based on the metric system. Only the U.S., Canada, and Mexico don't.

Polite Design was engaged to design the total identity system for Diana Vincent, a jewelry designer. The system included design of logo, stationery system, retail packaging, bags, print advertisements, and website.

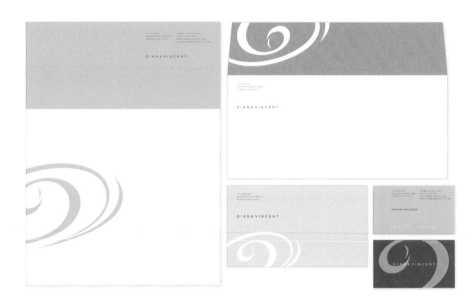

PROCESS: LETTERHEAD DESIGN

> Clarify use	> Determine need	> Finalize content	> Develop design
Letters, short and long	Corporate only	Best-case scenario	Use real letter
Contracts	Division letterhead	Worst-case scenario	Determine margins
Memos	Personal letterhead	Unify abbreviations	Show actual size
Invoices	Size	Tagline	Examine iterations
Forms		Regulatory information	Design envelopes
		Parent	
		Professional affiliation	

Letterhead design basics

Never design a letterhead without an actual letter on the page.

Never present a letterhead design without a real letter on it.

Take into consideration the location of the folds.

Get an ink draw on the paper that you have chosen.

Do a fax test.

Design a second sheet.

Research the right size for a foreign country.

Feel the paper, and identify the proper weight.

Find out biases regarding formats.

Provide templates for letter positioning, type style, and size.

Always test the paper and envelopes on a laser printer.

Look at recycled sheets.

Diana Vincent: Polite Design

Our design reflects the hallmark attributes of Diana Vincent's jewelry: simplicity, elegance, fluidity of form, and high quality artisanship.
Sonali Polite
Polite Design

The world of abbreviations

There are no universal abbreviations. Consistency is the rule.

Telephone

Phone
Tel
P
T
Voice
V

Facsimile

Fax
F

Mobile

Cellular
Cell
M
C

Email

email
e
(just address)

Website

Web
(just URL)

> **Specify paper**

Appropriate surface
Availability
Laser compatibility
Color

> **Determine production method**

Offset printing
Digital printing
Engraving
Foil stamping
Embossing
Letterpress
Watermark

> **Manage production**

Review proofs
Watch first run on press
Develop electronic templates

Business card

Each day millions of people say, "May I have your card?" This commonplace business ritual looks different around the globe. In Korea you show respect for a colleague by presenting a business card in two hands. In the Far East most corporate business cards are two-sided, with one side, for example, in Korean, and the other side in English. The Western-size business card is slowly becoming the standard around the world, although many countries still use variations of a larger card.

In the nineteenth century, Victorian calling cards were elaborately decorated, oversized designs to showcase a name. Today the designer is faced with so much information to include—from email to voicemail to mobile phone and 800 numbers, double addresses and domains—that the small business card is a challenge even for the most experienced designers. Information, by necessity, is flowing to the back side.

The business card is a small and portable marketing tool. The quality and intelligence of the information are a reflection on the card holder and her company. In the future a high-tech business card may double as an identification card and include a user's fingerprint or other biometric data.

A good business card is like a kick-ass tie; it won't make you a better person, but it'll get you some respect.

Sean Adams, Partner
AdamsMorioka

Mexico Restaurante y Barra: AdamsMorioka

PROCESS: BUSINESS CARD DESIGN

> Clarify positioning	> Determine need	> Finalize content	> Develop design
Revisit positioning goals.	Who uses a card?	Best-case scenario	Use real text.
Revisit competitive audit.	How frequent is the need?	Worst-case scenario	Show actual size.
Revisit internal audit.	What is the quantity required?	Unify abbreviations	Examine iterations.
Understand brand hierarchy.	What is the critical information?	Tagline	Consider the back.
		Regulatory info	Develop color strategy.
		Parent	
		Professional affiliation	

Business card design basics

Think of a business card as a marketing tool.

Make it easy for the receiver of a card to retrieve information.

Make it easy for new cards to be produced.

Minimize the amount of information, within reason.

Consider using the back as a place for more information or a marketing message.

Carefully choose the weight of the paper to convey quality.

Feel the paper and the surface.

Make sure that all abbreviations are consistent.

Make sure that the titles are consistent.

Make sure that the typographic use of upper- and lowercase is consistent.

Develop system formats.

Like the best packages, the best calling cards convey trustworthiness and WOW at once.

Tom Peters
Brand You

The overall idea for Mexico was lo-fi, bright, and cheap. Why have one vibrant business card if you can have many?

Sean Adams
Partner
AdamsMorioka

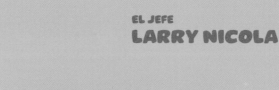

EL JEFE
LARRY NICOLA

**8512 SANTA MONICA BOULEVARD
WEST HOLLYWOOD CA 90069
310 289 0088 PHONE
310 289 0077 FAX**

> **Specify paper**

Appropriate surface
Weight
Availability
Color
Quality
Recycled

> **Determine production method**

Offset printing
Digital printing
Engraving
Foil stamping
Embossing
Letterpress
Watermark

> **Manage production**

Review proofs
Watch first run on press

Collateral

You are waiting for your café latte and see a set of brochures in a stylish rack. You go to the doctor, and each aspect of your health care has its own publication. You're in charge of making a buying decision at your office and your sales representative has a collection of information outlining their history, case studies, and advantages for selecting their product over a competitor.

The best collateral communicates the right information at the right time with a customer: discussing roasting techniques during that café latte; outlining surgery preparation before that big day; or sales literature that makes your company feel more confident about that big purchase.

TeleTech : Anabliss Design + Brand Strategy

We created a structured system for TeleTech that unified all sales collateral, clearly distinguished key lines of business and positioned the company as the leader in the business process outsourcing (BPO) arena.

Matt Coffman
President
Anabliss Design + Brand Strategy

PROCESS: COLLATERAL DESIGN

> **Revisit the big picture**	> **Design a cover system**	> **Determine typographic system**	> **Determine artwork**	> **Design color family**
Examine positioning goals.	Define grid for signature, content, and visuals.	One typeface family or two	Photography	Define set of approved colors.
Examine competitive audit.	Examine signature scenarios:	Title typeface	Illustration	Evaluate production methods to align color across media.
Examine internal audit.	Signature in primary and constant place	Cover descriptor typeface	Design elements	
Identify functional needs, i.e., how brochures are used and distributed.	Split signature	Header typeface	Collage	
Understand how collateral are produced within the company.	Signature not used on cover	Subhead typeface	Typographic	
Identify challenges.	Signature used on back only	Text typeface	Abstract	
	Signature used in secondary position with product name in primary position	Caption typeface	Identity derivative	

Collateral system basics

Unified collateral systems increase brand recognition.

Make it easy for customers to understand information and make buying decisions.

By making information accessible, a company demonstrates its understanding of its customers' needs and preferences.

Make it easier for sales teams to sell.

Effective systems allow for flexibility.

System standards should be easy for managers, design professionals, and advertising agencies to understand.

Systems should include flexible elements but not waver on clear, absolute standards regarding signatures.

Great design is effective only if it can be reproduced at the highest quality.

The best collateral is well written and presents appropriate amounts of information.

Systems should include a consistent call for action, URL, and contact information.

> **Choose standard formats**

U.S. sizes
International sizes
Consider postage
Consider electronic delivery

> **Specify paper**

Examine functionality, opacity, and feel
Examine price points.
Decide on family of papers.
Have dummies made.
Feel the paper.
Consider weight.
Consider recycled.

> **Develop prototypes**

Use real copy.
Edit language as needed.
Demonstrate flexibility and consistency of system.
Decide on signature configurations.

> **Develop guidelines**

Articulate goals and value of consistency.
Create grids and templates.
Explain system with real examples.
Monitor execution.

Website

Engaging content, sound, movement, and color create a walking, talking interactive company experience, bringing the brand personality to life. A website is the next best thing to reality, and in some cases it is more efficient, more user-friendly, and faster. The customer is in charge. The internet provides the customer with a no-pressure sales environment, and at the click of a mouse, a competitor is waiting.

The best websites understand their customers and respect their needs and preferences. A company's website should quickly answer these questions: "Who is this company? Why does anyone need to know? What's in it for me?" Expressing an authentic brand identity requires communication architects, information architects, designers, and engineers. Websites are increasingly used as portals for media tools. From logos to message points, downloading from a site enables employees to jumpstart marketing and communications from anywhere in the world.

Interactive experiences require nonlinear thinking, inviting interfaces, and creative intelligence.

Stella Gassaway, Visionary and Creative Principal
Stellarvisions

The number one myth is "Build it and they will come."
Richard Kauffman
Panoptic Communications

PROCESS: WEBSITE DESIGN*

> **Initiate plan**

Set goals.
Establish project team.
Identify audiences.
Define key messages.
Revisit positioning.
Set priorities.
Rough out project plan.
Define success.

> **Build groundwork**

Conduct competitive audit.
Gather data about audience.
Consider content sources.
Explore technological issues.
Assess resources for ongoing site updates.
Evaluate existing site.
Revisit goals + set strategies.

> **Define structure**

Outline content.
Map content.
Define logical relationships.
Create user personas and scenarios.
Postulate visitor's mental model.
Build wireframe prototypes.
Test prototypes.
Revise wireframes based on test results.

> **Prepare content**

Define editorial workflow.
Set editorial calendar.
Optimize content for search engines.
Identify existing content.
Rewrite text for web.
Commission new content, visual, or media assets.
Approve content, including legal sign-off.
Review content in screen context.
Edit and proofread text.

*Compiled by Stellarvisions

Characteristics of the best websites

Easy to use

Meets visitor expectations

Communicates visually

Keep site goals, audience needs, key messages, and brand personality central to each and every decision about the site.

Anticipate future growth. Measure, evaluate, change.

Site structure should not simply reflect organizational structure.

Begin site structure with content, not a screen design.

Do not force content into counterintuitive groupings.

Write content specifically for the web.

Conduct usability testing.

Observe etiquette. Alert visitors where special technology is needed, where a screen may load slowly, or where a link leaves your site.

Comply with ADA: arrange for visually impaired visitors to use software to read the site aloud or greatly magnify text.

At each stage ask: Is the message clear? Is the content accessible? Is the experience positive?

Confront internal political agendas that may sabotage site goals.

@issue journal: Pentagram

A lot of websites are morphing into weblogs with a blog component. @issue journal is a magablog—it's not a true blog because it is designed to look like an online publication, but it does feature new posts at the top.

Delphine Hirasuna
Editor
www.@issuejournal.com

> **Create visual design**

Color palette, tone, metaphor

Grid and element placement

Graphic elements and text styles

Navigational cues

Layouts of key screens

Anticipate display on various platforms.

Create visual objects for specific functions.

Integration of media

Prototyping and testing with users

> **Develop technical design**

Strategy for data integration

Static vs. dynamic screens

Content management option

Transaction flow design

Quality assurance testing plan

Security and scalability

Technical specifications

Prototyping and testing

Locking feature set

> **Finalize development**

Production of screen graphics

Development of HTML templates

Content freeze

Inserting content

Approval of beta site

Quality tests of beta site

User tests of beta site

Revisions based on test findings

> **Launch and maintain**

Promote site launch.

Complete style guide.

Develop maintenance plan.

Monitor logs and user paths.

Measure success.

Test ongoing usability.

Favicons

Favicons are miniaturized storefront signs that give brands an opportunity to attract attention and stand out from the crowd. They are the 16x16 pixel icons located in a web browser's address bar. If companies don't have a favicon, the browser's generic default icon will be next to the URL. Favicons are also visible next to the web page's name in a web user's list of bookmarks.

Favicons need to work within the extreme size constraints of the web address bar. One would think that telegraphing a unique identity in such a small low-res space would be impossible. It's not. The simplest boldest forms are immediately recognizable. Amazing.

We looked at 500 brands in 2008 and found that less than 50% had favicons.

Seize every opportunity to express who you are.

Blake Deutsch

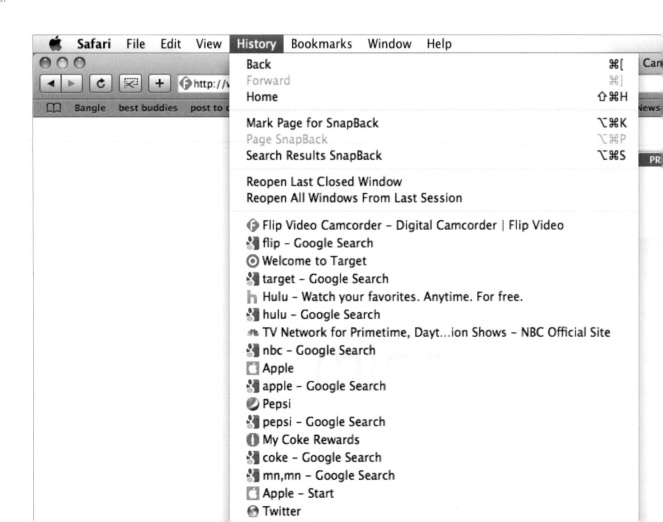

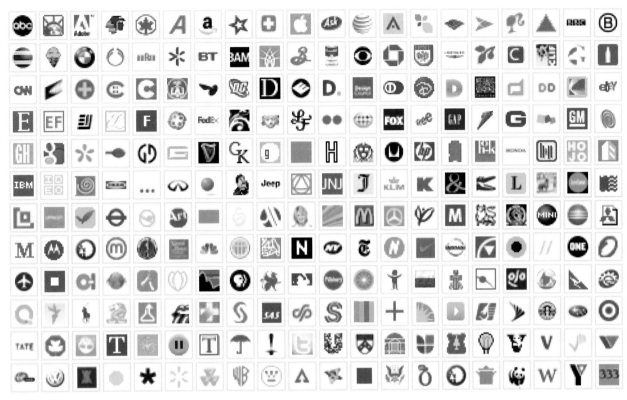

Left to right:
ABC
ACLU
Adobe
AeroMexico
Air Canada
Allstate
Amazon
American Girl
Apotek
Apple
Ask Jeeves
AT&T
Aveda
Bahamas
Bank of America
Bank of New York
Barbie
Bass Ale
BBC
B Corporation
Beeline
Ben & Jerry's
BMW
The Body Shop
Braun
Brinker Capital
British Telecom
Brooklyn Academy of Music
Brooklyn Botanic
Brooklyn Brewery
Campbell's Soup
CBS
Chase
Chicago Booth
Chrysler
Cigna
Clean & Clear
Clif Bar
Cloud Gehshan
Coca-Cola

CNN
Columbia Pictures
Crispin Porter
Cronan
Crosby Associates
Dairy Council
Danish State Railway
DC Comics
DeBeers
Dell
Deloitte
Design Council
Diners Club
Disney
Dominion
Dosirak
Duffy
Dunkin Donuts
Eastman Kodak
ebay
Economist
Eileen Fisher
Ernst & Young
Estée Lauder
Fallon
Fast Company
FedEx
Femina Photo + Design
Field Museum
Louise Fili Ltd.
Flickr
FORA.tv
Fox
Free Library of Philadelphia
GAP
Gatorade
Geico
General Foods
GM
Genomic Health
Good Housekeeping

Google
Grapefruit
Green Giant
Greteman Group
Gucci
Guinness
Guy Kawasaki
Gymboree
H&R Block
Harry Allen
Harvard
Herman Miller
Hewlett Packard
Hoeffler & Frere-Jones
HOK
Honda
House of Pretty
Howard Johnson
Hyatt
IBM
IDEO
Ignite
IKEA
Infinite Design
Infiniti
ING Direct
Itza Pizza
Jeep
Jon Bjornson
JNJ
Juicy Couture
KLM Royal Dutch
Kmart
Kort & Godt
Lacoste
Landor
Late July
Lev Lane
Library of Congress
LifeMark
Lippincott

Lipton
London Underground
Lufthansa
Main Line Art Center
Malcolm Grear
March of Dimes
Marriott
Martha Stewart
Bruce Mau
McDonald's
Mercedes
Mercy Corps
Meta Design
Merrill Lynch
MGM
Mini Cooper
Minolta
Mitsubishi
Monigle
Motorola
Mutual of Omaha
Muzak
National Guard
Natural History Museum
   of Los Angeles
NBC
Neptco
Nestle
Neutron
New York Jets
New York Times
Nickelodeon
Nike
Nissan
Northwest Airlines
The Olin Studio
Wally Olins
One
Oprah
Oslo Airport
Outward Bound

Owens Illinois
Panoptic
Paris
Parkinson's Disease
   Foundation
Patagonia
PBS
Philadelphia Museum of Art
Philadelphia Phillies
Pillsbury
Piperlime
Please Touch Museum
Poland
Presbyterian Church
Prophet
Providence Journals
Prudential
Qantas Airlines
Quest Diagnostics
QVC
Radio Free Europe
Ralph Lauren
Ritz Carlton
Rohm and Haas
Rolling Stones
Sacred Heart
SAS
Scandinavian Airlines
Schering Plough
Sears
Sherman Mills
Siegel + Gale
Smithsonian
SONY
Specialty Labs
Sprint
Starbucks
Subaru
Target
Tate

Thomas Jefferson's
   Poplar Forest
Timberland
Time Warner
TiVo
Tory Burch
Transamerica
Travelers Group
Turner Duckworth
Twitter
Unilever
University of Pennsylvania
University of Virginia
Univision
US Forest Service
USPTO
Vanderbilt
Vanguard
Velfina
Virco
Virgin Mobile
Volkswagen
VSA Partners
Vueling
Wallpaper
Walmart
Warkulwiz
Warner Bros
Westinghouse
Weyerhaeuser
Alina Wheeler
Ed Wheeler
White House
Whole Foods
Wild Kingdom
Williams-Sonoma
World Wildlife Fund
Wyeth
YMCA
333 Belrose Bar

Signage

From city streets and skylines, through museums and airports, signage functions as identification, information, and advertising. Effective retail signage increases revenues, and intelligent wayfinding systems support and enhance the experience of a destination.

In the eighteenth century, laws required innkeepers to have their signs high enough to clear an armored man on horseback. In the twenty-first century, cities and towns around the world routinely revise sign codes in order to create environments that support the image that a community wants to portray, and to regulate standards to protect public safety.

Signage can define a place and create a sense of community.

Keith Helmetag, Partner
C&G Partners, LLC

Signage helps people identify, navigate, and understand environments.

Alan Jacobson
Principal
ex;it

PROCESS: SIGNAGE DESIGN

> **Establish goals**	> **Build project team**	> **Conduct research**	> **Establish project criteria**
Determine project scope.	Client facilities manager	Site audit: environment	Legibility
Understand audience needs and habits.	Information design firm	Site audit: building type	Placement
Clarify positioning.	Fabricator	User habits and patterns	Visibility
Clarify function.	Architect or space designer	Local codes and zoning	Sustainability
Develop time frame and budget.	Lighting consultant	Consideration for the disabled	Safety
		Weather and traffic conditions	Maintenance
		Materials and finishes	Security
		Fabrication processes	Modularity

Signage basics

Signage expresses the brand and builds on understanding the needs and habits of users in the environment.

Legibility, visibility, durability, and positioning must drive the design process. Distance, speed, light, color, and contrast affect legibility.

Signage is a mass communications medium that works 24/7 and can attract new customers, influence purchasing decisions, and increase sales.

Exterior signage must consider both vehicular and pedestrian traffic.

Every community, industrial park, and shopping mall develops its own signage code; there are no universal codes.

Signage codes affect material, illumination (electrical), and structural choices; zoning or land use issues affect placement and size of signage.

Zoning constraints need to be understood prior to design development.

Permit and variance applications should include the benefit to the land-use planning scheme.

Signage requires a long-term commitment, and maintenance plans and contracts are critical to protecting the investment.

Developing prototypes minimizes risk by testing design prior to fabrication.

Signage should always complement the overall architecture and land use of a site.

Signage standards manuals include various configurations, materials, supplier selections, and production, installation, and maintenance details.

Flushing Freedom Mile:
C&G Partners, LLC

> Begin design schematic	> Develop design	> Complete documentation	> Manage fabrication + maintenance
Brand identity system	Begin variance process.	Complete working drawings.	Check shop drawings.
Color, scale, format	Prepare prototypes or models.	Construction, mounting, and elevation details	Inspect work.
Typography	Finalize content.		Manage fabrication.
Lighting	Create drawings or renderings.	Final specifications	Manage installation.
Materials and finishes	Choose materials and color samples.	Placement plans	Develop maintenance plan.
Fabrication techniques		Bid documents	
Mounting and hardware		Permit applications	
Placement			

Product design

The best products make everyday living easier and better, and fuse superior function, form, and brand. Think OXO, iPod, Google, Prius. Now products are also judged by their sustainability: Do I really need this? Will this product end up in a landfill? Is the company earth friendly and socially responsible? Satisfied consumers have become the new marketing department with blogs, Twitter, and texting. Disgruntled customers broadcast their dismay to the world through social media.

Behind every product innovation is a cross-functional team of experts who build on understanding customer needs, behavior, and desires. Research, design, human factors, and engineering experts work collaboratively with branding teams to satisfy unmet needs, build customer loyalty and lifelong relationships, and perpetuate the brand promise.

Excellent design provides superior function, performance, and value. Easy to understand and use, it delights the senses and stimulates desire.

Peter Bressler, Founder/Leader
Bresslergroup

Each day, a product lives the brand promise.

Mike Flanagan
Bresslergroup

PROCESS: PRODUCT DESIGN*

> Generative research	> Product definition/ planning	> Ideation	> Evaluative research	> Concept refinement
Clarify product brand strategy.	Assemble cross-functional development team.	Conduct multitier brainstorming.	Develop research methodology.	Synthesize customer feedback.
Conduct competitive analysis.	Develop user profiles.	Explore configuration options.	Recruit participants.	Refine the product specification.
Absorb client and secondary research.	Define key features and differentiators.	Explore 2D and 3D concepts.	Conduct customer concept testing.	Flesh out aesthetic and feature details.
Identify information gaps.	Clarify brand position.	Build models to prove concepts.	Analyze data.	Create user interaction logic.
Research new insights.	Refine formal product spec.	Refine concepts for team review.	Develop recommendations for refinement.	Engineer component resolution.
Analyze ergonomic and usability issues.	Build consensus with team.	Narrow range of concepts and refine.		Detail form and touchpoints.
Survey market trends.		Create testing presentation materials.		Refine product info and graphic system.
Search for any IP landmines.				Review 2D and 3D touchpoints.
Perform tech feasibility study.				

*Developed by Bresslergroup

Characteristics of the best consumer products

Anticipate customer needs and behavior

Express the brand promise

Deliver superior function, form, and value

Easy to use and easy to understand

Reliable, friendly service and support

Set expectation and desire for future products

Meaningful differentiation

Sustainable considerations in supply chain

Spark word-of-mouth referrals

Created by a cross-functional team

Consistent with pre- and post-sale touchpoints

Nielsen Kellerman Cadence Rowing Watch: Bresslergroup

The SRS product is an aesthetically integrated solar roof tile that generates electricity while looking and performing like a premium tile roof.

SRS Energy prototype tile: Bresslergroup

> Engineering development	> Evaluative research	> Production implementation	> Production support
Develop breadboards.	Validate product design:	Finalize production estimates.	Coordinate tooling fabrication.
Create manufacturing strategy.	Examine customer experience.	Complete mass production details.	Do formal review of first production parts.
Build detailed parts list.	Evaluate aesthetics, usability, functionality.	Fabricate final prototypes.	Achieve final approval.
Develop assembly design tasks.	Perform engineering analysis.	Codify design improvements.	Provide final production design changes.
Analyze high-risk features and interfaces.	Ensure standards compliance.	Perform engineering tolerance study.	Assist with final compliance testing.
Engineer for sustainability and cost optimization.	Review production strategy with manufacturers.	Finalize engineering documentation for tooling and production.	
Render mechanical, electrical, UI design in CAD.	Analyze results of testing.	Finalize tooling and production plan.	
Fabricate prototypes.	Create list of final changes.		
Conduct performance testing and customer validation.			

Packaging

Packages are brands that you trust enough to take into your home. We are continually comforted and cajoled by packaging shapes, graphics, colors, messages, and containers. The shelf is probably the most competitive marketing environment that exists. From new brands to extending or revitalizing existing product lines, considerations of brand equity, cost, time, and competition are often complex.

Packaging design is a specialty, and it routinely involves collaboration with industrial designers, packaging engineers, and manufacturers. In the food and pharmaceutical industry, it is regulated by the government. Package design is only one part of the puzzle involved in a product launch. Timetables include packaging approval and production, sales force meetings, manufacturing and distribution, and advertising.

First I bought it because it looked cool. Later I bought it because it tasted good.
Michael Grillo
Age 14

Packaging, the only brand medium experienced 100% by consumers, provides a higher ROI than any other branding strategy.
Rob Wallace, Managing Partner
Wallace Church

think

choose

change

Easy-to-understand icons reinforce Dell's commitment to sustainability on the new Dell Studio Hybrid™ box.

PROCESS: PACKAGING DESIGN

> Clarify goals + positioning	> Conduct audits + identify expert team	> Conduct research as needed	> Research legal requirements	> Research functional criteria
Establish goals and define problem.	Competitive (category)	Understand brand equity.	Brand and corporate standards	Product stability
Brand equity	Retail (point of sale)	Determine brand standards.	Product-specific	Tamper or theft resistance
Competition	Brand (internal, existing product line)	Examine brand architecture.	Net weight	Shelf footprint
Existing brands in product line	Packaging designer	Clarify target consumer.	Drug facts	Durability
Price point	Packaging engineer	Confirm need for product— does product benefit resonate?	Nutrition facts	Usage
Target consumer	Packaging manufacturers	Confirm language— how should benefit be expressed?	Ingredients	Packability
Product benefit	Industrial designers		Warnings	Fillability
	Regulatory legal department		Claims	

Packaging basics

Champagne in a can, tuna in a bag, wine in a box. The egg for me is still the perfect package.

Blake Deutsch

The shelf is the most competitive marketing environment in existence.

Good design sells. It is a competitive advantage.

Positioning relative to the competition and to the other members of the product line is critical for developing a packaging strategy.

A disciplined, coherent approach leads to a unified, powerful brand presence.

Structure and graphics can be developed concurrently. It is a chicken-and-egg debate.

Brand extensions are always a strategic tug-of-war between differentiation and coherence within a product line.

Consider the entire life cycle of the package and its relationship to the product: source, print, assemble, pack, preserve, ship, display, purchase, use, recycle/dispose.

Devise timetables involving packaging approval and production, sales force meetings, product sell in to stores, manufacturing, and distribution.

Developing a new structure takes a long time and is very expensive, but it offers a unique competitive advantage.

Studio Hybrid™ is Dell's greenest consumer desktop PC. Its packaging is made from 95% recyclable materials. A system-recycling kit is included to help preserve and protect the environment.

Marjorie Guthrie
Retail Packaging Manager
Dell | Experience Design Group

DELL: Wallace Church

> **Determine printing specifications**

Method: flexo, litho, roto

Application: direct, label, shrinkwrap label

Other: number of colors, divinyl, UPC code, minimums for knockouts

> **Determine structural design**

Design new structure or use stock?

Choose forms (e.g., carton, bottle, can, tube, jar, tin, blister packs).

Choose possible materials, substrates, or finishes.

Source stock and get samples.

> **Finalize copy + content**

Product name

Benefit copy

Ingredients

Nutrition facts/drug facts

Net contents

Claims

Warnings

Distributed by

Manufactured in

UPC code

> **Design + prototype**

Start with face panels (2D renderings).

Get prototypes made.

Narrow option(s).

Design rest of package.

Simulate reality: use actual structure/substrate with contents.

> **Evaluate solution + manage production**

In a retail/competitive environment

As a member of the product line

Consumer testing

Finalize files.

Oversee production.

161

Advertising

Since Silk Road traders described the benefits of jade and silk in lyrical song, merchants have created a sense of longing and entitlement by communicating about their products. Today we call it advertising and despite TiVo, social media, and the decline of print, it is still one of the ways consumers learn about new products, services, and ideas.

Our society has a love-hate relationship with advertising. Pundits issue warnings about its ubiquity and the cynicism of an increasingly skeptical audience. But who can resist the latest catalog or ignore sumptuous magazine ads? Advertising is influence, information, persuasion, communication, and dramatization. It is also an art and a science, determining new ways to create a relationship between the consumer and the product.

> Unless your campaign contains a big idea, it will pass like ships in the night.

David Ogilvy
Ogilvy on Advertising

I do not regard advertising as entertainment or an art form, but as a medium of information. When I write an advertisement, I don't want you to tell me that you find it "creative". I want you to find it so interesting that you buy the product. When Aeschines spoke, they said, "How well he speaks." But when Demosthenes spoke, they said, "Let us march against Philip."

David Ogilvy
Ogilvy on Advertising

PROCESS: ADVERTISING*

> **Conduct research**

Define objectives and target audience.
Review or develop brand vision and positioning.
Review past creative and results.
Analyze marketplace.
Review competition and trends.
Develop target archetypes.
Identify opportunities and unmet needs.
Review analysis and key insights.

> **Develop strategy**

Define strategic objective and customer benefit(s).
Weigh evolutionary vs. revolutionary approaches.
Define brand personality.
Revitalize positioning.
Validate priorities and assumptions.
Explore creative strategies.
Develop media strategy.

> **Develop creative**

Develop strategic design brief.
Define creative strategy.
Develop integrated theme.
Develop copy concepts.
Develop visual approaches.
Distill the best ideas.
Explore integration across media.
Establish marketing budget.

> **Test creative**

Determine testing approach.
Conduct consumer communication verification checks.
Modify concepts as necessary.
Develop production schedule.

*Developed by Ritter Strategic Marketing

Coca-Cola:
Turner Duckworth

**Branding is about
shifting perception.**

David Turner
Co-founder and Principal
Turner Duckworth

> **Develop media plan**

Develop alternative strategies.

Determine reach, frequency,
benefits, budgets.

Review and finalize plan and budget.

Place media buy.

Provide content to media.

Review media verification and invoices.

> **Manage production**

Assemble production specifications
and requirements.

Develop production schedule.

Review with client or test with
consumer.

Clear with legal.

Review, modify, and edit as necessary.

> **Implement campaign**

Communicate plan to client team.

Conduct road show for client
field outposts.

Launch integrated campaign.

Conduct consumer communication
checks.

Capture key learnings.

Document improvement opportunities.

Manage ongoing program.

> **Monitor impact**

Track impact across all media.

Compare sales activity to that of
prior campaigns.

Review costs relative to budget.

Assemble findings for discussion.

Modify campaign for future.

Environments

It's not unusual for the design and ambience of a restaurant to be a greater attraction than the culinary art, or for a financial services company to open a hip café to serve up good coffee and financial advice. Fabergé, the goldsmith known for the splendid jeweled eggs for the czar, was one of the first global entrepreneurs to understand that a well-conceived showroom appeals to customers and increases sales.

Exterior architecture represents yet another opportunity to stimulate immediate recognition and attract customers. In the 1950s, an orange tile roof in the distance sent an immediate and welcoming signal that there was a Howard Johnson's restaurant ahead. At the opposite

end of the cultural spectrum, the architecture of the Guggenheim Museum at Bilbao, Spain, is the brand and a powerful magnet that draws millions of visitors.

Architects, space designers, graphic designers, industrial designers, lighting experts, structural and mechanical engineers, general contractors, and subcontractors collaborate with client development teams to create unique environments and compelling experiences. Color, texture, scale, light, sound, movement, comfort, smell, and accessible information work together to manage perception in the environment.

Lippincott worked with McDonald's to refresh and update the restaurant design, creating a clean, modern, inviting environment for young adults and a wholesome setting for moms and kids.

Kathleen Hatfield
Partner
Lippincott

Seize every opportunity to create new experiences.

Blake Deutsch

McDonald's: Lippincott

Branded environment imperatives

Understand the needs, preferences, habits, and aspirations of the target audience.

Create a unique experience that is aligned with brand positioning.

Experience and study the competition, and learn from their successes and failures.

Create an experience and environment that make it easy for customers to buy, and that inspire them to come back again and again.

Align the quality and speed of service with the experience of the environment.

Create an environment that helps the sales force sell and makes it easy to complete a transaction.

Consider the dimensions of space: visual, auditory, olfactory, tactile, and thermal.

Understand the psychological effect of light and lighting sources, and consider energy efficiency whenever possible.

Consider all operational needs so that the client can deliver on the brand promise.

Understand traffic flow, the volume of business, and economic considerations.

Align merchandising strategies with displays, advertising, and sales strategies.

Design a space that is sustainable, durable, and easy to maintain and clean.

Consider the needs of disabled customers.

Apple store

We're starved for Wow! For experiences that coddle, comfort, cajole, and generally show us a darn good time. That's what we want for the money. I want decent vittles, mind you, but food we can get anywhere.

Hilary Jay
Director
The Design Center
Philadelphia University

Gucci has redesigned their retail experience. It's not a radical jump—it has to do with who they are, and it builds on their history with a new eye to the future—and a streamlined presence.

Trish Thompson
Fashion Consultant

Wherever I may wander
Wherever I may roam
When I walk into a Starbucks
I'm suddenly back at home.

Cathy Jooste
Global Citizen

Vehicles

Building brand awareness on the road is easier than ever. Vehicles are a new, large, moving canvas on which almost any type of communication is possible. Whether on an urban thruway at rush hour or a remote country road at sunset, the goal remains the same: make the brand identity immediately recognizable.

From trains, to planes, to large vans and small delivery trucks, vehicles are omnipresent. Vehicle graphics are experienced from ground level; from other vehicles, such as cars and buses; and from the windows of buildings. Designers need to consider scale, legibility,

distance, surface color, and the effects of movement, speed, and light. Designers also need to consider the life of the vehicle, the durability of the signage medium, and safety requirements and regulations that may vary state by state.

The Goodyear blimp and hot-air balloons are brand identities taking flight. Many vehicles carry other messages, from taglines and phone numbers to graphic elements and vehicle identification numbers. Simplicity should rule the road.

PROCESS: VEHICLE SIGNAGE

> **Plan**

Audit vehicle types.

Revisit positioning.

Research fabrication methods.

Research installers.

Receive technical specifications.

Get vehicle drawings.

> **Design**

Choose base color for vehicle.

Design placement of signature.

Determine other messages:
Phone number or domain
Vehicle ID number
Tagline

Explore other graphic elements.

> **Determine**

Fabrication methods:

Decal and wrap
Vinyl
Magnetic
Hand-painted

Get your motor runnin'
Head out on the highway
Lookin' for adventure
And whatever comes our way.

Steppenwolf

Vehicle types

Buses

Airplanes

Trains

Ferries

Subways

Container trucks

Delivery trucks

Helicopters

Motorcycles

Jitneys

Hot-air balloons

Blimps

Fresh produce from local farmers and wholesalers is delivered door to door by West Side Organics, inspiring their customers to "Save time, save gas, save the environment."

West Side Organics: Grapefruit

> **Examine**

Impact on insurance rates

Life of vehicle

Life of sign type

Cost and time

Safety or other regulations

> **Implement**

Create files done to spec.

Prepare documentation for installer.

Examine output.

Test colors.

Manage installation.

Uniforms

Clothing communicates. From the friendly orange apron at Home Depot, to a UPS delivery person in brown, a visible and distinctive uniform simplifies customer transactions. A uniform can also signal authority and identification. From the airline captain to the security guard, uniforms make customers more at ease. Finding a waiter in a restaurant may be as simple as finding the person with the black T-shirt and the white pants. On the playing field, professional teams require uniforms that will not only distinguish them from their competitors, but also look good on television. A lab coat is required in a laboratory, as are scrubs in an operating room, and both are subject to regulations and compliance standards.

The best uniforms engender pride and are appropriate to the workplace and environment. Designers carefully consider performance criteria, such as durability and mobility. The way an employee is dressed affects the way that the individual and her organization are perceived.

For employees, uniforms are a tangible, immediate, and highly visible way to demonstrate pride of ownership and commitment.

Adam Stringer, Partner
Lippincott

Vale is the second largest mining company in the world. After a wave of international acquisitions, the Brazilian company engaged Lippincott and Cauduro Associados to strengthen its brand globally with a clear identity and positioning. The branding team simplified the name to Vale, uniting all acquisitions under one brand.

Uniform performance criteria

Functional: Does the uniform take into consideration the nature of the job?

Durability: Is the uniform well made?

Ease: Is the uniform machine washable or easy to clean?

Mobility: Can employees do their tasks easily?

Comfort: Is the uniform comfortable?

Visibility: Is the uniform immediately recognizable?

Wearability: Is the uniform easy to put on?

Weight: Has the weight been considered?

Temperature: Does the uniform consider weather factors?

Pride: Does the uniform engender pride?

Respect: Does the uniform respect different body sizes?

Safety: Does the uniform adhere to regulations?

Brand: Is the uniform a reflection of the desired image?

Who needs uniforms?

Public safety officers
Security guards
Transportation personnel
Couriers
Bank tellers
Volunteers
Health care workers
Hospitality workers
Retail personnel
Restaurant personnel
Sports teams
Sports facilities personnel
Laboratory workers
Special events personnel

Methods

Off the shelf
Custom design
Custom fabrication
Embroidery
Screen printing
Patches
Striping

Uniform possibilities

Aprons
Belts
Pants
Shorts
Skirts
Turtlenecks
Golf shirts
T-shirts
Vests
Neckwear
Outerwear
Rainwear
Blazers
Blouses
Bows
Gloves
Boots
Helmets
Shoes
Socks
Tights
ID badges
Accessories
Scarves
Fleece
Windwear
Visors
Baseball caps
Patient gowns
Lab coats
Scrub apparel

Ephemera

A trade show is not a trade show without giveaways. The best booths give you canvas bags to store all your goodies, from squeezy stress balls, to commuter cups, to baseball caps, to mouse pads.

Ephemera is defined as objects with a short life, or more simply put, stuff. Companies frequently use marketing and promotion items.

Reproduction is rarely simple. Special techniques, such as embroidering a golf shirt or leather stamping a portfolio, usually require a custom signature that understands the needs of the production technique. The best way to control quality is to examine a proof.

Categories

Thank-you
Appreciation
Recognition
Special event
Trade show
Grand opening
Affiliation
Pride
Motivation
Production methods
Silk screening
Imprinting
Embossing
Foil stamping
Color filled
Engraving
Etching
Embroidering
Leather stamping

Whole Foods Market teamed up with Sheryl Crow to create a limited-edition reusable bag, in support of the Natural Resources Defense Council's Simple Steps program. These bags are made from 80% post-consumer recycled plastic bottles.

The possibilities

Alarm clocks
Albums
Aprons
Auto/travel stuff
Awards
Awnings
Badge holders
Badges/buttons
Bag clips
Bags
Balloons
Balls
Bandanas
Banks
Banners/pennants
Bar stuff
Barbecue stuff
Barometers/hygrometers
Baskets
Bathrobes
Batteries
Beauty aids
Belt buckles
Beverage holders
Bibs
Binoculars
Blankets
Bookends
Bookmarks
Books
Bottle holders
Bottles
Bottle stoppers
Bowls
Boxer shorts
Boxes
Breath mints
Briefcases
Buckets
Bulletin boards
Bumper stickers
Business card holders
Business cards
Calculators
Calendar pads
Calendars
Cameras
Camping equipment
Candle holders
Candles
Candy
Canisters
Cans
Caps/hats
Carabiners
Carafes
Cards

Cases
Certificates
Chairs
Christmas decorations
Cigars
Clipboards
Clocks
Clothing
Coasters
Coffeepots
Coin holders
Coins/medallions
Coloring books
Combs
Compact discs
Compasses
Computer stuff
Condoms
Containers
Cookware
Corkscrews
Cosmetics
Coupon keepers
Covers
Crayons
Crystal products
Cups
Cushions
Decals
Decanters
Decorations
Desk stuff
Dials/slide charts
Diaries/journals
Dice
Dishes
Dispensers
Doctor/druggist aids
Dog tags
Drink stirrers/sticks
Drinkware
Easels
Electronic devices
Emblems
Embroidery
Emergency first aid kits
Envelopes
Erasers
Exercise/fitness
Eyeglasses
Eyeglasses–3D
Fans
Figurines
Flags
Flashlights
Flasks
Flowers
Flying saucers

Flyswatters
Foam novelties
Folders
Food/beverages
Frames
Games
Gauges
Gavels
Gift baskets
Gift cards/wrap
Glass specialties
Globes
Gloves
Glow products
Goggles
Golf stuff
Greeting cards
Handkerchiefs
Hangers
Hardware tools
Headbands
Headphones
Headrests
Highlighters
Holders
Holograms
Horseshoes
Hotel amenities
Ice buckets
Ice packs
Ice scrapers
ID holders
Inflatables
Invitations
Jackets
Jars
Jewelry
Jewelry boxes
Kaleidoscopes
Kazoos
Key cases/tags
Key holders
Kitchen stuff
Kites
Labels
Lamps/lanterns
Lanyards
Lapel pins
Lawn/garden stuff
Leather specialties
Leis
Letter openers
License plates/frames
Lighters
Lights
Lint removers
Lip balm
Lipsticks

Liquid motion products
Locks
Luggage/tags
Lunch boxes/kits
Magnets
Magnifiers
Maps/atlases
Markers
Masks
Matches
Mats
Measuring devices
Medals
Medical information products
Megaphones
Membership cards
Memo cubes
Memo pads
Menus/menu covers
Metal specialties
Microphones
Miniatures
Mirrors
Money clips
Money converters
Mouse pads
Mugs
Musical specialties
Nameplates
Napkin rings
Napkins
Noisemakers
Office supplies
Openers
Organizers
Ornaments
Packaging
Pads
Pajamas
Pamphlets
Paper specialties
Paperweights
Party favors
Pedometers
Pen/pencil sets
Pepper mills
Pet stuff
Phone calling cards
Phones
Phone stuff
Photo cards
Photo cubes
Physical/therapeutic aids
Picnic coolers
Pictures/paintings
Pillows

Piñatas
Pins
Pitchers
Place mats
Planners
Plants
Plaques
Plates
Playing cards
Pointers
Poker chips
Portfolios
Postcards
Puppets
Purses
Puzzles/tricks
Radios
Rainwear
Recorders
Recycled products
Reflectors
Religious goods
Ribbons
Rubber stamps
Rulers
Safety products
Sandals
Scarves
Scissors
Scoops/scrapers
Scratch-off cards
Seals
Seats (folding)
Seeds
Sewing stuff
Shirts
Shoes/shoehorns
Shovels
Signs/displays
Slippers
Snow globes
Soap
Socks
Special packaging
Sponges
Spoons
Sports equipment
Sports memorabilia
Sports schedules
Squeegees
Stamp pads
Stamps
Staple removers
Staplers
Stationery/business forms
Stones
Stopwatches

Stress relievers
Stuffed animals
Sun catchers
Sun visors
Sunglasses
Sweaters
Tablecloths
Tags
Tape measures
Tattoos
Teapots
Telescopes
Thermometers
Tiaras/crowns
Ties
Tiles
Timers
Tins
Tissues
Toolkits
Toothbrushes
Tops/spinners
Toys/novelties
Travel stuff
Trays
Trophies/loving cups
T-shirts
Umbrellas
Uniforms
USB/flash drives
Utensils
Utility clips
Valuable paper holders
Vests
Vinyl plastic specialties
Voice recorders
Wallets
Wands/scepters
Watches
Watch fobs
Water
Weather instruments
Whistles
Wind socks
Wine stuff
Wood specialties
Wristbands
Wrist rests
Yo-yos
Zipper pulls

List provided by:
Advertising Specialty Institute

Managing assets: overview

Managing brand identity assets requires enlightened leadership and a long-term commitment to doing everything possible to build the brand. The mandate to build the brand must come from the top.

Brand is a living thing. It must be nurtured, attended to, and disciplined in order to survive and grow.

Bart Crosby
Crosby Associates

If management's commitment is tepid and the resources committed are minimal, the original investment will most likely deliver a dismal rate of return.

To the surprise of many clients, the brand identity process does not end after corporate letterhead and business cards are printed. This is when the work really begins. Because it takes quite a while to get to this point of visible accomplishment, many managers assume that the time, money, and energy spent thus far represent the majority of the investment. Wrong. This is just the beginning. Creating the brand identity was the easy part. Managing these assets well is harder.

Key initiatives

Conduct an internal launch.

Communicate with employees about the new brand identity.

Create standards and guidelines to ensure that all future applications adhere to the intention of the program.

Launch the new brand identity externally to key stakeholders.

Create accountability.

Identify those people who champion the brand.

Develop a checks-and-balances method to audit progress.

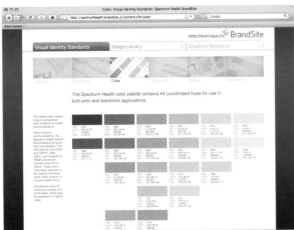

Spectrum Health in Grand Rapids, Michigan, distributed 15,000 new branding program overviews to its physicians and staff. The brand book encourages everyone to create an exceptional brand experience with all of the individuals and families that use Spectrum's healthcare facilities, its medical group, and health plan. Spectrum partnered with Crosby Associates to create the new brand identity system and tools, including an online brand center.

Spectrum Health: Crosby Associates

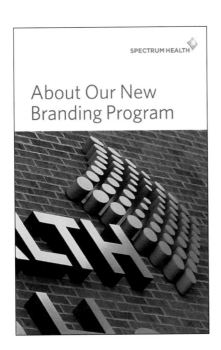

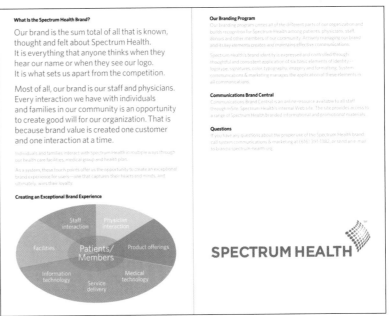

Changing brand identity

Rare is the person in an organization who embraces change. Introducing a new name and identity to an existing organization or to merged entities is exponentially more difficult than creating a brand for a new company. Changing brand identity means that whatever was on a manager's plate now doubles. The to-do list is extremely long, even in a small company. New brand identity implementation requires a vigilant strategic focus, advance planning, and obsession with detail.

Military mobilization skills come in handy, and boundless optimism helps. Typically, the director of marketing and public relations will oversee the change. In larger organizations an individual may be retained to focus exclusively on implementation. The skills required are knowledge of branding, public relations, communications, identity design, production, and organizational management.

Who needs to know?
What do they need to know?
Why do they need to know?
Does the change affect them?
How are they going to find out?
When are they going to find out?

Key pre-launch questions

Mutual of Omaha:
Crosby Associates

Biggest challenges

Developed by Patricia M. Baldridge, Vice President, Marketing and Public Relations, Philadelphia University

Time and money: planning enough advance time and an adequate budget

Deciding whether to go for a mega-launch or a phased-in launch

Internal buy-in and support

Keeping a strategic focus on all communications

Helping people make the connection from old to new

Honoring one's heritage while celebrating the new

Identifying the broadest list of stakeholders affected by the change

Helping people who have trouble with the change through a transition

Effectively communicating the essence of the brand within time and money constraints

Creating and maintaining message consistency

Reaching all audiences

Building excitement and understanding

Key beliefs

A strategic focus centers on the brand.

Brand identity can help to center a company on its mission.

A mega-launch means less chance for confusion and complications.

Clarity about key messages surrounding the launch is critical.

Go internal before you go external.

Once is never enough to communicate a new idea.

You need to sell a new name and build meaning.

Different audiences may require different messages.

Do whatever you can to keep the momentum going.

Recognize that an identity program is more than a new name or new logo.

Name change essentials

A sound reason for changing the name is the first and most critical step.

The change must have the potential to enhance, among others, the company's public perception, recognition, recruitment, customer relations, partnerships.

Accept the fact that there will be resistance.

Keep the momentum going by creating an air of excitement.

Targeted messages are better but cost more.

Applications affected by the new brand identity

Stationery, business cards, forms

Faxes, email signatures

Signage

Advertising

Website

Marketing materials

Uniforms, name tags

Customers, vendors, contractors

Directory listings

Voicemail, how you answer the phone

Managing brand identity change has the potential to enhance brand perception— by increasing awareness among constituencies, increasing preference, and building loyalty.

Patricia M. Baldridge
Vice President, Marketing and
Public Relations
Philadelphia University

Launching brand identity

Get ready. Get set. Launch. A launch represents a huge marketing opportunity. Smart organizations seize this chance to build brand awareness and synergy.

Different circumstances demand different launch strategies—from multimedia campaigns, company-wide meetings, and road tours, to a T-shirt for each employee. Some organizations execute massive visible change, including external signage and vehicles, virtually overnight, while others choose a phased approach.

Small organizations may not have the budget for a multimedia campaign. Smart organizations create a sales call opportunity to present a new card, or send a PDF announcement to each customer, colleague, and vendor. Others use existing marketing channels, such as inserting brochures with monthly statements.

In nearly every launch, the most important audience is a company's employees. Regardless of the scope and budget, a launch requires a comprehensive communications plan. Rarely is the best launch strategy no strategy, which is the business-as-usual or un-launch. Occasionally an organization may not want to draw attention from the financial community or its shareholders, so it may choose to do nothing.

The unveiling of a new brand identity is an emotional opportunity to energize employees around a new sense of purpose.

Rodney Abbot, Senior Partner
Lippincott

Sysmex: Lippincott

Photography: AHXUM Consulting

Strategic launch goals

Increase brand awareness and understanding among all stakeholders, including the general public.

Increase preference for the company, products, and services.

Build loyalty for the company.

Promote the new identity as a brand.

Create an emotional connection with stakeholders.

Positively influence your constituents' choices and/or behavior.

Comprehensive plan elements

Goals and objectives of the new brand identity

Communications activities supporting brand implementation

Timeline for implementation and budget

The way identity is aligned with company goals

The way identity is aligned with research

Target audiences

Key messages

Communications strategies, including internal communications, public relations, advertising, and direct marketing

Internal training strategy for employees

Standards and guidelines strategy

Methods

Organization-wide meetings

Press releases

Special events

Q & A hotline on website

Script of consistent messages

Print, radio, TV ads

Trade publications

Direct mail

Website launch

External launch basics

Timing is everything. Find the window.

Create consistent messages.

Target messages.

Create the right media mix.

Leverage public relations, marketing, and customer service.

Make sure your sales force knows the launch strategy.

Be customer-focused.

Schedule a lot of advance time.

Seize every opportunity to garner marketing synergy.

Tell them, tell them again, and then tell them again.

Internal launch basics

Make a moment. Create a buzz.

Communicate why this is important.

Reiterate what the brand stands for.

Tell employees why you did it.

Communicate what it means.

Talk about future goals and mission.

Review identity basics: meaning, sustainability.

Convey that this is a top-down initiative.

Make employees brand champions and ambassadors.

Show concrete examples of how employees can live the brand.

Give employees a sense of ownership.

Give something tangible, such as a card or a T-shirt.

Building brand champions

Engaging employees in the meaning of the brand and the thinking behind it is one of the best investments that a company can make. Organizational development consultants have long known that long-term success is directly influenced by the way employees share in their company's culture—its values, stories, symbols, and heroes. Traditionally the CEO and the marketing department were the most visible brand champions—individuals who understood and could articulate a company's core values, vision, and brand essence.

Companies all around the world are beginning to develop compelling ways of sharing the brand essence—from road shows, to online branding tools and guides, to special events. What was once a standards and guidelines toolkit for creative firms has evolved into a brand-building tool for all employees.

It's not just values. It's the extensive sharing of them that makes a difference.

Terrence Deal and Allan Kennedy
Corporate Cultures: The Rites and Rituals of Corporate Life

ARAMARK "Starman":
Interbrand

ARAMARK and the road show

Public companies routinely use road shows to bring their messages directly to key investors and analysts. Road shows are also an effective tactic for launching brand initiatives. ARAMARK chairman and CEO Joe Neubauer traveled to seven cities to speak to 5,000 frontline managers to launch his company's new brand and to align employees with the vision of the company. "If employees are excited and mobilized, then more than half the branding battle has been won," said Bruce Berkowitz, former director of advertising for ARAMARK. "Employees carry the company's culture and character into the marketplace."

ARAMARK worked with a meeting planning company to produce a one-hour road show. The show included a skit performed by Broadway actors and a multimedia presentation of the political, cultural, and economic milestones that gave a context for the company's metamorphosis. Neubauer reinforced key messages about the company's heritage and its leadership in the industry. His overarching message, "Employees are the heart of our success and convey our company's top-tier delivery of services," was supported by a new brandmark. Designed by the Schechter Group (now part of Interbrand), the mark embodies the star quality of the employees and supports the new brand promise of "managed services, managed better."

Managers were fully prepped on the new brand vision and strategy. They received an "Ambassador's Kit" that contained a company history, copies of the new advertising campaign, a merchandise catalog, and a graphic standards manual. In addition, the materials included a manager's checklist and a media launch schedule with explicit instructions on how to handle the launch, how to explain it to staff members, and how to implement the brand identity change. The CEO's presence and passion combined with accessible brand-building tools were a powerful combination that fueled ARAMARK's growth.

WGBH mission statement and video

The mission statement of WGBH, the Boston affiliate of the Public Broadcasting System (PBS), can easily be found on its website and is frequently seen in the signature block of employee email. It reads as follows: "WGBH enriches people's lives through programs and services that educate, inspire, and entertain, fostering citizenship and culture, the joy of learning, and the power of diverse perspectives."

A prominent and easily accessible mission statement is a simple tool that creates a sense of purpose and keeps employees focused on the vision. On the website, the mission statement is followed by a list of commitments that present the unified values of WGBH. In the "About Us" section, a QuickTime video describes the station as a window on the world and a storyteller to the nation, and cites its commitment to lifelong learning. When internal messages are aligned with external expression, the brand synergy created is evident and the result is profound.

Jenner & Block

Smart companies communicate about the brand to each employee. Crosby Associates designed a high-quality brochure for Jenner & Block that communicates the firm's mission and values, and displays how the brand is expressed through a variety of marketing communication channels.

The Little Red Book

In 1981, Scandinavian Airlines Group (SAS) distributed a small book to 20,000 employees. The purpose of the book was to simply and succinctly communicate the vision and strategy of the company at a time of organizational change. The book, well written and designed, not only informed the employees, but also inspired them to work toward the same goals.

Internal design teams

Internal design teams are the unsung heroes who work across organizational silos to build the brand and help design the customer experience, one touchpoint at a time. Increasingly, experienced design directors are joining senior management teams to oversee and build the brand, manage the design group, and identify specialists needed. Companies that value design as a core competency tend to be more successful in their marketing and communications.

Brand identity programs are usually developed by outside firms who have the right qualifications, experience, time, and staffing. The biggest mistake that external consulting firms and companies make is not including the internal

design group in the initial research phase. The internal group has insight into the challenge of making things happen. In addition, successful implementation of the program is dependent on the internal group embracing and implementing the system. The best companies have a roll-out program to ensure that all stakeholders across the company understand the parameters and rationale for the new brand identity. The internal team must have ongoing access to the external firm for questions, clarifications, and unforeseen circumstances. The external firm should come in for periodic reviews of new work, as well as participate in annual brand audits to ensure that brand expression remains fresh and relevant to the customer and prospect.

Internal creative teams need to seize their insider advantage by using deep knowledge of the brand to leverage their strategic value to the corporation.

Moira Cullen, Senior Director, Global Design
The Hershey Company

Act like an agency. Commit to excellence and innovation. Be entrepreneurial and market yourselves.

Lynn Whittemore
Design Director
HealthInk

The design team's level of growth is based on their ability to share knowledge through well-defined standards, training, and communication.

Emily Cohen
and Jen Miller
Cohen Miller Consulting

WGBH recognized that design needed to be a function that reported directly to the CEO.

Chris Pullman
Vice President of Design
WGBH

Characteristics and challenges

Essential characteristics

Managed by a creative or design director

Valued by senior management

Staffed by experienced designers (creative and technical expertise)

Multifunctional (experience across all media)

Multilevel experience (senior level and junior level)

Clearly defined roles and responsibilities

Clearly defined processes and procedures

Commitment to brand identity standards

Ability to be creative within a system

Ability to explain the rationale behind solutions

Open channels of communication with senior management and within the group

Systems to track progress and projects

Biggest challenges

Lack of clarity about the brand

Overcoming political hurdles

Getting access to senior management

Getting management's respect

Overcoming design-by-committee

Debunking the myth that high quality means high cost

Not being at the table when critical branding decisions are being made

Too much work for too small a staff

Organizational maturity level brand leadership
Model developed by Cohen Miller Consulting

Design groups within organizations often operate at and grow to different levels of maturity depending on the needs of their internal clients as well as their own internal capabilities.

Internal design department drives company priorities and brand vision, and leads development of brand standards. Brand standards are regularly updated and audited for usability. Brand adherence is measured.

Brand builders

Internal design team collaborates with external agency in brand development, and serves as primary counsel to executive team and clients in developing branding initiatives. Team includes dedicated brand ambassador role.

Innovators

External agency develops brand standards. Internal design department helps set company priorities and leads efforts based on brand knowledge. Creative directors monitor brand adherence.

Strategists

Internal design department designs and executes against brand standards, measures effectiveness, and adds value through best practices.

Advisors

Internal design department executes brand vision at request of business and against available brand standards. Standards are often outdated or lacking and adherence is informal.

Service providers

Brand books

Brand books, spirit books, and thought books inspire, educate, and build brand awareness. Brand strategy can't influence anyone if it stays in a conference room, in someone's head, or on page 3 of a marketing plan. The vision of a company and the meaning of a brand need a communications vehicle that is accessible, portable, and personal. Online brand sites are more frequently publishing "Who we are" and "What our brand stands for," in addition to standards, templates, and guidelines.

Timing is everything. Companies in the midst of organizational change need to convey "where the ship is going." Frequently, the brand identity process sparks a new clarity about the brand. Building awareness about how each employee can help build the brand is smart.

A spirit book is a compelling way to express the essence of a brand.

Ken Carbone, Principal
Carbone Smolan Agency

Superman

DC comics hired Little & Co. to design a brand book for licensees, retailers, and buyers to articulate the brand and to stimulate licensing opportunities.

Mutual of Omaha

Mutual of Omaha disseminated a poster designed by Crosby Associates to each employee that announced the revitalized brand identity and engaged everyone to take part in building the brand.

NIZUC brand book

NIZUC is an ultra luxury resort and complex of private residences located on Mexico's Yucatan peninsula. Alan Becker, the developer, brought in Carbone Smolan to create a unique brand platform prior to any architecture or building. The brand book expressed his vision and the brand promise, and helped Becker attract partners.

NIZUC: Carbone Smolan

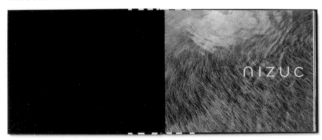

Standards content

Designing, specifying, ordering, and printing or fabricating elements of a new brand identity system are all dependent on a set of intelligent standards and guidelines. Good solid standards save time, money, and frustration. The size and nature of an organization affect the depth and breadth of the content and how marketing materials are conceived and produced in the future.

Following is an in-depth composite that can be used as a reference for building an outline. Usually printing and fabrication specifications accompany design specifications. Legal and nomenclature guideline considerations are essential. Some guidelines include order forms for business cards and other applications.

Kort & Godt online identity guide: Kontrapunkt

Contents

Standards + guidelines

Managing the consistency and integrity of a brand identity system is facilitated by intelligent standards and guidelines that are easily accessible to all internal and external partners who have the responsibility to communicate about the brand. Brand identity guidelines have become more accessible, dynamic, and easier to produce. The range of formats includes online standards, CDs, posters, fact sheets, PDFs, brochures, and binders. Now even the smallest nonprofit can provide streamlined standards, reproduction files, and electronic templates.

Building a brand is progressively viewed as the shared responsibility of each and every employee. Adhering to the guidelines requires discipline and vigilance. More importantly, it saves money, time, and frustration, and helps build the brand. The best branding tools communicate, "What does the brand stand for," in addition to providing brand identity information.

Adhering to the guidelines must unequivocally be a top-down priority.

Blake Deutsch

Who needs to understand what the brand stands for?

Everyone

Who needs access to guidelines?

Internal employees	External creative partners
Management	Branding firms
Marketing	Design firms
Communications	Advertising agencies
Design	Information architects
Legal	Technologists
Sales	Packaging design firms
Web gurus	Architects
Human Resources	Writers
PR	Co-branding partners
Product designers	
Anyone creating a presentation	
Customer service	

Types of standards

Online branding sites

The web has made it easy to consolidate brand management in one place, giving employees and vendors user-friendly tools and resources.

Marketing and sales toolkits

Companies that have independent distributors and dealerships need effective ways to control the look and feel at the point of sale. VSA Partners has created standards and marketing resources for Harley-Davidson that help independent dealerships achieve a distinctive and memorable retail presence through their exterior signage, retail displays, and advertising.

Identity standards manuals

Small companies produce limited-edition manuals using laser printers. The binder format allows changes to be made by replacing or adding pages. A CD that carries reproduction files and templates is placed in the back.

CDs

The CD, with its large storage capacity and portable format, is a great solution for those companies that cannot yet justify putting their standards online. Many companies are putting standards into a PDF format on a CD.

Media relations portals

Many corporations have downloadable logo files in the media relations section of their websites. These files are often accompanied by extensive legalese that outlines usage.

Online resources can help build brands
Developed by Monigle Associates

Communicate brand strategies and objectives

Provide help and best practices as opposed to rules (tools, not rules)

Save users time

Provide resources people need to participate in the brand-building process

Pull together often disparate subjects into one online resource center

Track user activity to help support future investments

Can reengineer many costly processes, reducing cost from strategy to implementation

Build consistent implementation

Demystify brand and identity systems

Characteristics of the best standards and guidelines

Are clear and easy to understand

Have content that is current and easy to apply

Provide accurate information

Include "what the brand stands for"

Talk about meaning of the identity

Balance consistency with flexibility

Are accessible to internal and external users

Build brand awareness

Consolidate all necessary files, templates, and guidelines

Promise positive return on investment contribution

Provide point person for questions

Capture the spirit of the program

Feature prototypes (best-in-class examples)

Online branding tools

The web has transformed brand management, consolidating brand assets and establishing 24/7 access to user-friendly guidelines, tools, and templates. Scalable, modular sites are always current, evolving as a company grows. Many sites feature brand vision and attributes, helping to build a shared vocabulary. Robust sites support strategic marketing, consistent communications, and quality execution. Initially envisioned to house logos and image libraries, sites now encompass brand strategy, content development guidelines, and web resources.

Creative firms and external vendors are assigned passwords to access key messages, logos, image libraries, glossaries, intellectual property compliance, and a panoply of smart resources and content. Sites may also be used for online ordering and transactions. Access to certain sections may be limited to user groups. The success of online branding tools is easily monitored through usage statistics. Additionally site monitoring tools are now validating the significant ROI results often realized using these tools.

Our brand center was integral to the successful launch of the Western Union global yes! campaign.

Gail Galuppo, Executive Vice President and Chief Marketing Officer
Western Union

Western Union is a global company, with employees and agents across 200 countries and territories. Having a centralized 'brand center' accessible through the web ensures that our teams—whether in Paris, Hong Kong, or Mumbai—have access to our brand guidelines and full library of marketing materials

Gail Galuppo
Executive Vice President
and Chief Marketing Officer
Western Union

PROCESS: ONLINE BRANDING SITE*

> Initiate plan	> Build groundwork	> Launch project	> Prepare content	> Design and program
Determine goals.	Review status of assets and standards.	Conduct launch meeting. Develop:	Determine author and status of content.	Identify interface and navigation style.
Identify brand management problems and issues.	Determine content approval process.	Site architecture map and functionality.	Set editorial style guidelines.	Develop and approve site interface.
Identify user groups and profiles.	Prioritize content and functionality.	Project online workroom Timeline and preliminary launch plan.	Develop content update plan if needed.	Initiate programming based on site map.
Identify stakeholders.	Research development options: internal and external.	User groups and user lists. Access and security plans.	Determine content file formatting and exchange requirements.	Develop system functionality.
Create project team and appoint leader.	Develop preliminary budget and timeline.	Determine IT requirements and hosting plan.	Secure final approval of content.	
Develop team roles, rules, and protocol.	Select site development resource.	Identify brand assets and cataloging scheme.		
		Define ROI measurements.		

*Developed by Monigle Associates

Characteristics of the best online sites

Educational, user-friendly. and efficient

Accessible to internal and external users

Build brand engagement

Consolidate brand management in one place

Scalable and modular

Offer positive return on investment contribution

Database-driven, not PDF-driven

Provide resources: signatures, templates, image library

Always current: new content and functions can be added to improve implementation of the brand

Build transactional elements into the site

Flexible in hosting and ongoing maintenance

Provide more rather than less information and resources

Content guidelines

Write concisely. Less is more

Outline carefully to create a logical order of information

Know the culture, and write accordingly

Use commonly understood terminology; do not use unnecessary "brand speak"

Provide examples and illustrations

Support site navigation

Don't underestimate the implementation and sustainability of your brand.

Mike Reinhardt
Monigle Associates

Western Union online branding site: Monigle Associates

> **Develop database**

Populate database with content and assets.

Program links and required functions.

Edit content and design by core team.

> **Prototype and test**

Core team reviews beta site.

Users test beta site.

Make modifications as necessary.

Approve site launch.

> **Launch**

Finalize launch plan.

Create communications and buzz.

Promote site launch.

Appoint brand champions.

Conduct special training sessions.

> **Monitor success**

Develop maintenance plan.

Assign administrator.

Assess usage trends and user reports.

Identify content updates and process.

Integrate technology and functional advances.

Assign budget for management and upgrades.

Define and measure impact.

Communicate successes.

Reproduction files

Maintaining the quality of reproduction in a world where tools are continually changing is an ongoing challenge. Users have urgent needs, different levels of proficiency, various software platforms, and a disparate understanding of digital files, color, and quality. An asset management system needs to be diligent about naming, organization, storage, retrieval, and overall usability of file formats.

The designer's responsibilities are to test all files in numerous formats and to develop a retrievable system that is logical and sustainable. The manager's responsibility is to determine who has access to files and how best to field all requests. It is no longer unusual to download logo files and images from a website's media portal. Clear legal guidelines, forms, and contact information help protect the assets.

You can't always get what you want, but if you try sometimes you might find, you get what you need.

The Rolling Stones

Finding your way around reproduction files

What type of image is it?

Is it a photographic image with continuous tones or is it a graphic image with solid color, crisp edges, and line art?

How is it going to be reproduced?

Professional printing, office printing, and screen display have different file requirements. Some documents may be viewed on screen or printed out.

What color space is needed?

Color information is included in a file and interpreted by the output device.

Professional printing techniques use spot color inks (such as Pantone®) or four-color process inks, which builds color out of cyan, magenta, yellow, and black (CMYK). Color inkjet or laser printers use CMYK toner.

Screens display color with red, blue, and green points of light (RGB). Hex numbers designate RGB colors for HTML code.

What program is being used?

It is important to know the program being used to ensure compatibility and to facilitate use of vector artwork whenever possible.

I can't open it!

Unless you are going to modify the artwork in a design program, image files should be inserted or placed, not opened.

I can't find it!

Files should be named as concisely and informatively as possible so they can be understood at a glance. Consistency is imperative for grouping common attributes and distinguishing unique ones.

File format basics

Vector graphics

Vector graphics are hard-edged images created in a drawing program. Because they are based on mathematically defined lines and curves, they can be manipulated and scaled without losing reproduction quality.

EPS *Encapsulated PostScript*

Vector graphics created in a drawing program are saved or exported as EPS files so that they can be placed into other applications.

The highest-quality output for graphic images with hard edges.

Printers must have Adobe® PostScript®.

When vector graphics are saved as TIF, JPG, or other bitmap file format, the hard-edged lines and curves are converted to pixels.

EPS files created in Adobe Photoshop® are bitmap images and will lose clarity when scaled or printed.

Raster or bitmap images

Raster or bitmap images are continuous-tone images that are constructed as a continuous mapping of pixels. These images cannot be scaled, rotated, or skewed outside of an image-editing application without the loss of reproduction quality.

TIF

Tag Image File Format

Highest-quality output for photographic images

Best bitmap version of hard-edged graphics—alternative to EPS when an Adobe® PostScript® printer is unavailable

Convenient for exchanging image files between computer platforms

JPG

Joint Photographic Experts Group

Compressed file format for on-screen viewing of continuous-tone photographs

Compression adds "artifacts" and smears text, lines, and edges

Not suitable for printing

GIF

Graphics Interchange Format

Compressed file format for on-screen viewing of graphics and images in HTML

Not suitable for printing

PNG

Portable Network Graphic

These are just a few of the most widely used formats.

File Format Matrix		Photographic images with continuous tone	Graphic images with hard edges
Printing	**Design software** Adobe Illustrator®, Macromedia Freehand®, CorelDRAW®, QuarkXpress®, Adobe InDesign®	TIF (PNG)	EPS
	Office software Microsoft Word®, Microsoft Excel®	TIF	TIF (PNG) Converts vector graphics to bitmap image
Screen	**Design software** Adobe ImageReady®, among others	JPG	GIF (PNG, TIF)
	Office software PowerPoint®	JPG	TIF (PNG)

Resolution

The resolution of digital imagery is measured in pixels per inch (ppi), the digital equivalent of dots per inch (dpi). The end use of the image is critical for determining the optimum resolution.

For printing, the higher the resolution the more detail and clarity there is to the image, and the larger the file is in terms of memory. Offset printing typically requires 300 ppi resolution.

For screen display, the pixels in the image map directly to the pixels on the screen. Images for screen display should be 72 ppi (Mac) or 96 ppi (PC), but the physical dimensions will be affected by the resolution of the display itself.

File naming conventions

File names should have no more than fifteen characters plus a three-letter file extension (.eps, .jpg, .gif, .doc) indicating what type of file it is.

Do not use uppercase, spaces, or special characters, such as "\ / : * < > ? ¦. Use a period only before the file extension suffix.

Create a system for organizing and identifying those variations of the artwork that are required for different applications, such as signature, color, subbrand entity, and file format.

Global metrics

In the early 1970s, most major countries, with the exception of the United States, adopted the metric system. The metric system is a decimal system of units based on the meter as the international standard unit of length. The meter is approximately equivalent to 39.37 inches. The benefit of the metric system is that it is more convenient and easier to calculate. Never assume that any U.S. company uses a standard size in their foreign branches until you have conducted a comprehensive audit.

Conversion formulas

to convert	multiply by
inches to centimeters	2.540
centimeters to inches	.394
inches to millimeters	25.400
millimeters to inches	.039
feet to meters	.305
meters to feet	3.281

Points and picas

12 points = 1 pica	
72 points = 1 inch	
6 picas = 1 inch	

Never assume that American standards hold true in other countries. Research, research, research.

Steff Geissbuhler, Partner
C&G Partners

Most business cards around the world are a universal size, the same as a credit card, easy to fit in your wallet.

Radio Free Europe/Radio Liberty broadcasts across 5 continents and 20 countries and in 28 languages, none of which are English.

Steff Geissbuhler
Partner
C&G Partners

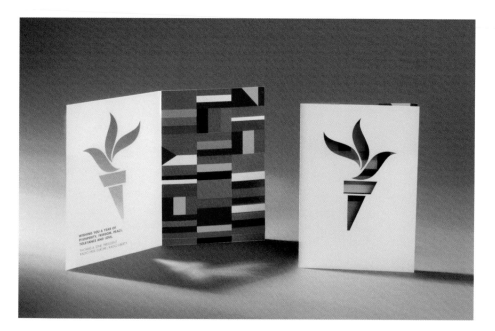

Metric business correspondence

A series

	mm	inches
A0	841 x 1189 (area=1m^2)	33^1/$_8$ x 46^3/$_4$
A1	594 x 841	23^3/$_8$ x 33^1/$_8$
A2	420 x 594	16^1/$_2$ x 33^1/$_8$
A3	297 x 420	11^3/$_4$ x 16^1/$_2$
A4	210 x 297	8^1/$_4$ x 11^3/$_4$
A5	148 x 210	5^7/$_8$ x 8^1/$_4$
A6	105 x 148	4^1/$_8$ x 5^7/$_8$
A7	74 x 105	2^7/$_8$ x 4^1/$_8$
A8	52 x 74	2 x 2^7/$_8$
A9	37 x 52	1^1/$_2$ x 2
A10	26 x 37	1 x 1^1/$_2$

B series

B0	1000 x 1414	39^3/$_8$ x 55^5/$_8$
B1	707 x 1000	27^7/$_8$ x 39^3/$_8$
B2	500 x 707	19^5/$_8$ x 27^7/$_8$
B3	353 x 500	12^7/$_8$ x 19^5/$_8$
B4	250 x 353	9^7/$_8$ x 12^7/$_8$
B5	176 x 250	7 x 9^7/$_8$
B6	125 x 176	5 x 7
B7	88 x 125	3^1/$_2$ x 5
B8	62 x 88	2^1/$_2$ x 3^1/$_2$
B9	44 x 62	1^3/$_4$ x 2^1/$_2$
B10	31 x 44	1^1/$_4$ x 1^3/$_4$

RA and SRA sizes for printing

RA sheets allow for extra trim
SRA sheets allow for extra trim and bleed

R A0	860 x 120	33^7/$_8$ x 48^1/$_8$
R A1	610 x 860	24^1/$_8$ x 33^7/$_8$
R A2	430 x 610	17 x 24^1/$_8$
R A3	305 x 430	12 x 17
R A4	215 x 305	8^1/$_2$ x 12
SR A0	900 x 1280	35^1/$_2$ x 50^3/$_8$
SR A1	640 x 900	25^1/$_4$ x 35^1/$_2$
SR A2	450 x 640	17^7/$_8$ x 25^1/$_4$
SR A3	320 x 450	12^5/$_8$ x 17^3/$_4$
SR A4	225 x 320	8^7/$_8$ x 12^5/$_8$

Metric C series envelopes

C0	917 x 1297	36^1/$_8$ x 51^1/$_{16}$
C1	648 x 917	25^1/$_2$ x 36^1/$_8$
C2	458 x 648	18^1/$_{16}$ x 33^1/$_8$
C3	324 x 458	12^3/$_4$ x 18^1/$_{16}$
C4	229 x 324	9 x 12^3/$_4$
C5	162 x 229	6^3/$_8$ x 9
C6	114 x 162	4^1/$_2$ x 6^3/$_8$
C7	81 x 114	3^3/$_{16}$ x 4^1/$_2$

Metric special-size envelopes

DL	110 x 220	4^5/$_{16}$ x 8^5/$_8$
C6/5	114 x 229	4^1/$_2$ x 9
C7/6	81 x 162	3^3/$_{16}$ x 6^3/$_8$

United States business correspondence

U.S. commercial envelopes

	inches	mm
6^1/$_4$	3^1/$_2$ x 6	89 x 152
6^3/$_4$	3^5/$_8$ x 6^1/$_2$	92 x 165
8^5/$_8$	3^5/$_8$ x 8^5/$_8$	92 x 220
7	3^3/$_4$ 3 6^3/$_4$	95 x 171
Monarch (7^3/$_4$)	3^7/$_8$ x 7^1/$_2$	98 x 190
9	3^7/$_8$ x 8^7/$_8$	98 x 225
10	4^1/$_8$ x 9^1/$_2$	105 x 241
11	4^1/$_2$ x 10^3/$_8$	114 x 264
12	4^3/$_4$ x 11	121 x 279
14	5 x 11^1/$_2$	127 x 292

U.S. A-style envelopes

A-2	4^3/$_8$ x 5^3/$_4$	111 x 146
A-6	4^3/$_4$ x 6^1/$_2$	121 x 165
A-7	5^1/$_4$ x 7^1/$_4$	133 x 184
A-8	5^1/$_2$ x 8^1/$_8$	140 x 206
A-long	3^7/$_8$ x 8^7/$_8$	98 x 225
A-10	6 x 9^1/$_2$	152 x 241

Research compiled by
Steff Geissbuhler, Partner,
C&G Partners

Extraordinary work is done for extraordinary clients.
Milton Glaser
Designer

3 Best Practices

Part 3 showcases best practices.
Local and global, public and private,
these highly successful projects
created by branding firms and design
consultancies inspire and exemplify
original, flexible, lasting solutions.

Case studies

The American Civil Liberties Union (ACLU) works to defend the Bill of Rights, mounting court challenges to preserve racial justice, human rights, religious freedom, privacy, and free speech.

Founded in 1920, the ACLU is a nonprofit, nonpartisan organization with 400,000 members and supporters. The national organization and its fifty state affiliates work in the courts, legislatures, and communities, handling 6,000 court cases a year. The ACLU is supported by dues, contributions, and grants.

Goals

Create a unified image for the entire organization.

Develop an integrated, sustainable, and meaningful identity system.

Connect the organization to ideas and ideals.

Differentiate from other public advocacy groups.

Communicate stature and stability.

Facilitate consistent communications.

We have to be one.
Anthony Romero
Executive Director
ACLU

We wanted to help the ACLU look like the guardians of freedom.
Sylvia Harris
Design strategist

Process and strategy: The ACLU set out to reach a broader constituency and build membership, and asked Fo Wilson Group to customize a team to build a unified, meaningful identity. The Fo Wilson Group, a design consultancy, was joined by Sylvia Harris, an information design strategist, and Michael Hirschhorn, an organizational dynamics expert. In the audit, the team found more than fifty logos. Every state affiliate had its own logo, website design, and architecture, with little connection to the national organization. Other advocacy organizations were studied, and Harris found that the "ACLU represents a set of principles, while most other advocacy groups represent a constituency." The team interviewed a wide range of stakeholders, including affiliates, communications staff, and members. The most frequently mentioned attribute that defined the ACLU was "principled," followed by "justice" and "guardian." A survey conducted in 2000 by Belden, Russonello & Stewart found that "over 8 out of 10 Americans (85%) had heard of the ACLU." The team realized that the ACLU identity needed to be recognized in a wide variety of arenas, from town halls to courtrooms and campuses.

Creative solution: The design directive was to capitalize on a highly recognizable acronym, and to connect ACLU principles and the spirit of freedom to the acronym. Fo Wilson Group designed a series of signatures with a contemporary logotype and expressive symbolism. Several options were tested for the modular system that used patriotic imagery. During the audit, the team found that the ACLU's original symbol from the 1930s was the Statue of Liberty, and it had been dropped in the 1980s. The Statue of Liberty tested the best, and although other advocacy groups used the symbol, the ACLU decided to return to its legacy and history. A unique photographic perspective of the statue's face was stylized, and a photographic signature was adopted to work in the digital environment. A range of applications demonstrated how the system worked, from website architecture to newsletters and membership cards. The flexible system needed to work for the national office, the affiliates, the foundations, and special projects.

Results: ACLU's leadership group championed the identity initiative from the early planning through the analysis, decision making, and roll out. The identity team conducted a series of phone conference presentations to roll out the new program with the affiliates. Educational programs for staff were conducted at the headquarters. The group was instrumental in getting forty-nine of the fifty affiliates to adopt the new identity system. The national organization paid to have new letterhead printed for the affiliates. Opto Design was retained to finalize the design system, produce all the preliminary applications, and develop an ACLU Identity Guidelines website. Membership has increased to its highest rate in its eighty-five year history, the budget has doubled, and the national staff has increased by 75%.

Although the ACLU had historically been strong in media relations, communications was a new function that was needed.

Emily Tyne
Communications Director
ACLU

With a complex national organizational model such as ACLU, it is important to strategize thoughtfully how to gather input, test out ideas, and roll out new plans across the 50+ offices nationally.

Michael Hirschhorn
Organizational dynamics expert

National identity

Affiliate identity

Foundation identity

Amazon.com seeks to be the world's most customer-centric company, the place where people discover anything they want to buy online.*

Originally an online bookstore, Amazon.com is positioned as the "web's biggest retail store," selling music, software, toys, tools, electronics, fashion, and housewares. Founded in 1994, the company has 30 million customers and ships to 150 countries.

Goals

Create a unique and proprietary identity.

Maintain the brand equity of the original identity.

Position Amazon.com as customer-focused and friendly.

Modify the core identity for global domains.

*Jeff Bezos
Founder and CEO
Amazon.com

Why did you name your company Amazon?

Earth's biggest river. Earth's biggest selection.

Jeff Bezos
Founder and CEO
Amazon.com

Process and strategy: In 1999 Amazon.com retained Turner Duckworth to redesign its brand identity. Amazon.com's positioning as a customer-focused, friendly company was the core of its mission and values. The challenge was to create a unique and proprietary identity that maintained what Amazon.com believed were its brand equities: lowercase type in the logo, and an orange swoosh underneath the name. Turner Duckworth immersed itself in the brand, spent a lot of time on the website, and examined competitor sites. The firm also analyzed what makes a logo effective or ineffective on the web. "Our goal was to infuse personality into the logo, and to create a compelling idea that would convey the brand message," said David Turner, head of design.

Creative solution: The design team developed distinct visual strategies at the first stage; each one emphasized a different aspect of the positioning brief. The final logo design was an evolutionary leap from the old logo. The central idea behind the new logo reflected the client's business strategy of selling more than just books. The design team connected the initial *a* of "amazon" to the *z*. This approach clearly communicated "Amazon.com sells everything from A to Z." The graphic device that connects the *a* and the *z* also speaks to the brand positioning: customer

focus and friendly service. This device forms a cheeky smile with a dimple that pushes up the *z*. The brown shipper box packaging was considered at every stage of the logo design.

Turner Duckworth designed custom lettering for the wordmark and made the "amazon" more prominent than the ".com." The typography was designed to give the logo a friendlier and unique look. The design team also designed a full alphabet so that Amazon.com could update its international domains, currently in the United Kingdom, Germany, France, and Japan. The project was completed in eight weeks.

Results: Jeff Bezos, the CEO, founder, and visionary, was involved at every presentation and was the key decision maker. Amazon.com had determined that it would execute a "soft launch" of the new identity. The new brand identity was not announced to the press or highlighted on its website. Sensitive to the perceptions of customers and Wall Street analysts, the company felt it was important that Amazon.com did not appear to be a "different" company.

In 2005 Amazon was named the fourth fastest growing brand in the world, with a 35% compounded growth rate in brand value between 2001 and 2005, according to *Brand Republic*.

Access to the key decision maker, and in particular to the visionary of a company, certainly makes our work easier. Not only does it accelerate the feedback, development and approval processes, but it also allows us to ask questions of the visionary and hear unedited answers.

Joanne Chan
Head of Client Services
Turner Duckworth

Apotek wants to be your local health center. We offer an independent, professional, and highly professional service.

The Association of Danish Pharmacies has state-regulated and independently operated pharmacies that provide cost-controlled prescription medication, as well as health information for the citizens of Denmark. As of 2009, there are 449 pharmacies, which operate as independent business entities.

Goals

Create a unified, simple, flexible design program for the pharmacy of the future.

Use design to improve the user experience.

Differentiate from commercial competition.

Establish a clear brand.

Remain true to the heritage.

We recognize that design is central to long-term strategic changes.
Gitte Nørregaard
Marketing Coordinator
Association of Danish Pharmacies

Process and strategy: The Association of Danish Pharmacies' directive was to rethink and design the identity of the pharmacy of the future. Kontrapunkt's multidisciplinary team interviewed a number of pharmacists about their vision and strategies for the future, and conducted ethnographic studies of the role of pharmacies in people's lives. Consumer psychologists and designers observed users inside pharmacies to examine their experience. Due to their long history, these pharmacies are not perceived entirely as commercial entities but more as cultural institutions. Kontrapunkt and the Association determined that true differentiation and brand value would be achieved if the pharmacies were perceived as more than a purveyor of pharmaceuticals. Kontrapunkt's strategy was to change the pharmacy experience from being about illness to being about health.

Creative solution: The new strategy led to an intensive design phase, and a brand personality guided by the attributes of noncommercial, scientific, precise, and calm. Apotek means pharmacy in Danish; Kontrapunkt decided to let the name stand alone as a wordmark. The brand architecture needed to accommodate the master brand as well as the local pharmacy location. Pharma, a modern and highly legible typeface, was designed

by Kontrapunkt, for all consumer touchpoints from signage to advertising. The brand's color palette was limited to black and white, and used an orange-red highlight for important information. One of the biggest system challenges was that many of the pharmacies were housed in buildings of significant cultural heritage. Signage in Denmark is heavily restricted; it was critical to preserve architectural integrity and achieve a degree of consistency. The system created a cohesive brand image across multiple touchpoints including print, digital, media, and signage. Guidelines and digital design templates were developed and distributed.

Results: The new brand image puts the focus on health maintenance and the health of Denmark's citizens. It dramatically differentiates Apotek from its commercial competitors, and strives to position the pharmacies as the preferred health center. From the pharmacies' perspective, this system establishes a brand promise and common direction; it reduces the conflicts between being a public health system and being a retailer of health products. This strengthened the union amongst the pharmacists and also gave customers a better use experience. The design program was voluntary; by early 2009, 80% of Apotek's pharmacies had signed up for the program.

Prescription envelope

The successful initial public offering marked a new beginning for Assurant. The company is focused on being a premier provider of specialized insurance products and related services.

Assurant provides specialty insurance and insurance-related services through its four key businesses: Assurant Employee Benefits; Assurant Health; Assurant Solutions; and Assurant Specialty Property. After operating as the North American independent arm of Fortis Insurance N.V. for twenty-five years, the company changed its name in connection with its initial public offering in 2004.

Goals

Design a new brand identity.

Collaborate with the in-house creative team.

Create an ad campaign to launch a new name and brand identity.

ASSURANT®

Our name and logo may have changed, but our strategy and values have not.

J. Kerry Clayton
President and CEO
Assurant

Process and strategy: Assurant formed a brand leadership council that worked closely with the president and the CEOs of the individual companies. This council provided strategic leadership, research, and direction to the Carbone Smolan Agency about brand aspirations and structure. The new brand needed to send a strong signal to the business and investment community and distance itself from its parent, Fortis, a Belgo-Dutch multinational corporation.

The identity was to be the first tangible representation of the company and had to be completed in a very compressed time frame. Carbone Smolan Agency conducted an intensive, "rapid response" creative session to get stakeholders to agree quickly about how best to represent the brand visually.

Creative solution: Assurant's new logo design consists of three brightly colored and tightly woven bands, which symbolize the integration of the three core strengths of the company: highly disciplined risk management expertise, customized technology, and long-term client partner-

ships. The ad campaign, with its theme of "bringing clarity to complexity," was visually rendered by using dynamic photographs of common objects that are simple demonstrations of complex laws of physics, such as a yo-yo for gravity. These objects were colored in the Assurant palette to strengthen their visual connection to the new brand identity.

Results: Assurant launched a national advertising campaign to promote its new name and brand identity in national media, including *The Wall Street Journal.* Carbone Smolan Agency created the fundamental brand identity tools and trained Assurant's internal creative staff to use them. Ken Carbone, principal, conducted a "creative summit" to evaluate the implementation of the new identity, already in use on thousands of applications. Cross-company brand design board members provide feedback about what is working and suggestions for the future evolution of the brand identity. An online branding site helps Assurant employees and agencies manage brand consistency and stay on message.

We wanted a branding firm that would create the basic building blocks for our internal creative group to implement in the future. Our employees bring in-depth knowledge as well as passion to our new brand.

Cathy Feierstein
Vice President
Organizational Learning
Assurant

We believe in beauty with a purpose. Our ingredients must be not only high-quality, but high-integrity. We are dedicated to changing the way the world does business.*

Aveda is a beauty line that uses environmentally sound ingredients in its hair care, skin care, makeup, perfume, and lifestyle products, available at 5,800 spas and salons in 26 countries. Aveda was founded in 1978 by Austrian artist and environmentalist Horst Rechelbacher and acquired by Estée Lauder in 1997.

Goals

Develop a new makeup line from an authentic source.

Connect beauty, the environment, and well-being.

Create an aesthetically pleasing packaging solution with 100% recycled materials.

*Dominique Conseil
President
Aveda

This Aveda Uruku packaging combines aesthetic excellence and environmentally sensitive engineering.

Process and strategy: Aveda prides itself on using botanicals and plant minerals derived from authentic sources. It also views outsourcing to developing communities as a way of giving back. This philosophy led to a collaboration with an indigenous tribe in South America, the Yawanawa. The western Brazilian tribes use a reddish pigment, derived from the urukum palm tree, to adorn their bodies. Aveda collaborated with the Yawanawa to organically grow the tree, fostering the community's economic and cultural survival. After rigorous research and development, Aveda developed a new line of products using the red uruku pigment derived from the trees. The resulting makeup line, free from any synthetic dyes and fragrances, was called Aveda Uruku makeup. Aveda's environmental concerns required a packaging solution created entirely from recycled materials that was also aesthetically pleasing. To accomplish this vision, Aveda's design and marketing team approached Harry Allen and Associates.

Creative solution: Harry Allen's primary goal was to find an eco-friendly material that would make an attractive package and be compatible with Aveda's existing compression molds. Allen approached Material ConneXion for a packaging solution that matched the Aveda philosophy. After checking the available options of environment-friendly materials, Allen selected post-industrial polypropylene made of flax chide, a type of plastic with a woody texture for the cap. A collaboration of Aveda's design team and Harry Allen resulted in a highly styled lipstick case that was refillable and had a pleasing, earthy feel. Recycled aluminum was used for the metal base. The packaging was constructed from molded fiber clamshell made of 100% recycled newsprint, applying the process used to make egg cartons.

Results: The packaging design was environmentally sensitive and low cost. Aveda designed a print and web campaign to introduce the Aveda Uruku makeup, to tell the story of the Yawanawa tribes. The product and communications were aligned at every step with Aveda's morals and ideals. Aveda won several accolades for its frontline efforts to create recyclable and renewable cosmetic packaging. In 2002, the Aveda Uruku makeup line won the International Package Design Award "Cosmetic Category Leader."

Customers are increasingly aware that you can look beautiful and make a difference.

Chris Hacker
Former SVP
Global Marketing and Design
Aveda

Aveda was the first beauty company to use bottle and jars with up to 80-100% post-consumer content.

Reuters

Beeline believes in life on the bright side. We aim to help people delight in the pleasure of communications, and to always feel free anytime and anywhere.

Beeline is the trademark of VimpelCom Group which provides voice and data services through a range of wireless, fixed, and broadband technologies. Founded in 1992, VimpelCom was the first Russian company to list its shares on the New York Stock Exchange. As of 2008, its total number of active subscribers in Russia and the CIS was 57.8 million.

Goals

Stand out and raise the bar.

Set a new standard for modern Russia.

Renew customer understanding.

Become the market leader.

Build a sense of pride and belonging.

Билайн™

play

live life

stand out

Photography: Jim Naughten

Process and strategy: In 2005, the Russian mobile communications market was approaching saturation, especially in Moscow. The principal players were competing for the leading position in the market and there was no clear point of differentiation between them. The competitive audit revealed that marketing and branding in the mobile communications sector was focused mostly on technology rather than people. Wolff Olins was engaged to create a new brand identity that would build an emotional bond with consumers in order to retain loyalty. The other prerequisite for the new brand was to provide an outward-looking, more modern face that would help the company prepare for regional and international expansion. The competitive audit also revealed that the market in general was cluttered and noisy. The opportunity for Wolff Olins was clear—create a brand that could stand out and cut through the noise. The brand team worked closely with Beeline's marketing team in Moscow to deliver a brand that was bold and that delivered maximum impact.

Creative solution: Inspired by the company's strategy, Wolff Olins developed a working platform to focus the work. "Beeline inspires me to live life to the fullest" was the idea used to drive all aspects of the creative work visually and tonally. The solution was not just a logo but a complete and coherent language that was flexible and universal, that captured the imagination of different audiences across Russia and that transcended cultural and social barriers. Visually, it was an invitation to see life with imagination, illustrated by the use of black and yellow stripes in an individual and ownable way. The new tagline, "Live on the bright side", informed the tone for the new brand's personality. Brightness, friendliness, simplicity, and positive emotions would be the new attributes the revitalized brand would embrace. A new brand identity system, communications style guidelines, and an image library were created to get the company ready for the launch. Wolff Olins was also commissioned to create the launch campaign.

Results: The new brand had a big impact in the market and the business. By the end of 2005, revenues at Beeline were up by 40%, market capitalization had also increased by 28% and ARPU (average revenue per user) was up by 7%. Since relaunching the brand, Beeline has independently been ranked as the most valuable brand in Russia for four consecutive years. During this time the company has expanded its operations to neighboring countries such as Kazakhstan, Uzbekistan, Ukraine, Tajikistan, Georgia, and Armenia, as well as countries further afield as Cambodia. Beeline has also extended its product portfolio from mobile to data, fixed line, and mobile TV services.

BP has transformed from a local oil company into a global energy brand. We need to reinvent the energy business, to go beyond petroleum.

The 1998 merger of British Petroleum and Amoco created one of the world's largest oil and petrochemical groups, providing its customers with energy for heat and light, fuel for transportation, retail services, and petrochemical products.

Goals

Develop a brand identity that would unite BP Amoco's employees from two merged companies.

Signal to the world that the merged company is a new strong global brand.

Align the company's business with its external expressions and its internal culture.

Create an online resource and other tools to ensure that actions are aligned with BP's core values.

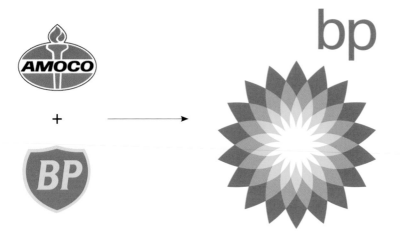

In a global marketplace, branding is crucial in attracting customers and business. It is not just a matter of a few gas stations or the logo on pole signs. It is about the identity of the company and the values that underpin everything that you do and every relationship that you have.

Lord John Browne
Former Group Chief Executive
BP

Process and strategy: Landor Associates began by reviewing BP Amoco's existing research and conducting new research on the equity of the existing brands. Landor used a rigorous process to affirm what makes the brand unique, compelling, and differentiated. This included one-on-one interviews with senior managers and culminated in an off-site workshop called Brand Driver. During this workshop senior managers and marketing executives worked collaboratively to substantiate the core values and attributes of the new brand. It led to the affirmation of the already emerging values (performance, innovation, green, and progressive) and a commitment to transform the organization and transcend the petroleum sector.

Creative solution: Landor developed a brief that distilled BP's brand essence for its creative team. After assessing the strengths and weaknesses of numerous naming options, Landor made a strong recommendation to retain the BP name, based on its significant equity, high-quality perception, and global heritage. The theme "Beyond Petroleum", developed by Ogilvy & Mather, was recommended as a central concept to unify all actions, behaviors, and communications for the BP brand. It signaled a BP imperative to go beyond conventional ways of thinking and doing.

Landor designed a series of visual strategies. The CEO and senior management chose the helios strategy, which tested strongly against the qualities of progressive, forward-thinking, innovative, and environmental. The helios trademark shifted the paradigm of how the petroleum industry should look and feel.

Results: Ensuring that 100,000 employees in 100 countries understood how to align their actions with BP's core values was key to the new strategy. Landor developed a series of employee workshops to engage employees in the new vision, and to engender discussions about ways to live the brand in their daily lives. The Brand Centre, an online resource for guidelines, demonstrates how the brand is used throughout BP and helps each employee play a part in building the brand. BP's ongoing commitment involves annual surveys to monitor the brand's impact externally on business performance, and relations with consumers and communities, and internally on brand perception, employee morale, and job satisfaction.

Branding is not about checking the box and moving on. Brands are living, and breathing—they need to be embraced, monitored, and adapted.

Andrew Welch
Landor Associates

BP has 28,500 service stations and over 90,000 employees worldwide.

California Academy of Sciences is a natural history museum, aquarium, planetarium, four-story rainforest, and research laboratory all under one living roof. We offer visitors a new way of exploring the key questions of life on earth.

The California Academy of Sciences is a multifaceted scientific institution committed to leading-edge research and educational outreach, and to engaging and inspiring the public. Located in San Francisco, the 154-year-old nonprofit institution houses the Steinhart Aquarium, the Kimball Natural History Museum, a four-story rainforest, and the Morrison Planetarium.

Goals

Revitalize the institution's visual identity and brand voice.

Design a comprehensive program.

Deliver a comprehensive visitor experience that complements the state-of-the-art facilities.

Increase recognition and attract new visitors and members.

Strengthen brand equity.

CALIFORNIA
ACADEMY OF
SICENCES

We're an un-museum. In the past, natural science museums had thick walls and high columns, and they were about history. We're the inversion of that. Light streams in and the Academy is full of life.

Greg Farrington, Ph.D.
Executive Director
California Academy of Sciences

Process and strategy: In fall 2008, the California Academy of Sciences unveiled its iconic new building that exists beneath a 2.5-acre living roof. The $488 million all-green, LEED® Platinum Certified museum was designed by Renzo Piano and houses a four-story rainforest, a natural history museum, an aquarium, a planetarium, and research facilities. Pentagram was engaged to design an identity and visual system that celebrates the Academy's dynamic, thriving, and interconnected experience, and complements its state-of-the art facilities.

The comprehensive identity system needed to include collateral, development, and membership materials; interior and exterior signs, banners, and donor walls; newsletters, membership cards, visitor maps; and more. Pentagram's Kit Hinrichs and Laura Scott worked closely with the Academy's senior leadership team, building architects, and other design consultants, to create a cohesive brand experience to increase recognition, visitation, membership, and support.

Creative solution: Taking inspiration from the building's architecture, the Academy's new identity reinforces the cyclical nature of the natural sciences, and is often described as "The Fabric of Life." Everything was designed to have an unexpected element of discovery and engagement—like a photograph with a twist or scale larger than life, or the 21' diameter logo at the entryway inset into the ground so children can trace its outline with their feet. For the development newsletters, the theme "Life Stories" was

created; oversized newsletters brought to life stories of people who have infused their passion into or been impassioned by the Academy, be they staff, donors, docents, enthusiasts, volunteers, researchers, scientists, aspiring scientists, or wide-eyed kids. Pentagram also created a series of donor walls. The major donor wall is a permanent installation of 388 six-inch-square glass blocks, a modern take on scientific "specimen boxes" that have been etched with names of major contributors. True to its sustainability mission, every element is designed with environmental responsibility in mind; membership cards are printed on recycled plastic and issued for the lifetime of the member, and visitor maps are printed on recycled paper and designed to be reused.

Results: The new California Academy of Sciences has been met with unprecedented local, national, and international enthusiasm. Membership has grown to over 75,000 in the first six months (up from 16,000 in 2004 when the Academy closed for reconstruction). Attendance has far exceeded its ambitious opening goals and, just five months after the opening, the Academy celebrated its one-millionth visitor.

Donor wall

We created Cereality® to celebrate the very personal nature of enjoying a good bowl of cereal, anywhere, anytime. Cereality transforms the way people think about cereal.*

Cereality Cereal Bar & Cafe is the first quick-serve restaurant concept entirely focused around brand-name cereals. The company was launched in 2003 by David Roth and Rick Bacher. It was acquired in 2007 by a prominent, multibrand restaurant portfolio company.

Goals

Build an iconic brand experience, not a store.

Invent, test, and refine various retail formats.

Generate brand awareness and diversified revenue streams.

Position brand for acquisition.

*David Roth, Rick Bacher
Co-founders
Cereality

People have relationships with cereals. Not just to a grain, not just to a flake, but to a particular branded product. And this business was inspired by an observation that those relationships are very, very strong, very particular and very personal. And so, why not create a retail business that really celebrates those relationships. And our attitude was, don't try and build it, just find it, and celebrate it.

David Roth
CEO and Co-founder
Cereality

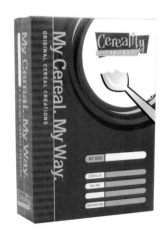

Process and strategy: The co-founders decided to combine their expertise in brand management, marketing, design, and food to build a unique branded experience. The big idea is simply "all cereal, all day, all ways." An early investor, Quaker Oats, provided Cereality with R&D. AC Nielsen marketing research revealed that cereal was the third best-selling item after milk and soft drinks. Ninety-five percent of Americans eat cereal. Cereal is both a snack and a meal other than breakfast. The founders recruited a world-class team from the foodservice and retail industries to turn their vision into a profitable business; this was not a run-of-the-mill start-up.

Creative solution: Rick Bacher designed the multicolored logo and the imaginative, light-filled environment, described by the press as "Seinfeldesque." Customers order a custom blend of favorite cereals from pajama-clad Cereologists™. Cereal is served in a "milk-tight bucket," a container inspired by Chinese take-out containers. Behind the counter, cereals are kept in wood and glass kitchen cabinets.

A bright red sofa offers a comfy rest, and the farm table seating twelve people is often the choice of a local book club or a birthday party. On Saturday mornings the first family to arrive gets to choose the cartoons shown on the flat screen TV. Cereality merchandise is sold: striped cotton pajamas that declare "Captain of Crunch" or "United Flakes of America," baseball caps, and cool mugs. Everything is branded, and all names are trademarked from Cereality Bars™, to Cereality Bites™ and Slurrealities™, otherwise known as smoothies.

Results: Four years after launching their business, the founders proved the concept's viability. Cereality had seven company-owned stores, 26 franchised locations under contract, more than 8,000 unsolicited franchise inquiries, and an arsenal of strategic alliances and licensing deals when it was acquired by Kahala Corp., the parent company of Cold Stone Creamery and Blimpie in 2007. The founders launched their next venture, an innovation, brand strategy, and design firm called Get Stirred Up.

Cereality has energized the cereal category.

Mary Dillon
Former President
Quaker Oats Company

Cereal is served in a "milk-tight bucket"– a container inspired by Chinese take-out containers.

Striped cotton pajamas that declare "Captain of Crunch," baseball caps, and cool mugs are all sold at the café.

Chambers Group's coaching model, 7Chambers, connects the head, heart, and spirit for individuals groups, organizations, and communities across race, gender, sexual orientation, and culture.

Founded in 2005, Chambers Group is a leadership development firm specializing in executive development, individual and team coaching, and integrating diversity and human capital planning. The founders, Dr. Barbara Riley and Dr. Delyte Frost, have been consultants to Fortune 100 companies for 25 years. Chambers' Leadership Matrix guides leaders in implementing change, achieving power, and realizing measurable results.

Goals

Express the vision of a new firm.

Create an identity that is fluid and expressive.

Communicate dynamic experience.

Differentiate the offerings.

Achieve balance between business discipline and spiritual values.

\|/||| Chambers Group

We always imagined we could attain a visual identity as rich as our view of the world.

Dr. Delyte Frost
Dr. Barbara Riley
Founders
Chambers Group

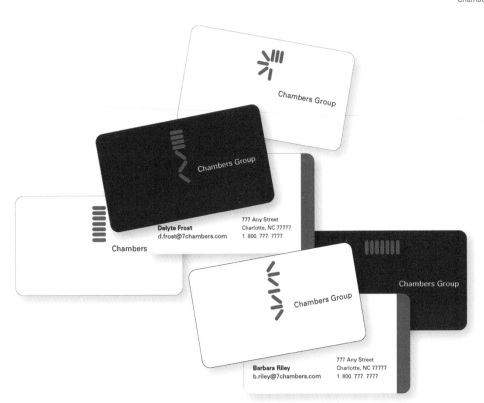

Process and strategy: Chambers Group needed to find a way to balance the social justice and spiritual values of the partners with a strategic business model that would appeal to large companies. Chambers Group's process with Stellarvisions began with a series of conversations that explored the idea of connecting head, heart, mind, and spirit. During these initial meetings, Chambers was evolving and designing its coaching and leadership models. Stellarvisions created a series of personas and scenarios of senior managers and HR professionals who would either choose or refer Chambers Group. These personas activated intensive discussions about the essence and dynamics of the Chambers process, and the needs and perceptions of Chambers clients. The creative team and the partners collaborated to identify unconventional ways to communicate with a broader audience. The number 7 had implicit, explicit, and ancient etymology that was important to the partners.

Creative solution: From the inception of the conversations, Stella Gassaway, firm visionary and creative director, wanted the identity and the web presence to embody the intense, individual, enlightening, and empowering experience of working with the Chambers Group. Stellarvisions immersed itself in thinking through a different cultural space: Jacob's Ladder, the I Ching, yin and yang. The identity needed to express the integration of life and work, and the endless cycle of learning and living. Gassaway instinctively knew that the identity would comprise a wordmark and an avatar. She designed a series of interchangeable elements—called the elements of change—which are integrated into the coaching process itself as well as into the communications of the company. The website mimics Chambers' coaching process: a series of questions leads the visitor on a journey and calls on visitors to engage and make choices. Chambers makes people feel safe, heard, and seen. The website uses images and metaphor and is not text heavy.

Results: The meaning and the formation of the elements of change are in constant transformation and engender lively discussions. The new business was launched in 2005 with an invitation to 7+1 Intensive, a year-long process for intensive change: A multicultural group of women will meet for three days a month for eight months. The business launched Chambers into a bright future, with consulting contracts in place for a year out. Unlike most consulting groups, the physical becomes spiritual, the yin and yang of Chambers. In 2008, the founders published their first book, *Are You Ready for Outrageous Success?*

conscious

context

choice

courage

competence

confidence

create

Leadership Matrix intelligence quotients

IQ	Knowledge Intelligence
EQ	Emotional Intelligence
TQ	Thinking Intelligence
DQ	Diversity Intelligence
PQ	Purpose Intelligence
JQ	Job Intelligence
SQ	Spiritual Intelligence

City Church Eastside is a church for the local neighborhood, telling the story of the Christian faith and promoting social healing and cultural renewal.

City Church Eastside is located just east of downtown Atlanta, in the middle of a small grouping of unique, local, and culturally rich neighborhoods where residents live, work, and play all in the same community.

Goals

Tell the story of the neighborhood church.

Promote the concept of community living.

Create a unified brand system to include future neighborhood congregations.

The Eastside is the cradle of the civil rights movement and still today issues a clarion call not just for racial reconciliation but for a unity that eclipses race, economics, and social stratification.

Scott Armstrong
Lead Pastor
City Church Eastside

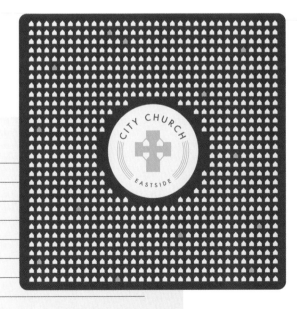

216

Process and strategy: Scott Armstrong, the founder of City Church had lived in the Eastside for several years before planting the church in order to gain a rich understanding of the people he would be serving as well as the spiritual ethos of the community. The vision was to be a reflection of the eastside community, which meant not growing to be a large church, but rather to be a network of small churches serving the local communities.

Matchstic joined the process with Armstrong and his launch team to set up a brand architecture that would allow for growth and the eventual launch of several small neighborhood churches. The name City Church Eastside was chosen as a way to speak to the cultural renewal of the city and establish common ground for future City Church locations.

Creative solution: The central idea behind the City Church identity reflected the unique vision of the church being focused on serving the local neighborhood. Matchstic created a pattern of simple houses that would be used as a graphic device to tell the story of community. A cross is the central icon of the Christian faith, but it needed to be used in a way that was unique to

City Church and its story. A Celtic cross provided a more appropriate graphic foundation, in which there are two lines intersecting with a circle around the center. Matchstic used the two lines of the cross to represent two streets intersecting. The negative space created by the circle was replaced by four houses, thus communicating the idea of a church at the center of a neighborhood. The symbol was placed in a circle with the name and neighborhood around it to accomplish the goal of making it scalable to other neighborhood churches.

Results: The solid foundation of the City Church Eastside brand identity gave the pastor and his launch team a representation of their shared vision and passion. A year after launch they outgrew their place of worship and moved into a larger facility. But more than raw attendance numbers, the church continues to focus its efforts on local community groups caring for the neighborhoods in which they live. City Church plans to launch their second local church within the next three years.

Once a year, Matchstic provides one deserving nonprofit organization with an entire brand makeover free-of-charge. Our goal is to substantially increase the non-profit's efforts and establish brand recognition within their community. Additional service providers joined us to partner on City Church Eastside.

Craig Johnson
Partner
Matchstic

Photography: Caleb Chancey

Coke brings joy. It's happiness in a bottle.
Let's find the truth and celebrate it.

The Coca-Cola Company is the world's largest beverage company. Founded in 1886, the company offers more than 2,800 products in over 200 countries, it has over 90,000 associates and 300 bottling partners. On an average day, 1.2 billion people around the world have a Coca-Cola product. Coca-Cola, the soft drink, is the best-known product and brand in the history of the world.

Goals

Make Coke feel happy, fresh, and honest again.

Visually leverage the trademark's iconic, enduring values.

Drive compelling, cohesive 360 brand experiences.

Evoke meaningful and memorable consumer connections.

Re-establish Coke's reputation as a design leader.

We had to bring forward what was true about the brand.

Moira Cullen
Former Group Director
Strategic Design
Coca-Cola North America

Principles of iconic brands
Developed by Turner Duckworth

Confidence to be simple

Honesty (no overpromising)

In tune with the current culture

Highly considered use of icons

Attention to details

Process and strategy: Coca-Cola is the most valuable and recognized brand in the world. Its trademark and contoured bottle design are ubiquitous cultural icons. In late 2005, Pio Schunker, head of the Creative Excellence Group at Coca-Cola North America, engaged Turner Duckworth to deliver against the brand idea that Coke brings joy. Schunker then appointed Moira Cullen as the Strategic Design Director to manage the project. The team reported to Katie Bayne, the Chief Marketing Officer, who oversees all marketing initiatives. The design goal was to make Coke feel happy, fresh, and honest again. The process began with analyzing Coke's heritage and visual assets, and demonstrating how leadership brands use design and visual identity to achieve a competitive advantage. There was agreement that Coke's identity had become cluttered, uninspiring, and static. Given the rapid pace of change in today's consumer society, the team felt that Coke's identity needed to be dynamic and constantly relevant to the culture. Turner Duckworth identified five principles of iconic brands to guide the design thinking.

Creative solution: Turner Duckworth focused on Coke's iconic elements that no other brand can own: the white Spencerian script on a red background, the contoured bottle, and the dynamic ribbon. Turner Duckworth showed what the design of "Coke brings joy" looks like and feels like across multiple touchpoints from cups to trucks and environments. Turner Duckworth examined the entire visual identity toolbox: trademarks, icons, color, scale, symbols, patterns, forms, typography, and photography. At various stages of the process, designs were sent into research to verify that they were aligned with company strategy.

The new bold and simple design strategy leveraged the trademark's enduring and emotional appeal. The design has the simplicity, confidence, and flexibility to work in different environments and media. It was designed to be in tune with the culture. The value of design leadership was discussed with key decision makers. The new design guidelines were developed and posted online for suppliers, creative partners, and design centers around the world.

Results: The revitalized visual identity has made the brand relevant to a new generation, reconnected with people who grew up with the brand, and increased sales. Coke received a number of global awards including the coveted Design Grand Prix at the Cannes Lions advertising festival and the Gold Lion for its new aluminum bottle. The new design strategy gave Coke a leadership position in design that was undoubtedly an influence on Pepsi's recent radical redesign.

The secret to making work like this happen is passion, persuasion, and perseverance.

David Turner
Principal
Turner Duckworth

219

Eimer Stahl is a trim, agile firm with extraordinary client relationships that uses advanced technology and strategic insight to quickly mobilize to big firm capacity.

Eimer Stahl Klevorn & Solberg LLP (Eimer Stahl) is a national litigation firm in Chicago founded in 2000 to resolve the largest, most complex legal matters for America's corporations. It performs securities and antitrust work, multidistrict environmental and product liability litigation, and high-stakes contract disputes. The four founding partners left an established global legal firm to create a different kind of law firm.

Goals

Build recognition for the new law firm and transcend the category.

Articulate a differentiated brand strategy and positioning.

Create a visual identity system across media.

Establish a fluid, effective, strategic marketplace communication system.

When we formed Eimer Stahl in 2000, we set out to create a different kind of law firm—one that would deliver outstanding results for clients, but take a more personal, creative approach to getting there. And that's what we've done.

Nate Eimer
Managing Partner
Eimer Stahl

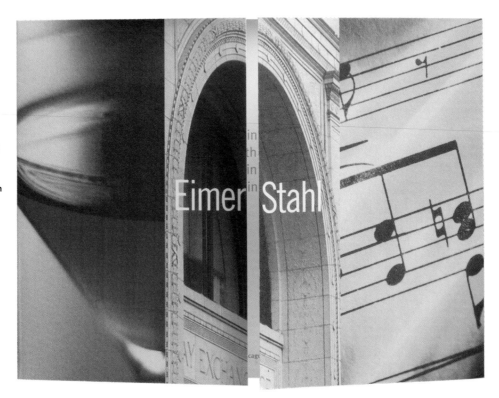

Process and strategy: Unlike traditional litigation firms, Eimer Stahl wanted to make litigation more cost-effective, more successful, and more enjoyable. Despite their stellar individual reputations, the partners acknowledged that launching a new small law firm was a risk. None of the partners had ever created a new company. They retained Crosby Associates to help them develop a brand value proposition, a mission statement, a positioning platform, and an identity.

Crosby Associates facilitated an off-site meeting with the founding partners to discuss the new firm's goals, philosophy, personality, and unique strengths. Joining Crosby's team was Cheryl Slover-Linett, a strategist and joint facilitator. The team drafted a list of key marketing strategy deliverables, using a hierarchy of brand values and associated client benefits. After the partners' agreement, Crosby began to design.

Creative solution: Crosby designed a very confident, streamlined sans serif logotype and applied a new sensibility across media. Dramatic black-and-white photography is used in the website and in the firm brochure. A marketing system was designed to be sent out regularly to clients and other lawyers. The format, a 4" x 5" gatefold card, is used consistently regardless of the announcement or invitation. But the mailing is always a surprise. The first one was an invitation to a Rolling Stones concert for the band's opening event. Others include newsworthy announcements, such as an open house or a firm anniversary.

Results: Being a small firm with a big firm capability has proven to be a successful strategy. Eimer Stahl was named one of the best boutique firms in the country by *The American Lawyer*, and Crain named it the best law firm in Chicago in 2004. Crosby Associates developed a launch plan to help Eimer Stahl implement its new brand in the legal marketplace. The firm has doubled in size since its founding, from twenty-five attorneys to fifty. Marketing is integral to growth.

Crosby has designed a system for us that continues to bring our message to the market, in a way that is clever, appropriate, and differentiated.

Nate Eimer
Managing Partner
Eimer Stahl

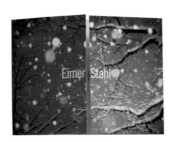

FedEx embodies a twenty-first century vision based on a common information interface for all global customers, applying one brand link to a broad spectrum of transportation and logistics services.

FedEx provides a wide range of business, logistics, and transportation services to customers and businesses in 220 countries and territories through its network of independent operating companies. Six million packages are now delivered each business day—a feat achieved through continuous innovation. FedEx was founded in 1973 by its visionary chairman and CEO, Fred Smith.

Goals

Conduct worldwide research and analysis.

Position FedEx as a global provider of time-sensitive material.

Collaborate on articulating brand attributes.

Design a new identity and brand architecture.

Facilitate cross-selling.

Develop a brand management resource tool.

Corporation

Express

Ground

Freight

Custom Critical

Trade Networks

The success of FedEx branding has been driven by smart instinct, swift decision making, and compelling execution, with the role of research often being to validate and provide executional guidance.

Gayle Christensen
Managing Director
Global Brand Management
FedEx

Process and strategy: In a relationship that began in 1993, Landor Associates has co-created two generations of branding transformations for FedEx. The original identity, Federal Express, became a potential impediment to building a global business. By the early 1990s, the company was known as "FedEx" and, unlike the former name, could be said easily by customers who did not speak English. Landor emphasized the organization's global scope, reliability, and speed with a new brand line, "The World on Time," and launched FedEx as the primary verbal and visual identifier. The bold new identity was applied to thousands of uniforms and packages, and fleets of planes and vehicles.

Beginning in 1998, the parent company of FedEx, originally called FDX Corp., acquired a string of shipping and logistics companies to provide transportation, supply chain, and information system services. Each retained its brand name.

Creative solution: Landor began to examine new brand architecture and verbal branding that would make it simpler for customers and prospects to understand the global scope of FedEx and its range of capabilities.

The new brand architecture unified the independent companies under the powerful FedEx brand, accompanied by clear language to differentiate each company service: FedEx Express, FedEx Ground, FedEx Freight, FedEx Custom Critical, and FedEx Trade Networks. Each operating company was also color-coded. This approach was aligned with Fred Smith's vision and requirements to build independent companies that could collectively compete under a strong global brand and symbolize one touchpoint for customers everywhere.

Results: Conversion to the new brand architecture involved a large capital investment during a period of complex organizational and technological change. Landor developed a comprehensive brand resource management website for FedEx, designed to make the core meaning of the brand resonate with employees and creative marketing teams. With more than 3,000 downloads, this website houses the brand assets of all FedEx operating companies. It features a global brand management feedback and approval loop—when a marketing piece is designed and submitted, it is tested against the core brand attributes, and the sponsoring manager receives feedback within 36 hours.

The consumers themselves had evolved the brand to FedEx. It had become the Kleenex and the Coke of its category.

Clay Timon
Former CEO
Landor Associates

Feng is an homage to the serenity and passion of the Asian culture. It delights guests with beauty, a heightened sense of discovery, and unprecedented service.*

Feng is an Asian-inspired luxury retail experience in Kansas City, Missouri, that features runway fashions by Asian and other international designers, an eclectic collection of designer shoes and accessories, home furnishings, specialty teas, and a unique offering of children's clothing, toys, and collectables.

Goals

Create a one-of-a-kind retail experience.

Celebrate the beauty of Asian fashion, theatre and culture.

Generate appreciation of Asian design and aesthetics.

Support local and global causes through the retail venue.

*Beth Zollars
 Proprietor
 Feng

Feng essence:

Look east
Past the horizon
Reflections dance as one
Butterfly dream

Process and strategy: Beth Zollars founded Feng to share her lifelong passion for Asian culture and fashion. Beth spent several years collecting Asian artifacts. Her background in visual merchandising and experiential retail as the corporate director of sales and marketing for Tiffany & Co. provided a solid platform to begin the early phases of ideation for her new retail concept. She began her process with a comprehensive vision session. Her audit of the potential collections of Asian designers established the foundation to build the positioning platform and brand promise. She engaged Willoughby Design to create a unique brand experience that would celebrate the beauty of Asian fashion, theatre and culture, and translate it throughout the retail environment, product design, and communications. Feng customers are offered runway styles exclusive to Feng in Kansas City.

Creative solution: Willoughby designed the Feng experience to deliver a rich sensory journey that fuses luxury retail and the best of Asian culture. Custom interiors and great attention to detail like fresh flowers, aromatic teas, and ambient music create a sense of discovery and anticipation as guests meander deeper into the store, exploring the space and entering partially hidden rooms and chambers. All elements of the identity, including the gift packaging, were designed to extend the retail experience and be reminiscent of the store's discovery and hidden beauty. Feng's patrons have an eclectic sense of style and are looking for one-of-a-kind items. Feng offers them an otherworldly experience near the place where they live.

Results: Feng opened its doors in 2006, and enjoyed favorable media attention, including a visit from Project Runway's Tim Gunn. Philanthropic support has been a driving force. Beth Zollars, who was named Woman of the Year by *KC Magazine* for her many contributions to the Kansas City community, hosts many events at the store to support local and global causes. The store was profitable in year one and continues to grow through word of mouth. Zollars' focus will be to continue to grow the business organically and to open new Feng retail experiences when the time is right.

A 250 year-old Ming porcelain vase next to Vintage China jeans. Feng is about juxtaposition.

Beth Zollars
Proprietor
Feng

Distilling the essence of an Asian aesthetic into a distinctive luxury retail experience that is universal in appeal is what makes it work.

Ann Willoughby
President
Willoughby Design

FORA.tv provides videos of the world's top thinkers discussing the most important social, political, cultural, technological, and ethical issues that face the world today.

FORA.tv gathers the web's largest collection of unmediated video drawn from live events, lectures, and debates at the world's top universities, think tanks, and conferences. Founded in 2005 by Brian Gruber, FORA.tv presents provocative, big-idea content for anyone to watch, interact with, and share.

Goals

Ignite debate on the world's greatest ideas.

Inform and inspire the viewer with big idea content.

Establish FORA.tv as an online thought leader.

Stimulate exploration of the vast collection of programming.

Create brand tools.

Every day, it is apparent that the future of the web is being driven by video and social experiences. The online video audience is predicted to double to nearly one billion viewers in the next three years, and we are constantly striving to provide the smartest content available in a world of limit-less choice.

Blaise Zerega
CEO
FORA.tv

The World is Thinking.

Process and strategy: Initially Cronan partners Michael Cronan and Karen Hibma were engaged to design the brand, create the top line brand messages, and oversee the next-gen user interface. Brian Gruber, the founder, had just completed the proof of concept for the start-up, built his core team, and had his early content partners in place. He was ready to ignite his new company and wanted to brand components to help him get to the big league quickly. Cronan conducted brainstorming sessions and extensive interviews, and charted all the strategic relationships, stakeholder objectives, and key messages. This methodology, called Brand Ecosystem, helped the FORA.tv management team set strategic priorities. The new tagline, The World is Thinking, summarized the key strategy: present extraordinary big idea public forum content within a branded platform in a way that provided the viewer with a clear, unmediated, and unique experience.

Creative solution: Cronan's brief was to brand FORA.tv as a worldwide media company. The scope of the project involved everything from brand tools to the user interface feature, program and product naming, banner ads, event concepts, and even included presentation decks created while consulting with and advising the CEO. The brand aspires to express the liveliness, agility, and editorial professionalism of international news outlets like CNN and BBC. Cronan designed a globe as a community of multicolored windows to suggest diverse content, and myriad conversations readily available anywhere, anytime. The globe graphic is glowing and designed to give the impression of activity conveying that "the lights are on at FORA.tv." The "O" in the wordmark FORA.tv world becomes a globe. The globe graphic can also be used as a separate brand element when necessary.

Results: FORA.tv is becoming a respected category leader online and continues to establish itself everywhere people are meeting to discuss world-changing ideas. Its popularity and recognition as one of the smartest websites on the internet continue to accelerate. Viewership is expanding impressively, larger and more widespread content partners and sponsoring brands have come onboard, and FORA.tv's recognition has attracted more top-level internal team members including a new CEO, CMO, and SVP of Product Development. The founding CEO has become the Executive Chairman and Cronan has become FORA.tv's Designer Emeritus.

The world is thinking and wants to exchange world-changing ideas.

Brian Gruber
Founder
FORA.tv

FORA.tv attracts a smart, affluent and engaged audience that cares about the big news and current events of the day

Aaron Griffiths
Executive Creative Director
Ogilvy NY

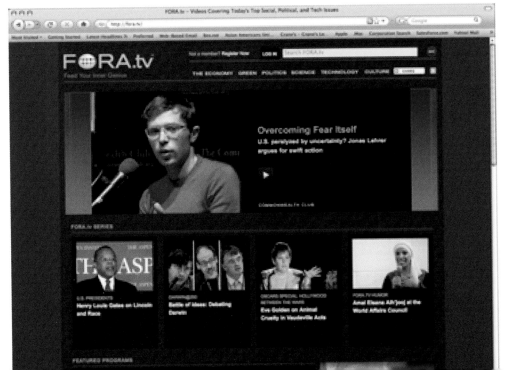

GE is imagination at work. GE people worldwide are dedicated to turning imaginative ideas into leading products and services that help solve some of the world's toughest problems.

GE is a diversified infrastructure, finance, and media company taking on the world's toughest challenges. From aircraft engines and power generation to financial services, medical imaging, and television programming, GE operates in more than 100 countries and employs more than 300,000 people worldwide.

Goals

Better share GE's brand strategy and the brand story.

Create collaboration and sharing tools.

Make it a true brand center.

Shift focus from guideline compliance to brand engagement.

Our goal was to share GE's brand strategy and create an engaged community of brand advocates.

Ivan Cayabyab
Global Brand and Digital Manager, GE

Process and strategy: GE has a history of brand focus. "For GE, imagination at work is more than a slogan or tagline. It is a reason for being," says Jeffrey R. Immelt, CEO. It has been diligent about protecting its brand assets (name, trademark, tagline) and its monolithic brand architecture is applied consistently across sectors and around the world. Continuous improvement requires that existing processes and tools be reevaluated periodically to be sure they are clear, state-of-the-art, and engaging. In 2008, the GE Brand Management staff began a process to validate current practices and recommend improvements. This started with surveys of GE Brand Center users to determine issues and opportunities moving forward. The results identified several areas for improvement, including how information is organized and searchable; cataloging of resources such as logo, image and template files; integration of best practices; and establishing a platform with expansion capabilities. Executive support was secured to move into a site enhancement project that would shift the focus from guideline compliance to brand engagement.

Creative solution: GE partnered with Monigle Associates to develop the next generation GE Brand Center. The initial steps for the project were focused on integrating the summary of the survey results into a scope of work document that would deliver an enhanced experience for users and improve brand management processes. Specific functions and content were identified, as well as future phase modules to extend the site over the long term. The project required collaboration with agencies as well as GE's design team. The new configuration includes a more robust brand strategy section, enhanced guidelines and policies, new search functionality to distribute brand assets, a best practices library, project management tools to collect new creative services projects and manage them through implementation, and a content management system to facilitate site updates by GE Brand Management team members and agencies.

Results: The GE Brand Center was relaunched in February 2009, supported by a significant communications campaign to build awareness and usage. The site is generating consistently positive reviews from both power and occasional users. Feedback validates that key improvement objectives have been met. Of particular value is the best practice sharing that educates and inspires our creative processes. Site usage is up 25% compared to peak usage patterns of the previous site. Other metrics track efficiencies in creative services project submissions, distribution of brand assets, most popular content, and overall ROI contribution of the site. Additional modules are in development to extend the site to new levels of value for GE employees and agencies.

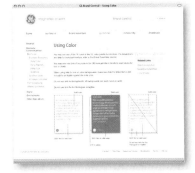

When the Good Housekeeping Seal was first introduced in 1909, we were protecting consumers from tainted food, and advocacy remains our mission today.

Founded in 1885, Good Housekeeping is a trusted name for providing essential information about food, diet, and consumer products. The Good Housekeeping Seal itself has long been known by consumers for its quality reassurance on a wide range of consumer goods.

Goals

Redesign seal to commemorate Good Housekeeping's 100th anniversary.

Revitalize the seal to better reflect the company's heritage.

Develop a classic look that will stand the test of time.

The Seal has been a cornerstone of the Good Housekeeping brand, and, along with the Good Housekeeping Research Institute and the magazine itself, has made this the most trusted brand in America.

Rosemary Ellis
Editor-in-Chief
Good Housekeeping

July 1909

December 1911

December 1913

July 1929

November 1941

June 1962

July 1975

1997

Process and strategy: The Good Housekeeping Research Institute (GHRI) was formed before there was an FDA and a Pure Food and Drug Act. As an early proponent of consumer protection, the Good Housekeeping magazine created testing labs to evaluate products for their readers. Products advertised in the magazine that bear the seal are tested by GHRI and are backed by a two-year limited warranty.

To celebrate the 100th anniversary, Good Housekeeping commissioned a new seal to be drawn by Louise Fili Ltd. The Director of Brand Development, Sara Rad, wrote a brand brief, searched through the archives to uncover the seal's history, and organized a small team of decision makers. There had been a total of eight different designs of the seal since 1909. "Good Housekeeping was seeking an update that would seamlessly combine its classic history with a modern type aesthetic. The goal was to design this one to last a long, long time."

Creative solution: The Seal's many revisions have always been a reflection of the style of the times. Right from the start, Louise Fili and the committee at Good Housekeeping knew they wanted the Seal to convey a timeless quality. According to Fili, "I wanted the Seal to look as though it had always been there—classic but not retro. And in a style that exudes reassurance and trust." Having done design makeovers for many companies, she learned that a lot can be changed, as long as at least one element stays the same. In this case it was immediately apparent to her that the oval needed to stay, as well as the star, if possible. Fili also revisited the typeface in this makeover, opting for Neutraface—a classic set of letterforms based on the work of the famed modern architect, Richard Neutra. The design process also took into consideration that the Seal would be reproduced in dramatically different scales and media.

Results: The new and improved Good Housekeeping Seal made its debut on the Today Show, on a float at the Macy's Thanksgiving Day Parade, as well as on a billboard in Times Square, all in the same week. The magazine planned an entire year of Seal-related features for their 25 million readers. To honor the Seal's birthday, the doors of GHRI in New York City were opened to the public so that consumers could see firsthand how Good Housekeeping evaluates everything from electronics to vacuums to clothing on their state-of-the-art testing equipment.

I wanted the seal to look as though it had always been there—classic but not retro. And in a style that exudes reassurance and trust.

Louise Fili
Louise Fili Ltd.

Heavy Bubble is a service for career artists to create a do-it-yourself website to display their work. For visual artists marketing is painful and technology is scary —Heavy Bubble is disarming and fun.

Heavy Bubble was founded in 2008 by artist Stella Gassaway in response to the need she saw among her career artist friends. Artists sign up for monthly subscriptions to Heavy Bubble services, which include website design and hosting and other marketing tools.

Goals

Choose a great name.

Create a flexible visual vocabulary.

Develop language to support the brand.

Offset the technology intimidation factor.

Heavy Bubble. You just have to smile when you say it!
Damini Celebre
Artist

The brand is about supporting artists, helping them advance their careers, getting their work before new audiences, and presenting it effectively.
Stella Gassaway
Founder
Heavy Bubble

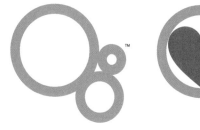

Process and strategy: As an artist, Gassaway is very aware of the need within the artist community. Very few can afford to hire a professional to create a website or help with marketing. They have been dependent upon ineffective low-cost solutions: awkward templates, amateur-built sites they cannot update, artist portals where they get lost in the clutter. Heavy Bubble gives an artist their own site that is easy to update and templates that keep the focus on the artwork.

Heavy Bubble needed to become visible in artist communities around the country. Gassaway recruited opinion-leaders from her artist network as bubble agents. The tangible advantages of the websites—connections with galleries, sold work—made the agents enthusiastic and reputable advocates. While supported by targeted advertising and sponsorship of art events, artist-to-artist recommendation remains Heavy Bubble's most consistent source of new subscribers. Heavy Bubble is pacing marketing efforts so that demand does not adversely affect the quality of customer service.

Creative solution: The answer to "What does Heavy Bubble mean?" is listed at the heavybubble blog as: "heavy is substantial, bubbles rise to the surface." This ex post facto definition aside, the investigation sought a name that 1) had an available URL, 2) was memorable, and 3) made people smile. Heavy Bubble is paradoxical, unexpected, and fun. The tagline "makes me happy" is supported by a casual, reassuring tone in communication: "Awesome! We're excited about floating your trial bubble." A straightforward

descriptive tagline "websites for artists" is used where the identity appears in a foreign context. To be ultimately searchable, both forms of the name are used: Heavy Bubble and heavybubble.

In her role as a designer and principal of Stellarvisions, Stella Gassaway designed a simple and playful identity for Heavy Bubble. Three connected bubbles—large, medium, and small—represent the three levels of web presence offered.

Results: The reaction to Heavy Bubble has been overwhelmingly positive. Artists from California and Arizona to Alabama and Pennsylvania have subscribed. On Twitter, heavybubble is followed by major art institutions and artists and galleries from Liverpool to New York.

The name spawned many terms: support emails from tinyheavybubble.com, bubbleRAP newsletter, bubblePRESS email marketing for artists, hug-a-bubble valentines. The inherent contradiction of the heavy (serious artwork) and bubble (light tone) begins to work on more and more levels.

electronic mail : bubbleRAP

website : www.heavybubble.com

blog : blog.heavybubble.com

twitter : www.twitter.com/heavybubble

Herman Miller stands for a better world around you—whether you are a customer, employee, investor, or community member.

Herman Miller, Inc. designs, manufactures, and distributes furnishings, interior products, and related services for office, healthcare, home, and higher education environments. It sells worldwide through its sales staff, dealer network, independent dealers, and the internet. Herman Miller, a $1.6 billion public company, was founded in 1905.

Goals

Improve the performance of human habitats.

Reduce composite footprint on the environment.

Reach environmental sustainability goals by 2020.

Focus on design innovation and quality.

Building a better world is not so much a goal as an everyday fact of life.
Brian Walker
CEO
Herman Miller

Eames Molded Plywood Chair, designed 1946

Left: The Herman Miller Greenhouse received the LEED Pioneer Award (Leadership in Energy and Environmental Design) in 2000. The design combined a manufacturing plant with office space.

Right: Over 100 Herman Miller employees were involved in every aspect of building a Habitat for Humanity house.

Process and strategy: The things that matter to Herman Miller—design innovation, high-performance office systems, and seating—have co-existed with environmental advocacy for decades. Products from the 1950s are still in use today. D.J. DePree, the founder, required all new sites to be 50 percent green space, and in 1953 said, "Herman Miller shall be a good corporate steward of the environment." In the late 1980s, a group of employees pushed senior management to take a strong position on the environment. In 1989, the group formed what became the Environmental Quality Action Team (EQAT) to formulate and monitor environmental policy. In 1993, Herman Miller collaborated with architects, engineers, developers, builders and product manufacturers, nonprofits, and government agencies to co-create the U.S. Green Building Council, to find ways to get people to build more sustainably. The group's biggest contribution was setting up LEED standards, designed to boost green-building practices.

Creative solution: Becoming a sustainable business is intrinsic to Herman Miller's spirit, value system, and heritage. This commitment is demonstrated by its numerous green building facilities, its design process and products, its management's benchmarks, and environmental education. In 2003, the Mirra was the first chair designed from the ground up to meet Herman Miller's stringent Design for the Environment (DfE) protocols, which focus on creating economic value while simultaneously valuing the environment. It is made of a minimal number of parts and is easily disassembled for recycling. The new Embody chair is 96 percent recyclable and PVC free.

Herman Miller communicates regularly and across media about "Perfect Vision," a broad initiative that sets significant sustainability targets for the year 2020, including: zero landfill, zero hazardous waste generation, 100% green electrical energy use, and 100% of sales from DfE-approved products. Even the business cards are used to communicate the things that matter most—from a better world to transparency and sustainability goals.

Results: The CEO's scorecard includes environmental goals. As of January 2009, Herman Miller is 50 percent of its way to Perfect Vision 2020. My Studio is the first office furniture system product to be designed according to the McDonough Braungart Design Chemistry (MBDC) Cradle-to-Cradle Design protocol. It is 69 percent recyclable and is made from 30 percent recycled materials. Herman Miller's fuel savings program helped employees carpool using a web-based clearinghouse and offered a company-sponsored rebate to help employees buy fuel-efficient cars and bicycles.

Mirra, designed 2003

We're working to get to zero landfill, zero hazardous waste generation, zero VOC emissions into the air, and zero process water emissions by 2020.

A better world matters at Herman Miller.

Bri

Presi

brian_

616 654

616 654 5

375 West 4   Street   OFFICE

Holland MI 49423 5341

Herman Miller Inc

PO Box 302   US MAIL

Zeeland MI 49464 0302

HermanMiller

Hot Wheels encompasses speed, power, performance, and attitude—the basis of all brand expressions.

Hot Wheels® die-cast cars were introduced in 1968. The brand has become a global lifestyle property that celebrates all things fast and automotive for kids and collectors everywhere. The brand is owned by Mattel, Inc., the world's largest toy company.

Goals

Redesign packaging system.

Communicate core brand attributes of speed, power, performance, and attitude.

Create a system to work across all packaging sizes and configurations.

Simplify shopping process for consumers.

Good design needs to be accountable—it needs to be consistent, logical and deliver basic principles that can be maintained long term.

Matt Petersen
VP Design
Mattel

Hot Wheels brand style guide

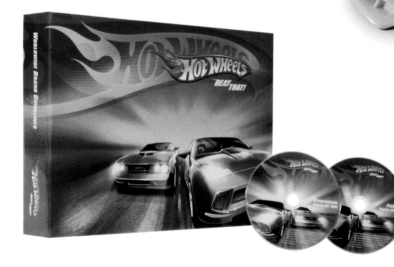

Over 41 million children have collected Hot Wheels cars. The typical adult collector owns 1,550 cars on average.

Process and strategy: Every two seconds, a Hot Wheels car is sold somewhere in the world. The brand's marketing team recognized that their packaging needed to do a better job of helping parents quickly find the toys their kids were asking for by name that they had seen on TV. In addition, the creative team, led by riCardo Crespo, believed that the consumer shopping experience should be streamlined. The internal team took the lead on the redesign. Speed and performance were the drivers. Because the team was familiar with the brand and culture, they were best qualified to solve the problem quickly. The team of a creative director and three art directors worked closely to design and evaluate creative solutions across the breadth of the line. Upper management was brought in for feedback during the process. Three packaging concepts were tested with consumers. Results were used to confirm instincts rather than define them. The entire creative process took about a month.

Creative solution: The team's focus was to help their target consumer quickly navigate pertinent information. Every decision, from the hierarchy of information, color, and scale to typography, was considered in relationship to the long-standing core brand attributes of speed, power, performance, and attitude. The team began by amplifying and brightening their signature blue.

A new italicized font, named Beat That, was commissioned by the team to convey speed and movement. The product name, set in Beat That, was enlarged and angled to draw the eye. Below it, a bright red band carries succinct information to explain the product. The scale of the logo was increased. The center illustration was invigorated with more active imagery and brighter colors. The photograph of the product was enlarged to give the shopper a better idea of what was inside the box. Its location was standardized. After the system was finalized, Crespo did a road show around the world to explain the new packaging system to key creative partners, retailers, and licensors.

Results: Since the redesign, Mattel has seen increased sales as well as satisfaction from retailers. The system has been incorporated into the brand style guide, and shared with licensors as well as in-house teams. Cross-functional teams use the font, colors, and general style in internal communications and presentations, unifying the brand. The company is looking at leveraging in-house talent and a simplified process to redesign packaging as a benchmark for other brands. Internal collaboration, expertise, and passion measurably improved the customer experience.

HP invents new technologies and services to drive business value, create social benefit, and improve the lives of people everywhere.

HP was founded in 1939 by inventors Bill Hewlett and Dave Packard in a wooden garage in Palo Alto, California. Seventy years later, HP is the 14th largest company in the world, with more than one billion customers and 321,000 employees operating in more than 170 countries on six continents. Their products range from home printers to large printing systems, from mobile computers to powerful workstations, and from storage and servers to software and services.

Goals

Develop a program to drive marketing excellence.

Share best practices across all regions, businesses, and departments.

Recognize and motivate high achievement.

Turn successful projects into learning materials.

Our investment in innovation is an investment in growth.

Mark V. Hurd
Chairman, Chief Executive Officer and President

The design learning loop

Success increasingly depends on returns on talent. Companies that aim to innovate—not sporadically but serially—need to invest in a culture of innovation.

Marty Neumeier
President
Neutron

DESIGN
ACTIONS, PROCESSES, AND MESSAGES TO ALIGN WITH GOALS

ARTICULATE
ORGANIZATION'S GOALS, STRATEGIES, AND VALUES

ASSESS
ALL DESIGN OUTPUT THROUGH ANNUAL COMPETITION

TEACH
ACQUIRED LEARNINGS AND SPREAD NEW DESIGN SKILLS

RECOGNIZE
WINNING TEAMS AND EXTRACT THEIR LEARNINGS

Process and strategy: In 2002, after its merger with Compaq, HP had three organizational mandates: Introduce a new collaborative culture; change the company from product-driven to brand driven; and talk to customers in a single, clear voice. Twenty-two international teams were assembled to examine every customer touchpoint. Over 18 months, HP developed an online brand center with new standards, templates, and brand tools to facilitate the alignment of product design and external communications with the company's revitalized brand values and business goals. A curated photo library was also launched.

Finally, HP trained 3,000 marketers and 1,000 agency professionals in the application of these elements. Armed with new tools and knowledge, internal and external teams were able to forge a single voice from two disparate cultures. All that remained was a method for sustaining and building this success over time.

Creative solution: Neutron and HP designed a simple program that creates a "flywheel of increasing returns." Dubbed the Circle Awards, it combines an internal competition, a recognition system, a global brand audit, and an educational program into one initiative. It works like this: 1) employees execute brand-related projects, which they enter into an annual competition; 2) internal and external teams select the winners; 3) the winners are recognized at a gala awards ceremony at an off-site location; and 4) winning projects are turned into learning materials that are uploaded to an online brand center.

The competition not only provides a framework for recognition, but also serves as an annual brand audit, allowing visibility into regions, departments, and business units that need additional help. Help can take the form of focused training, educational tours, or regional events that employ educational materials from the competition. Since everyone in the company builds on the success of the highest achievers, each year the bar is raised, and each year the culture becomes more collaborative, more creative, and more brand-savvy.

Results: In 2007 the program provided crucial continuity through a change of leadership, and under CEO Mark Hurd it serves as a central mechanism for unifying the brand effort across otherwise siloed business units, regions, and departments. Entries are collected and judged online, and brand training is delivered through an online brand center. Since the Circle Awards began, HP has grown from 128,000 employees to 321,000 employees, which effectively doubles the importance of the program. HP's brand valuation grew 18% between 2004 and 2009.

CIRCLE:

Consistency

Innovation

Relevance

Collaboration

Learning

Effectiveness

Circle Awards exhibit; winners are also posted on HP's intranet

Trophies are awarded to best in category. With each year the level of design and innovation has improved, as employees vie for the coveted glass cube.

IUNI Educacional private colleges will educate the future workforce of Brazil, bringing innovation and pride to the central west, north and northeast regions of the country.

IUNI Educacional is a private institutional holding group based in São Paulo, Salvador, and Mato Grosso, Brazil. It owns and administers 19 higher education institutions and has close to 55,000 students. Its colleges are based in the midwest, north, and northeast regions of Brazil. It was founded in 1988 by the University of Cuiabá (UNIC).

Goals

Create a strong, unified brand for a holding group of colleges.

Name the group and create a visual identity system.

Build synergy and culture between the colleges, and between the academic and administrative groups.

Position the group for growth and future acquisitions.

More than a new brand, the creation of IUNI seeks to be responsible, integrated, and strong as we grow our group.

Rodrigo Galindo
Chief Executive Officer
IUNI Educacional

Process and strategy: In 2007, The University of Cuiabá (UNIC) was a holding group that owned five private colleges that had 35,000 students. The management group, led by CEO Rodrigo Galindo, aspired to become one of the top five university groups in Brazil. UNIC retained two branding firms to work together to reposition its brand, illuminate a new future, and build synergy between the various colleges. Per Creare Branding was responsible for strategy and liD Brand + Experience was responsible for naming and visual identity. The consultants conducted a rigorous process and involved the management, the academic staff, and both existing and prospective students in the different regions served. Interviews, surveys, and workshops were conducted with more than 1,000 stakeholders. The goal for this phase was for management and academic staff to clarify their shared mission, vision, attributes, competitive advantage, and personality. The brand essence that was co-created was, "Experts in management, passion for education."

Creative solution: Staff from all of the colleges were involved in the branding process. Unilateral agreement on the brand and its DNA, its values, its points of difference, it attributes were critical to the success of this initiative. liD Brand developed

more than one hundred names and narrowed down the list to three different strategies. Each name strategy was presented to the decision makers with an identity design strategy. Typical applications were used to demonstrate the difference of each strategy. It was determined that a short name was ideal. The name IUNI was created from a word that meant junior. Another meaning was "one university" to emphasize the unity of the group of schools. The bold and energetic logo and color reflected the brand attributes of young, confident, and forward-looking. Because of the spelling of the name, the logo can also be read upside down!

Results: The launch generated extensive media exposure and numerous interviews with the CEO were broadcast. Since the new brand launch, Group IUNI has acquired five more colleges and 15,000 more students. The academic staff and the management of the colleges have a new confidence, pride, and commitment to IUNI. They feel part of a larger whole that is dedicated to the highest quality education in Brazil. An intranet was created to encourage ongoing dialogue and information sharing between colleges. The website development was managed by IUNI's director of marketing and the site was built by the IUNI's IT department.

From the beginning of the process, the CEO's vision was the seed of the big idea and the one who inspired others to live the brand promise.

Antonio Roberto de Oliveira
liD Brand + Experience

Unilateral agreement on the brand and its DNA, its values, its points of difference, and its attributes were critical to the success of this project.

Wandy Cavalheiro
Per Creare Branding

Everything begins with the customer. We focus on all elements of our customer's traveling experience. When we say that we will make it easy for our customers, we mean it.*

DSB (the Danish state railway system) embarked on a retail initiative for their subbrand, Kort & Godt, creating a new concept in travel kiosks to sell not only tickets, but also coffee, pastry, fresh salads, newspapers, and other products to fast-moving travelers. Each day, a half million journeys are taken on DSB, which provides rail service within Denmark and across international borders.

Goals

Create a visual identity for the retail concept and subbrand.

Express the value "Making it easy."

Develop a distinct expression in the public space.

Develop signage, advertising, packaging, and products.

*Keld Sengelov
Chief Executive Officer
DSB

Kort & Godt

DSB believes that good design is good business. Kort & Godt is an integral part of DSB. Although our retail brand requires a unique graphic personality, it also needs to reflect the DSB program and distinctiveness.

Pia Bech Mathiesen
Director of Design
DSB

Innovation is not about technology alone. It is about understanding real-world people and creating products and services that fulfill human needs in new and better ways.

Kontrapunkt

Process and strategy: When in 2003, DSB decided to create a more customer-friendly environment in railway stations, they repurchased the DSB kiosks. Kontrapunkt worked closely with DSB to create a new branded concept, combining the purchase of tickets and convenience products in one shop. This strategy was an extension of DSB's consumer promise, "Making it easy." Kort & Godt was a subbrand of DSB and needed to co-exist with the DSB logo and identity system. The project began with a full-day briefing from DSB on the project, followed by an internal brainstorming session on the concept of the kiosk. The creative team determined that the success of the concept depended on fast service as well as a range of great products. Transparent walls and upscale positioning were central to the brand's easy and accessible image.

Creative solution: The new logo used a specially designed, expanded version of DSB's Via typeface to underscore the link with DSB. Photography of real people using DSB and Kort & Godt in public places was art directed and photographed. A new color palette was developed from DSB's identity program and applied to environment and products. Red signals hot food and beverages while green is for cold products. The simple and flexible signage system was designed to be easily adapted to the variety of architectural styles in the stations. It comprises vertical banners and transparent horizontal bands. The transparency of the facades signals openness, and enables the public to look into the shops through dot patterns of colored foils.

Results: DSB views the Kort & Godt shops as an important and tangible expression of their customer commitment to better standards of comfort and convenience. Research has shown that the shops have influenced customer satisfaction and the new subbrand has also resulted in increased revenues.

DSB values

Makes it easy

We make it easy for customers and for each other.

Committed

We identify opportunities.
Value-adding
We add value for our customers.

Efficient

We will become even better at what we do.

Responsible

We acknowledge our responsibilities.

Photography: Claus Løgstrop

Kort & Godt means "fast and easy."

243

Merging a passion for naturalist illustration with the day-to-day needs of a household, Laura Zindel integrates techniques from the Arts and Crafts movement with modern industrial design practices.

Laura Zindel Design is the collaboration of artist, designer, and ceramicist Laura Zindel and her husband, Thorsten Lauterbach. Laura and Thor, along with a small staff of artisans, create fine ceramics, dinnerware, textiles, paper products, and gift items from the converted barn of the Partridge House, a farmhouse located in Guilford, Vermont.

Goals

Reposition the brand.

Develop a distinct and versatile visual identity.

Transform perceptions from a craftsperson to a design maven.

Develop a platform for multi-product brand development.

Build a web presence to support the positioning goals and enable online retail activity.

LAURA ZINDEL
GUILFORD · VERMONT

Certain objects carry a personal history from generation to generation. "Crazy Uncle Larry bought that peculiar spider platter, and we just can't seem to part with it"—our products aspire to live in people's lives that way.

Laura Zindel
Founder & Principal
Laura Zindel Design

Process and strategy: Laura Zindel had been making wholesale handcrafted ceramic tableware for more than a decade from a small studio in San Francisco, selling her products mainly through word of mouth and national craft fairs. Having achieved national and international acclaim with celebrities, retailers, and upscale restaurants among her clientele, she engaged longtime friend and designer Jon Bjornson to help reposition and elevate her brand. Along with Laura's husband and business partner Thor Lauterbach, the team examined the company's operations, wholesale clients, retail customers, market segment, and competitive set. Their goal was to launch a new identity in tandem with the launch of a new line of production dinnerware, while also building a platform for increasing retail sales, entering new houseware product categories, and engaging financial and manufacturing partners for expanding production.

Creative solution: Noting the explosion of individual designers reaching name recognition through mass-market retailers, Bjornson recommended a name change from Zindel Ceramics to Laura Zindel Design, and acquired the URL laurazindel.com. A versatile symbol was developed that recalled antique colophons, referencing the creativity, craftsmanship, and uniqueness of Zindel's work. Known for her graphite illustrations, a drawing of a partridge was also created, emblematic of the 1778 farmhouse they now occupied in Vermont. For her signature, the two symbols were combined with a contemporary font with industrial roots, carrying the name of the small town in Vermont where the company is based. A basic marketing package was created, with look and feel reflecting the simple color palette and subdued warmth and beauty of her products.

Results: During the International Gift Show, held semiannually in New York, Zindel successfully launched her new line, attracting hundreds of wholesale clients, licensing partners, and manufacturing companies, including ABC Carpet & Home and Barneys.

The idea of an individual artist or designer building and leveraging a brand has never been more relevant or viable.

Jon Bjornson
Brand Strategist

The Library of Congress collects, preserves, and provides access to knowledge; sparks human imagination and creativity; and recognizes and celebrates achievement.

The Library of Congress is the de facto national library of the United States, and the research arm of the U.S. Congress. The largest library in the world, its collections include over 100 million books (in 470 languages), manuscripts, maps, legal materials, sound recordings, films, prints, and photographs. It also consists of a series of specialized centers, such as the U.S. Copyright Office.

Goals

Express the Library's essential identity.

Unify and integrate the communications of its many divisions and activities.

Complement and reinforce the Library's overall brand strategy.

Animation storyboard, "Books give us wings."

Process and strategy: Few people understand the scope and reach of the Library of Congress, which is composed of many parts, some of which have their own identities. In mid-2006 an overall branding study was undertaken by an internal Brand Working Group and Fleishman-Hillard. The year-long study defined a comprehensive brand message architecture. Chermayeff + Geismar was then retained to develop a complementary new visual identity program that would better represent this complex institution.

Having worked on various Library projects for over a decade, Chermayeff + Geismar had some familiarity with the institution. Nevertheless, a comprehensive visual audit was undertaken, and interviews were conducted with twelve senior representatives of the major constituent entities. The interviewees included all the members of the Brand Working Group, the committee charged with overseeing the project. It was at the end of this process that the project goals were clearly defined.

Creative solution: Chermayeff + Geismar's solution was two-fold: As the centerpiece of the new identity system the firm created a bold symbol that joins the essence of a book and the American flag to represent the national library. The symbol also suggests the idea of a diverse array of programs, services and activities flowing from a central core, and the flowing shape subtly suggests wings. When it came to the wordmark, the firm recommended dropping the word "The," enabling the name to be set in two justified lines.

Chermayeff + Geismar initially presented quite a few alternative symbol concepts, some based on the idea of a light or torch as a metaphor for knowledge, but ultimately recommended the book/flag design because no other library or organization could claim the marriage of a book and the American flag as its identifier.

The animation was created after the symbol had been chosen to help illustrate the slogan "Books give us wings."

Results: The result is a consistent and coherent identity system that centers on a bold symbol that is meaningful, easy to understand, and easy to remember. Because of the visual strength of each of the logo's elements (the symbol and the word mark), multiple arrangements (lockups) are possible while maintaining a consistent sense of identity.

A comprehensive style guide was created as an essential tool for the semi-autonomous units of the Library of Congress.

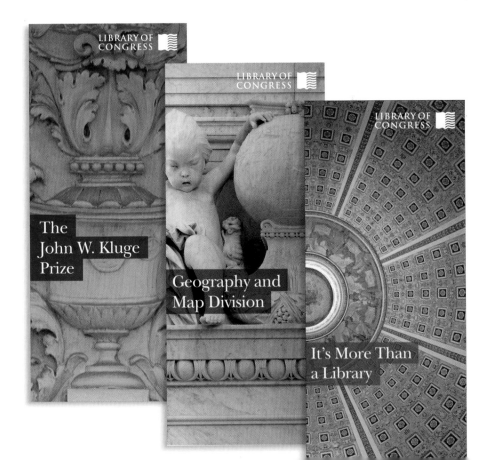

Properly implemented, the new identity should be an effective tool in helping the Library achieve its goal of communicating as one enterprise connected by a unified vision.

Tom Geismar
Chermayeff + Geismar

No other library could claim the marriage of a book and the American flag as its identifier.

Sagi Haviv
Chermayeff + Geismar

The Museum of Modern Art seeks to create a dialogue between the established and the experimental, the past and the present.

Founded in 1929, the Museum of Modern Art (MoMA) in New York is dedicated to being the foremost museum of modern art in the world. Central to its mission is the encouragement of an ever-deeper understanding and enjoyment of modern and contemporary art by the diverse local, national, and international audiences that it serves, from scholars to young children.

Goals

Design a bold, contemporary system.

Create a powerful and cohesive institutional voice.

Design an organized and flexible system across web, print, and environmental applications.

Underscore the museum's leadership in design.

MoMA

The new integrated design and marketing system underscores MoMA's leadership role in the field of design. The bold palette and the dramatic cropping of images exemplifies the spirit of this iconic institution.

Paula Scher
Partner
Pentagram

Process and strategy: MoMA has one of the most recognizable logotypes in the museum world. Originally designed by Ivan Chermayeff in 1964, the Franklin Gothic No. 2 logotype was redrawn in a new custom typeface named MoMA Gothic by Matthew Carter in 2004. Although the core identity itself is bold and iconic, the overall application across web, print, and physical environment has not been cohesive or visionary like the museum itself. The marketing advisory committee of the museum identified revitalizing the communications system as a priority. The museum engaged Pentagram to design a more powerful and integrated comprehensive system. "While the MoMA logo is iconic, it alone is not enough to continually carry the spirit of the institution," said Paula Scher, partner and lead designer for this project.

Creative solution: To create an attitude that modernizes the institution's image, Scher designed a complete methodology for the new system that works at any scale, from an exterior banner to a print advertisement in the newspaper. A strong grid was designed for the uniform placement of images and type. Each quadrant of a page or a banner has a specific function. And for

the first time in museum history, artwork is being cropped to maximize visual impact and marketing. A bold, singular image is selected as the signature focus of an exhibit, and is visually accompanied by a text block that features upcoming events. The logotype, always black on white, is used vertically when possible, and always bleeds off an edge. MoMA Gothic is the primary font for all typography in all applications. The system is very flexible. On applications like banners and billboards, type and images are used in multiples, creating a dynamic pattern against the urban landscape.

Results: The new system is being used for MoMA's institutional and public communications, including brochures, banners, the website, and other materials. Individual exhibitions will continue to have their own identities, used in catalogues, websites, and exhibition graphics. Julia Hoffman, Creative Director for Graphics and Advertising at MoMA, and her internal team have institutionalized the new system and have brought the system to life in applications from large banners and subway posters to the website. MoMA at long last has an identity system that carries the spirit of its iconic institution.

This project is one of a series of innovative initiatives conceived by a new marketing advisory committee established by MoMA in January 2008. The committee, comprised of local advertising and design professionals, advises the Museum on new avenues of communication and ways to diversify and engage with its audience. The committee is chaired by Ted Sann, MoMA honorary trustee.

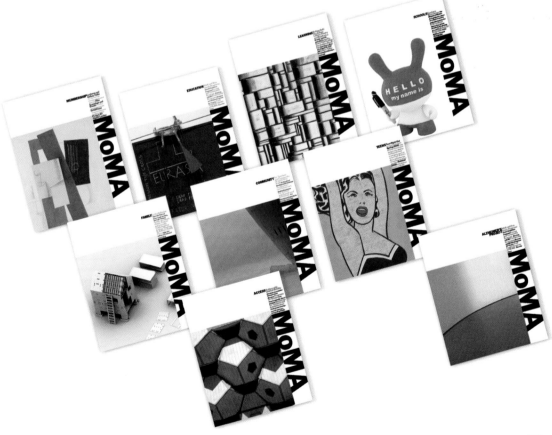

The New School stands for critical thinking and civic engagement; creative, disciplined, and collaborative self-expression; fearless participation in the debates of the day; and a willingness to embrace change.*

After World War I, The New School became a strong voice of new political and artistic thought. Based in New York City's Greenwich Village, the university houses eight schools and more than 8,000 undergraduate and graduate students. In 2003 Bob Kerrey, former senator of Nebraska, became its president.

Goals

Bring The New School's brand to life.

Develop a consistent naming structure for the university, divisions, and programs.

Create a clear core positioning strategy.

Develop a memorable voice.

Develop simple visual and writing guidelines.

*Bob Kerrey
 President
 The New School

THE NEW SCHOOL
A UNIVERSITY

We eschew the cautious and predictable in favor of the courageous and bold.
Excerpt, The New School Vision

THE NEW SCHOOL FOR GENERAL STUDIES

THE NEW SCHOOL FOR SOCIAL RESEARCH

MILANO THE NEW SCHOOL FOR MANAGEMENT AND URBAN POLICY

PARSONS THE NEW SCHOOL FOR DESIGN

EUGENE LANG COLLEGE THE NEW SCHOOL FOR LIBERAL ARTS

MANNES COLLEGE THE NEW SCHOOL FOR MUSIC

THE NEW SCHOOL FOR DRAMA

THE NEW SCHOOL FOR JAZZ AND CONTEMPORARY MUSIC

Process and strategy: Project Mirror's central goal was to provide a coherent, accurate portrayal of the university's identity. In an intensive two-year research study, Siegel+Gale interviewed a cross section from all eight schools, which included trustees, deans, faculty, administration, and other stakeholders. An invitation to participate in a web-based email survey was emailed to 1,800 students, faculty, prospects, alumni, and board members. An in-depth communications audit was conducted. The data collected was rich in narrative responses. Numerous dichotomies were identified. Although the school was known worldwide and each of the schools had significant reputations, the school's eight divisions bore no resemblance to each other or the parent. There was also no schoolwide catalog. Coherent key differentiators that were relevant to all of the schools were developed.

Creative solution: Siegel+Gale developed a new naming system for the eight schools so that the brand architecture was coherent. "No longer are we a collection of interesting schools; we are a university," remarked President Kerrey. The new visual identity is a wordmark in and out of focus; the wordmark is not fixed but has multiple states to exemplify a school that is active and alive. The design team wanted to embody the unconventional, edgy, and dynamic qualities of the school in a program that is kinetic, dynamic, and nontraditional.

Results: Every effort has been made to engage the entire community in the vision, identity, and positioning of the university. The website has the entire project dynamically presented, including the research process and findings, the strategy, and the identity examples. The transformation was well covered in the press, and new student enrollment is up 16% overall and up close to 23% at the undergraduate level.

Project Mirror is much more than a marketing effort—it not only defines our identity to the world, it helps us lay out what sets us apart from other institutions of higher education.

Bob Kerrey
President
The New School

The New School's positioning expresses what they stand for, what sets them apart, and why that's relevant to their constituencies.

Alan Siegel
President
Siegel+Gale

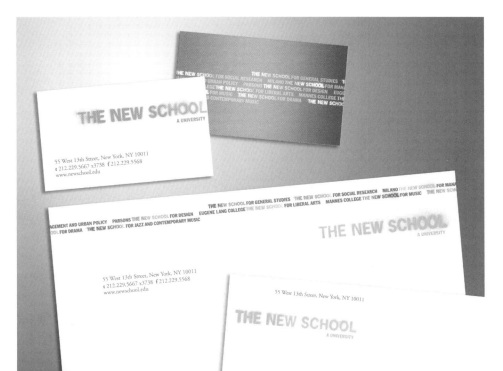

NIZUC reflects the ancient Mayan belief that in the beginning, nothing existed but sea and sky. NIZUC is where the Mayan culture embraces the 21st century.

NIZUC is an ultra luxury resort property and complex of private, modernist residences located on Mexico's Yucatan Peninsula. Its world-class architecture, preservation of the wild, natural landscape, and level of service redefine luxury in a region filled with legends of Mayan civilization.

Goals

Envision a lifestyle brand.

Distinguish from other world- class luxury destinations.

Attract world's best partners.

Establish a strong brand before opening.

We wanted it to be Mayan without being thematic.

Alan Becker
Developer
NIZUC

Photography: Quentin Bacon

Process and strategy: Soon after Alan Becker, NIZUC's developer, purchased the 28-acre estate of the former Mexican president, he began a search for a hotel operator. He interviewed a number of international upscale hotel management companies who were more interested in extending their brand equity than developing a vision for his site's unique attributes. "We wanted to be Mayan without being thematic;" Becker envisioned the architecture to reflect the culture and heritage of the Mayan civilization.

Becker brought in Carbone Smolan to create a unique brand platform to establish the core ideas from which all other decisions and partnerships would emanate. Becker and Carbone Smolan collaborated over the next nine months to understand conceptually and visually what the soul of this new ultra luxury destination would feel like and look like. The theme was "Mayan culture brought into the 21st century." This branding-first approach was considered a radical departure in the hotel industry.

Creative strategy: The luxury destination exists on a peninsula, Punta Nizuc, which inspired the name. Carbone Smolan began the creative process by designing a modern Mayan glyph as the brandmark. The iconic strong form lent itself to creating beautiful patterns and facilitated the design of objects of desire, from amulets to soaps and cookies. The second phase of the process was about creating images that captured the soul and experience of a destination that was not yet built. Led by Design Director Carla Miller, the creative team packed 22 boxes of props and flew down to Mexico with a staff of designers, stylists, models, and a photographer. Seven 18-hour days created a series of images that celebrated beauty, magic, design, high-end luxury, and otherworldliness. These images were then designed into a brand book that illuminated the essence of the destination.

Results: The NIZUC branding process channeled the vision of the developer. It enabled Alan Becker to attract renowned hospitality guru Adrian Zecha from Amanresorts, who in turn brought in architect Jean-Michel Gathy and Indonesian interior designer Jaya Ibrahim. Last year, advertisements began appearing in magazines depicting sand, surf, and, in one case, a model wearing a mysterious silver amulet. Establishing a brand platform and a branding-first approach has worked from an investment perspective as well as a marketing perspective.

Design was at the heart of our process. We needed to create a place before there was a place. We needed to capture the experience of NIZUC.

Leslie Smolan
Partner
Carbone Smolan

Barack Obama's 2008 U.S. presidential campaign sent a message of hope, change, and "Yes We Can" to the citizens of the world.

Barack Obama is the 44th President of the United States. He was the 2008 Democratic candidate and the first African-American to hold the office. His historic 22-month campaign galvanized media attention and set off an unprecedented, worldwide grassroots social media campaign.

Goals

Develop a bold visual identity for an American presidential candidate.

Express the candidate's vision and core values.

Build brand recognition in a competitive field.

Transcend traditional political campaign strategy.

There was a strong sense from the beginning that the campaign represented something entirely new in American politics.
Sol Sender
Sol Sender LLC

Photo: Darren Abate

John Slabyk created extensions of the symbol for different constituencies.

Process and strategy: In February 2007, Barack Obama announced his candidacy for U.S. president. Media outlets from all over the world were clamoring for assets, and speed was imperative. Mode Project, a Chicago-based firm working directly for David Axelrod, Obama's chief political strategist, retained Sol Sender and his firm Sender LLC to design the campaign identity. Mode initiated the process by stating clearly what the campaign stood for: "Change, reform, unification, a new day, a new beginning."

To gain more insight into the vision of the candidate, Sender read Obama's two books, *The Audacity of Hope: Thoughts on Reclaiming the American Dream* and *Dreams from My Father: A Story of Race and Inheritance.* Sender's firm also conducted an audit of presidential campaign branding over the past one hundred years to determine how far the identity should depart from traditional, patriotic visual language. In the end, Sender believed that it was critical to convey timeless American values, while simultaneously breaking new ground.

Creative solution: Like the candidate, the identity needed to be inclusive of Americans of all political stripes, races, and creeds. "It was not about the blue states versus the red states; it needed to be about one united America," said Sender. After examining a number of primarily typographic approaches, the campaign decided on an iconic symbol based on the letter "O"—the first time in American campaign history that a symbol was used. Radiating from the counterspace of the blue "O" is a soft, white glow, symbolizing the dawn of a new day. The foreground of red and white stripes further reinforces the patriotic theme. The simplicity of the symbol facilitated use on a variety of applications, including bumper stickers, banners, buttons, lawn signs, and the campaign website. Interim guidelines were created for the campaign's strategic design, social media, and branding teams, who proceeded to build a dynamic and cohesive system.

Results: Barack Obama's messages of hope and change were clear, distinct, and inspiring—qualities that charged the "O" symbol with a deeper level of meaning that resonated with citizens the world over. So popular was the Obama symbol that people made it their own, spontaneously applying it to everything imaginable. Citizen-generated tributes spread through social networking sites, effectively creating the twenty-first century's first impromptu, grassroots presidential campaign. The symbol became an integral part of a social media campaign that forever changed the face of American politics.

Sender and his design team, Andy Keene and Amanda Gentry, were able to create at the speed of light because a powerful, bold idea was clearly articulated in the beginning of the process.

Photo: Megan Paonessa

Thousands of iterations everywhere: Facebook, Twitter, cupcakes, cookies, human sculptures—we had never encountered anything like it in U.S. political history.

Sol Sender
Sol Sender LLC

The Olympic Games celebrate human spirit and achievement, and challenge the athletes of the world to be the best they can be. The festival itself transcends the politics of a fractured world to focus on our shared humanity.

Four billion people watched the 2004 Olympics on 300 different channels. Events were simultaneously streamed into mobile phones and websites. Dormant for 1,500 years, the games were revived in 1913 by Baron Pierre de Coubertin, who designed the five colored interlocking rings Olympic trademark.

Olympic Games: Baron Pierre de Coubertin, 1913

Below, from left to right:*

Tokyo 1964:
Unknown

Mexico 1968:
Lance Wyman, Pedro Ramirez Vásquez, and Eduardo Terrazas

Munich 1972:
Otl Aicher

Montréal 1976:
Unknown

Moscow 1980:
Vladimir Arsentyev

Los Angeles 1984:
Deborah Sussman and Jon Jerde

Seoul 1988:
Seung Choon Yang

Barcelona 1992:
Jose Maria Trias

Atlanta 1996:
Landor Associates

Sydney 2000:
Mark Armstrong

Athens 2004:
Wolff Olins

Beijing 2008:
Guo Chunning

*IOC/Olympic Museum Collections

TOKYO 1964

Munich1972

GAMES OF THE XXIVTH OLYMPIAD SEOUL 1988

Barcelona'92

Atlanta 1996

Process and strategy: Olympic Games help host countries boost tourism, build new infrastructure, and display their brand globally. The host country gets special rights to use the Olympic logo owned by the International Olympic Committee. Traditionally each country designs its own proprietary trademark and mascot to garner greater attention and marketability, helping sell products and attract corporate sponsors. Some countries, such as China and Greece, held global competitions that drew thousands of entries. Experienced world-class design firms are needed to ensure that the identities are graphically powerful and can be reproduced across thousands of applications. Designers are also needed to envision the look and feel of the Games, the environmental graphics, and everything from the medal design to the sports icons to the interactive multimedia displays.

Creative solution: The best Olympic trademarks engender pride, express a cultural difference, and look great on television and mobile phones. The challenge is to capture the spirit of the Olympics and combine it with the distinctive culture. Like other icons, the best ones have a strong central idea. The Athens 2004 emblem is an olive branch wreath, designed to express the heritage and legacy of the ancient Games in a color inspired by the Aegean sea and Greek sky. The Beijing 2008 script is inspired by bamboo carvings from the ancient Han Dynasty.

Results: The increasing breadth and reach of the Olympic Games have made them a powerful platform for building brands for the cities and countries that host them, the corporations that fund them, and the athletes who aspire to celebrity status. The symbols of the Games are reproduced hundreds of millions of times across a wide range of media and engender pride and ownership. The identities are traditionally launched in a large multimedia event.

The ever-existing challenge for each Olympics is not only to re-emphasize the original ideals, but also to be part of a process of moving them into the future.
Wolff Olins

Montréal 1976

Игры
XXII Олимпиады
Москва
1980

Games of the XXIIIrd Olympiad Los Angeles 1984

ΑΘΗΝΑ 2004

We are the Park Angels of Charleston—the historic, the proud. And we come together to improve, to preserve, and to share our parks in a way that's worthy of our beautiful city.

The Park Angels are the volunteers of the Charleston Parks Conservancy (CPC) in Charleston, South Carolina, who actively take a special interest and ownership in their city parks. The Park Angels is also a movement that connects people to the past, people to people, and people to their parks. CPC was founded in 2007 by Darla Moore.

Goals

Raise awareness and generate excitement in the community and among volunteers and donors.

Work with the City of Charleston to create a unique private/public partnership to support the parks.

Create an outlet for caring citizens who want to make a difference.

Instill a sense of ownership among the citizens of Charleston.

The Park Angels movement has given rise to a whole new way of defining support. It has opened a window for the community to give back to one of our most important resources—our parks.

Jim Martin
Executive Director
Charleston Parks Conservancy

Park Angels is a movement of people coming together in the name of their public spaces.

Robbin Phillips
Courageous President
Brains on Fire

Process and strategy: Charleston, South Carolina, is a 300-year-old city, rich with pride and heritage. The Charleston Parks Conservancy partnered with Brains on Fire to start a grassroots movement within the Charleston community to revitalize the more than 120 city parks. The identity firm's qualitative research revealed that there was no centralized documentation about public parks. The stories that did exist were personal, and passed on by word of mouth. The city could no longer fund the needed upkeep, and residents wouldn't respond to a basic call for a tree planting or cleanup day.

Brains on Fire developed a strategy to reframe the conversation about how the parks fit into people's lives and interests, either from a horticulture perspective and passion, or simply creating life memories.

Creative solution: To get park lovers involved, Brains on Fire set out to form deep relationships, and the Park Angels were born. The firm created separate but complementary identity and online community sites, and recruited and trained six Lead Park Angels. Lead Angels would serve two-year terms, and be responsible for responding to citizen concerns and suggestions, recruiting new Park Angels, and coordinating improvement efforts. The Lead Park Angels are featured prominently on the highly interactive website. Use of social media tools, including Facebook and Twitter, helps them connect people to people, people to the past, and people to the parks—both online and off. You can see the Park Angels on YouTube and Flickr, or help write a park Wiki and post on a messageboard. Dog lovers are encouraged to post their pups and become "Bark Angels." The Charleston Parks Conservancy was the first such organization to elevate its volunteers by allowing them to help guide the direction of the organization and serve as its public face.

Results: A transformation has taken place. There are no more barriers between the residents of Charleston and their parks. Now, neighborhoods are reaching out to the Park Angels to inquire how to beautify their parks. Education classes on the horticultural history of the parks are filled to capacity on a monthly basis, and more and more park lovers—from Gen Y to Boomers—are actively volunteering in their parks. The Charleston Parks Conservancy is taking the burden off of the city and has allowed the community to engage on a personal, grassroots level.

Virtual Wallet makes it easy and fun for the Gen Y crowd to plan and save money, pay bills when and how they want, and track their finances virtually. Better still, it can help eliminate worry.

PNC is a diversified and global financial services organization that spans the retail, business, and corporate markets. The retail-banking segment provides deposit, lending, brokerage, trust, investment management, and cash management services to approximately 2.9 million consumer and small business customers in the eastern United States (2008).

Goals

Understand how Gen Y views banking + money management.

Support Gen Y mental modes and lifestyles.

Create simple, direct, intuitive tools and interface.

Optimize banking activities.

Engage and delight users with simplicity, clarity and on-demand access.

Encourage financial savings and planning.

Gen Y specifically is the mass market of the future. It's the first generation to grow up with the internet. We're trying to respond to the unique ways they want to do business.

Tom Kunz
Senior Vice President
E-Business, PNC

By 2017, Gen Y will outnumber any other generation.

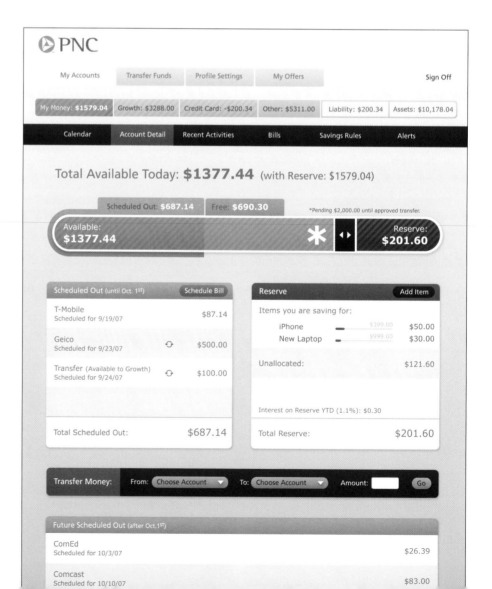

Process and strategy: Eager to make lifelong customers from the emerging Generation Y market, PNC came to IDEO to develop and refine their financial service offerings for a market that is made up of 70 million young, tech-savvy consumers. The design team began by understanding how members of Gen Y view banking and feel about money and managing their finances. These initial observations revealed that members of Gen Y embed technology into their lives and expect seamlessness, constant access, and fluidity from digital platforms.

Observations also uncovered two distinct user archetypes: those who embrace technology but are selective of how and when they use it, and those with a voracious appetite for digital content. These insights and archetypes became the basis for a design language for a banking service intended to engage users with simplicity, clarity, and on-demand access. The service would need to not only provide relevant tools for users, but also address the range of emotions associated with money and finances.

Creative solution: IDEO's result is "Virtual Wallet," a family of banking products that provide customers with seamless access to their finances and intuitive, tangible, and direct control of their money. Centered on electronic transactional banking, it is designed to both promote and optimize banking activities with features and visualizations that support the mental models and lifestyles of its Gen Y customers. The suite

includes a personal banking website that combines rich visualizations and contextual information to communicate the implications and relationships among financial data.

Graphics, behaviors, and exclusions were all carefully chosen using insights from Gen Y customer observations. The website features include a money slide bar to graphically indicate available funds, a "Savings Engine" that helps customers establish rules around spending, and a playful instant transfer feature named "Punch the Pig." In addition, Virtual Wallet includes a mobile application based on the same design language and structure as the website, simply adapted for small screens.

Results: Virtual Wallet customers are provided with an enticing experience that is still in line with the structure of the bank's existing offers. The highly visual interface helps customers plan and save money, pay bills and track finances virtually, which in turn, minimizes mistakes and creates a more confident money manager. Within two months of the service's launch, PNC customers opened thousands of Virtual Wallet accounts, with 80 percent of the new business coming from the targeted younger demographic, according to *BrandWeek*. The average visit to the Virtual Wallet site has been well above average, and retention has also exceeded PNC averages.

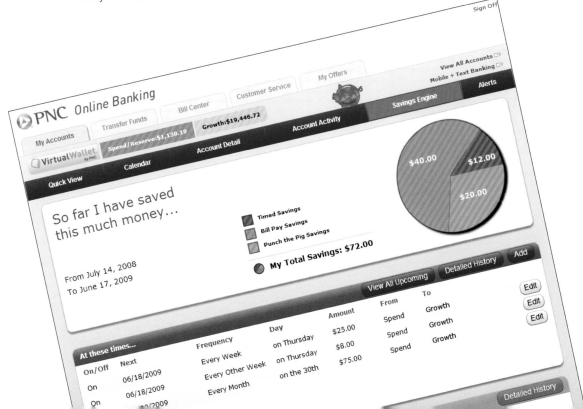

The two major branches of the Presbyterian Church, separated since the Civil War, were reunited in 1983, and a seal, also referred to as a symbol, to represent this unification was needed.

The Presbyterian Church has 2.3 million members, more than 10,000 congregations, and 14,000 ministers in the United States. An eight-person task force comprising theologians, pastors, educators, an artist, and a musician was responsible for determining what theological ideas and images should be incorporated into the new symbol.

Goals

Design a symbol that represents the church's mission.

Design a symbol that is emotive and evocative.

Reflect the ordered and structured nature of the church.

Suggest the vitality of the church.

Integrate theological images and ideas.

Represent the unification of two branches.

I worked on possibilities all day, every day, and most of every night. I dreamed about the symbol during whatever time was left to sleep.

Malcolm Grear
CEO
Malcolm Grear Designers

The Cross

The Pulpit

The Fish

The Fire

The Dove

The Cup

The Book

The Triangle

Process and strategy: The task force, led by John M. Muldar, Ph.D., conducted a national search for a designer and, after interviewing forty-six firms, chose Malcolm Grear Designers. The task force had extensive theological and philosophical discussions around which images should be included in the seal. Grear's studio brought in Martha Gregor Geothals, Ph.D., a historian and artist trained in theology, to give a historical perspective on the history and meaning of Christian symbols.

The primary goal was the creation of a design that would have an emotive and evocative character, suggesting the vitality of the church's mission. The design, however, needed a level of formality to reflect the ordered and structured nature of the church. The seal also needed to serve as a symbolic statement of the unification.

Creative solution: What seemed like an impossible goal for any experienced designer evolved into a design process that generated close to 4,000 sketches. Grear was obsessed with finding an answer, but initially he thought he could never develop a design that would incorporate more than three of the theological ideas.

After an exhaustive exploration, Grear was able to incorporate eight ideas in the design of the mark: the cross, the pulpit, the fish, the fire, the descending dove, the cup, the book, and the triangle. Grear's recommendation to the diverse task force received unanimous approval, but that was only the first step. The church's charter required the General Assembly, composed of 2,500 individuals, to vote on it.

Results: The General Assembly staff developed a powerful video presentation about the seal and its meaning. The assembly gave Grear and Geothals a standing ovation, and the rest is history. It represented the first unanimous vote in the history of the Presbyterian Church. The story of the process was documented in a book written by Muldar, and the church's website contains an in-depth explanation of the meaning of the elements.

The seal has been applied to an endless variety of entities, from stained-glass windows, church bulletins, and Bibles, to informational signage and clothing. More than twenty years after the initial design, the Presbyterian Church leadership returned to Malcolm Grear Designers to request a redesign of its website and the creation of branding guidelines.

The design has proved to be a simple but eloquent statement of the Presbyterian Church's heritage, identity, and mission. I have used the seal to teach people the meaning of the Presbyterian tradition, and I have been intrigued by the way the seal itself engages people's imagination—it helps them understand the content and imagery of the Bible and the abstractions of doctrine and theology.

John M. Muldar, Ph.D.

Our business philosophy has never changed: take a long-term view of the market, find value in markets others overlook, and do the right thing.*

Founded in 1992, Preferred Unlimited is a privately held, diversified investment firm with a portfolio of more than $1.5 billion in assets. Preferred specializes in the acquisition of value-add investments across a broad spectrum of asset classes including natural resources, commercial real estate and development land, and existing operating companies.

Goals

Reposition the brand of a highly successful real estate company.

Develop a name and visual symbol to reflect the company's mission, values, and its "work hard, play hard" culture.

Focus the company's brand on its entrepreneurial soul.

Build a differentiated web presence.

Own the name 'Preferred.'

*Michael O'Neill
Founder & CEO
Preferred

I have two folders on my desk: my business plan and my charities. I make no distinction as to either's immediate importance throughout the course of any given day.

Michael O'Neill
Founder & CEO
Preferred

People want to be entertained. I think our website clearly expresses exactly who we are, what we do, and what we believe—in a way that is unlike anything in our industry.

Michael O'Neill
Founder & CEO
Preferred

Process and strategy: Preferred Real Estate Investments had worked with Jon Bjornson as its design consultant for nearly a decade when the company approached him to join its senior management team. Bjornson joined Preferred as its creative director in 2005, and embarked on a two-year process to reposition the company's brand.

Preferred had an extensive track record rehabilitating large, outmoded industrial properties into vibrant commercial office campuses throughout the Mid-Atlantic region. Preferred also had a long history of charitable activity, with a focus on community revitalization and youth education. With a constant eye on market fluctuations, and led by a visionary CEO, the company was seeking investment opportunities in new markets, and on a national scale, but its perception as a commercial 'rehab' specialist hindered its ability to successfully position the company with sellers and financial institutions. It had a lengthy and generic name and a niche it wished to broaden.

Although the company had surpassed 15 years in business, it was clear that its most successful business relationships centered around its energetic, youthful style; its hard-working, business-savvy, and charitable culture; and its aggressive, innovative approach to structuring capital investments.

Creative solution: Working with senior management and in-house legal counsel, the company name was changed to Preferred Unlimited, Inc., referencing both its "anything is possible" personality and its repositioning as a holding company for private equity investments. The company also negotiated the purchase of the URL preferred.com, and adopted the communicative name "Preferred." A stylized "P" logo, derived from the symbol for infinity, was designed to support a logotype referencing speed, youth, and sport. A marketing program, inspired by a collection of words describing Preferred's brand characteristics, was applied to stationery, signage, press kit, internal communications, interior office artwork, presentations, proposals, charitable ads and sponsorships, and ephemera.

Working with Dan Marcolina and Marcolina Design, a website was created to mirror the company's people, culture, and entrepreneurial spirit in a transparent, unexpected and entertaining way, unlike any of its competitors.

Results: The brand established an energized new look to bridge the company's transition to a broader, national presence, and provided an entry point for its employees, partners, and clients to understand the company's mission, purpose, and culture. Preferred successfully completed several national acquisitions, in a turbulent economic climate, and fostered new relationships with sellers, investors, and financial partners. The company also continues its charitable mission as an unswerving priority.

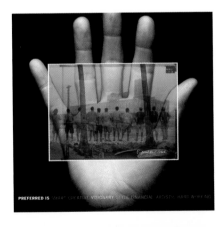

Working on the client side for two years was probably my most valuable experience as a designer. Client discovery and immersion are ephemeral in comparison to becoming a part of the fabric of a company's culture, knowing its people, and understanding the driving forces behind its business.

Jon Bjornson
Brand Strategist

(RED) embraces brands and empowers you, the consumer, to choose products that raise money for the Global Fund to help eliminate AIDS in Africa.

(RED) is a global licensed brand created in 2006 to raise money for and awareness of AIDS in Africa. Formed by U2 frontman Bono and Bobby Shriver, (RED) works with partners to create and market (RED) products. A portion of the sales of these products goes directly to the international NGO Global Fund, an acknowledged expert and world leader in financing the fight against AIDS.

Goals

Harness the power of the world's greatest companies to eliminate AIDS in Africa.

Develop a new business and brand model.

Develop a source of sustainable private sector income for the Global Fund.

Make it easy for consumers to participate.

Inspire partner companies to participate.

(RED) was born from friendship and anger, ambition and heart, and the sheer will to make the impossible possible.

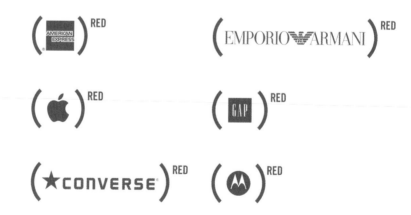

Process and strategy: Harnessing the private sector and partnering with successful global brands to eliminate AIDS in Africa was the big idea conceived by Bono and Bobby Shriver. Bono calls it "conscious consumerism." Their new business model had three overarching principles: deliver a source of sustainable private sector income to the Global Fund, the acknowledged leader and expert in financing the fight against AIDS; provide consumers with a choice that made giving effortless at no extra cost; and generate profits and a sense of purpose for partner companies. Brand partners pay a licensing fee for use of the (RED) brand, which they then use to manage and market their (RED) products. The fee does not infringe on the amount of money sent to the Global Fund. Wolff Olins was engaged to work with Bobby Shriver and his team to paint a vision of the new brand and develop a strategy to attract founding partners, and to create a unique brand expression that allows (RED) to interface with iconic brands in a way that allows them to be themselves, but also to be (RED).

Creative solution: Wolff Olins built the brand around the idea that (RED) inspires, connects, and gives consumers power. The design team needed to create a brand architecture that showcases the participating brand and, at the same time, links that brand to the power of (RED). The identity system needed to be immediately recognizable and work across media, in marketing and on product. Although making the products the color red was not a requirement, many of the participating businesses extended the idea of (RED) to the product. Apple created red iPod Shuffles and iPod Nanos. In the UK, there is a (RED) American Express card that gives money to the Global Fund each time a consumer makes a purchase. All bear the (product/brand) RED lockup.

Results: Within the first five weeks of the US launch, the (RED) brand registered 30 percent unaided awareness. (RED) partners delivered $45 million to the global fund in one year (more than was received from the private sector in the previous five years). This is enough money to give 290,000 people life-saving drugs for one year. By spring 2009, (RED) had raised $130 million, which is enough to buy AIDS drugs for more than 800,000 people for one year.

Two thirds of people affected with AIDS in Africa are women and children.

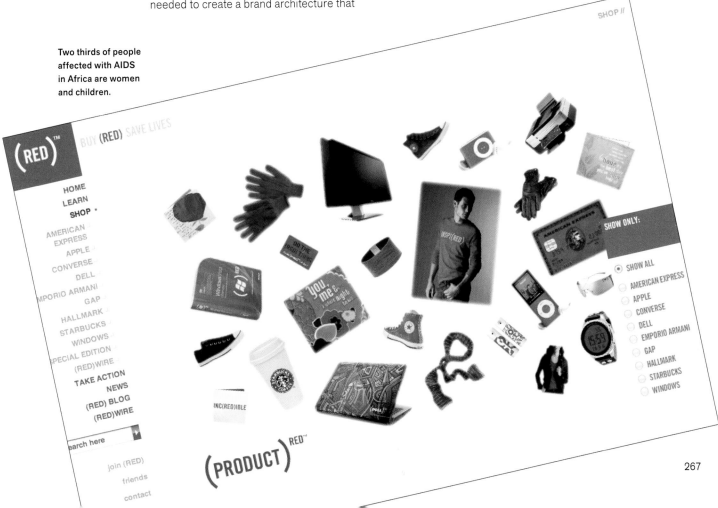

267

Long known for its élan, Saks Fifth Avenue exists for the discerning shopper with a penchant for unmitigated style and outstanding service.

Saks Fifth Avenue, a subsidiary of Saks Incorporated, is a high-end department store specializing in clothing, footwear, beauty products, and housewares. Formed in 1898, they operate 53 stores across the U.S.

Goals

Revitalize brand presence.

Design distinctive, easily identifiable iconic identity.

Create flexible program to work across multiple applications.

Build on brand equity.

Energize the category.

The updated logo gives us a modern look that is sure to resonate with our customers and contribute to the resurgence of Saks Fifth Avenue.

Steve Sadove
CEO
Saks Incorporated
Fashion Week Daily,
December 11, 2006

Process and strategy: Saks approached Pentagram in 2004 to design an identity program that would encompass its signage, advertising, direct mail, online presence, and packaging. The Saks leadership team was eager to send a signal that the then-106-year-old retailer was looking to the future—its stores offered constant change and surprise as well as superlative quality. Director of Marketing Terron Schaefer desired a ubiquitous and iconic identity that would be instantly recognizable across a busy street.

Saks, unlike Tiffany, had never had a signature color, and unlike Burberry, no signature pattern. The current logo, used for the last decade, and its gray-on-gray packaging had done little to advance the brand's high-fashion profile. An audit revealed that Saks had used literally dozens of logos since its founding in 1898. Many were variations on the same theme: cursive writing, sometimes casual, sometimes Spencerian. The classic script, redrawn by Tom Carnese and used in packaging designed by Massimo Vignelli, was still the one that customers remembered.

Creative solution: Pentagram began the creative process with conversations about visually inspiring art and cultural artifacts. Early creative sessions at Saks made it clear that the bold, energetic paintings of Franz Kline and Barnett Newman continued to resonate, and Pentagram's Michael Bierut began looking for "a way to get that kind of dramatic scale and energy into the program." Bierut took the cursive logo, redrew it with the help of font designer Joe Finocchiaro, and placed it in a black square. He then subdivided that square into a grid of sixty-four smaller squares that could be visually shuffled and rearranged to form an almost infinite number of variations, calculated at almost a 100 googols! A googol is a one with one hundred zeros after it.

Results: Fashion is about constant change and the new black-and-white identity is organic and unpredictable. When scaled up and used on packaging, the reconfigured patterns are still immediately recognizable and remain dramatically differentiated from other high-end retailers. Pentagram designed over forty different packages in the program, from jewelry boxes to hatboxes and gift cards, and four sizes of shopping bags. In the new program, no two of these are alike, yet they all go together. The quality embodies Saks signature style.

We tried to signal continuous change, the essence of fashion, but also convey the timelessness you get in familiar packaging, like the Tiffany blue box.

Michael Bierut
Partner
Pentagram

Embodying the philosophy of celebrated sushi chef Kazunori Nozawa, sugarFISH offers a dramatically simplified prix-fixe menu. The freshest catch. Great sushi. Everyday prices. New experience.

sugarFISH™ by Sushi Nozawa offers traditional sushi of the highest quality in a fun, casual setting in Marina Del Rey, California. Opened in 2006, the restaurant is a collaboration between Kazunori Nozawa, renowned chef, and Jerry Greenberg, technology and new media entrepreneur, both of whom are passionate about making authentic food available to everyone.

Goals

Change the way Americans think about sushi.

Extend the brand equity of a master chef and his philosophy.

Build on quality that is exceptional and uncompromising.

Embody a simple, real, and eye-opening experience.

Combine old school values with new school vision.

With sushi, it's all about the details.
Kazunori Nozawa

Process and strategy: The business partners aspired to change the way Americans think about sushi, combining age-old Japanese craftsmanship with a whole new dining experience. In the Japanese tradition, sushi is a celebration of the purity of ingredients and the skill of chefs in selecting, cutting, and presenting them. Celebrated sushi chef Kazunori Nozawa cleaves to the Japanese tradition of *omakase,* or "trust in the chef."

Brand strategy sessions were a collaboration between Jerry Greenberg and Clement Mok, designer and digital pioneer. The brand promise, "Surprisingly good food at a fair price that's quick and easy," was at the center of the new business that would build on chef Nozawa's legendary status, and two decades of top Zagar ratings for his restaurant in Studio City. The name sugarFISH was created since Nozawa is known for his "melt in the mouth" sushi. The menu, while always changing to reflect what's fresh, would be dramatically simplified. Diners choose from three core selections, called Trust Me's. It's a prix-fixe menu with tax and gratuities included. No surprises on the cost. Anticipation on the top three selection.

Creative solution: Clement Mok managed all points of customer interaction and experience including interiors, web, print, packaging, web, and signage to insure that the spirit of sugarFISH was communicated at each touchpoint. He designed a kaleidoscopic big eye tuna brandmark that sparkles with delight and a look and feel language of abstract sea bubbles. He engaged Zaudhaus to develop and build the site. Unlike other sushi restaurants, the design is modern and casual—the chic bar is not a traditional sushi bar since the chefs are in the back. Updated menus are shown on vertical monitors, a counterbalance to the sea bubble wall and the organic shape of the bar. Curbside take out service has been branded sugarFLIGHT. Each Trust Me selection is served in a specially designed white recyclable bento box with dressing and garnish instructions for customers to create their own mini sugarFISH experience.

Results: Since opening, sugarFISH has received rave reviews, significant press coverage, and a loyal following. Chef Nozawa's son, Tom, and Jerry Greenberg are already looking to expand the restaurant to other cities. The new restaurant continues to build on Nozawa's mythical status and the uncompromising quality of his sushi. The prix-fixe menu as well as the dramatically simplified selection has been a great success with value-conscious sushi-loving consumers. Leveraging long-term relationships with the best Japanese importers and fish purveyors and eliminating the middleman to maximize quality and contain costs has made this business model work. Trust me! Delight me. Yes.

Every day Chef Nozawa assembles menus that he calls, quite simply, Trust Me.

Superman

The Superman brand goes deeper than the shield. Authentic. Powerful. Proven. The mark of a hero.*

Superman, the brand, is owned and licensed by DC Comics, a subsidiary of Time Warner, and the largest English-speaking publisher of comic books in the world. Superman, the Man of Steel, a cultural icon and multimedia superhero since his 1938 debut, appears in comic strips, movies, television programs, toys, children's clothing, and thousands of other products.

Goals

Protect Superman's brand equity.

Clarify brand attributes.

Stimulate licensing opportunities with licensees, retailers, and buyers.

Preserve and grow the iconic value.

*Excerpt, *Superman Brand Book*

Whether it's our internal people, our retail partners, or our licensing partners, people are starting to understand that Superman is more than just a piece of artwork.

David Erwin
Executive Creative Director
Licensing
DC Comics

Process and strategy: The release of the 2006 movie *Superman Returns* and the brand extensions were designed to saturate the media and the marketplace. David Erwin, Executive Creative Director of Licensing for DC Comics, wanted to ensure that their leading superhero was a well-defined brand that licensees, retailers, and buyers understood and respected. DC Comics hired Little & Company to articulate the Superman brand and stimulate licensing opportunities. The brand book needed to demonstrate that the brand was far greater than the Superman logo. In order to insure a pipeline of quality products aligned with the brand's aspirational attributes, the book also needed to reverberate with quality and inspiration. The creative team included designers, writers, researchers, and archivists.

Creative solution: The *Superman Brand Book* is an impeccably designed and produced sixty-page hardcover book that feels like a limited-edition collector's volume. Iconic imagery is juxtaposed with a strong, confident voice and writing. Hold the book in your hands, and the cover reads *Indestructible* while the reader is reintroduced to Superman's inherent heroic qualities, the attributes that define the brand. Turn the book upside down, and the cover reads *Inspirational* and the book demonstrates how the brand can inspire people of all ages to be superheroes in their own lives. In a spread that features a collage of past and present Superman images, the text reads, "A hero for modern times no matter how often these times are reimagined."

Results: Five thousand copies were distributed to the employees of Warner Bros. (DC Comics licensing agent), and to targeted retailers. Bryan Singer, the director of *Superman Returns*, used the brand book to help shape his character development. The book's popularity has propelled the printing of an additional 7,500 copies. DC Comics is proceeding with a family of brand books, including Batman and Wonder Woman.

> **Our goal was to inspire marketers, designers, and licensees to incorporate the big ideas behind the Superman brand. Strength. Invincibility. Courage.**
>
> Mike Schacherer
> Design Director
> Little & Company

Inspirational

Woven throughout the fabric of our culture.

Indestructible

He doesn't need his cape to fly. Only his will.

Tate reinvented the idea of a gallery—from a single institutional museum, with a single institutional view, to a branded collection of experiences offering many different ways of seeing.

In the 1990s, Tate was referred to as "The Tate," implying that it had just one location. Three galleries were as architecturally diverse as their collections, which encompass international contemporary art, as well as British art from the 1500s. The opening of the fourth gallery in 2000 provided the impetus to transition Tate from an institution lead to a brand lead organization.

Goals

Unify the brand without losing each gallery's distinctive properties.

Distinguish diverse locations for visitors.

Express the theme, "one Tate, yet many Tates."

Articulate a forward-thinking, global, and accessible approach to art.

Position the Tate experience as culture, art, entertainment, and enjoyment.

Tate has moved from being a gallery to being a space where people can experience art, meet, think, learn, and eat.

Marina Willer
Creative Director
Wolff Olins

The challenge for any museum is to find a way of combining content, building, and experience to tell a coherent story.

Marina Willer
Creative Director
Wolff Olins

Tate Museums
Tate Modern
Tate Britain
Tate Liverpool
Tate St. Ives

Process and strategy: Tate retained Wolff Olins to create a new brand to unify the collections and the four museums. Extensive interviews were conducted to clearly define Tate's opportunity and ambition. Research among visitors and nonvisitors revealed that in the United Kingdom, more people visit museums than attend football matches. Wolff Olins helped Tate discover and articulate its central brand idea.

"Look again, think again," invites visitors to reconsider the experience of a gallery. It also challenges Tate to reevaluate how it speaks to the public about art. The new brand strategy simplified the names of the four museums and dropped the definite article. What was known as the Tate Gallery or London Millbank became Tate Britain.

Creative solution: Instead of one unchanging symbol in a prescribed color consistently applied across all media, Wolff Olins created four dynamic wordmarks, each to be used interchangeably all using the name "Tate" in uppercase lettering and appearing in various degrees of visual focus. The fluidity of form reflects the essence of Tate's point of view.

Allowing flexibility within a unified identity, the design conveys transformation and nonconformity. Tate's luminous and expansive color palette is unpredictable and fresh. In addition Wolff Olins designed a custom-designed typeface called "Tate," which is used for all signatures, for the signage system, and in exhibition signage.

Results: The new brand broadened the appeal of Tate's museums, illuminated the four locations, and positioned Tate globally. From the day it opened, Tate Modern was a huge success, attracting double its target visitor numbers, and becoming the most popular modern art gallery in the world. After seven years, Tate's overall annual visitor numbers had tripled, to 7.7 million. As the Observer wrote in May 2005, Tate "has changed the way that Britain sees art, and the way the world sees Britain."

Large billboards that hang in Turbine Hall of Tate Modern advertise existing and upcoming exhibitions. Illuminated exhibition signage at Tate Modern can be read from across the Thames, and exhibition banners hang ceremoniously between the columns at Tate Britain. Wolff Olins designed an online brand toolkit, ensuring that all agencies involved with Tate are in sync with the program.

A successful brand is all about detail. Every facet of a brand must be apparent in an organization's communications, behavior, products, and environment.

Brian Boylan
Chairman
Wolff Olins

Thomas Jefferson's Poplar Forest was a pursuit of happiness. Between the ages of 66 and 80, Jefferson went to the octagonal retreat he designed to rekindle his creativity and escape the crowds at Monticello.

Poplar Forest was designed during Jefferson's tumultuous second term as U.S. president. Sold by his grandson, the house and plantation fell into private hands for 160 years. In 1984, The Corporation for Jefferson's Poplar Forest began the rescue, repurchase, archeological study, and meticulous restoration of this national historic landmark.

Goals

Reposition Poplar Forest as a national treasure.

Illuminate the genius of Thomas Jefferson.

Create an emotional connection with visitors and supporters.

Differentiate Poplar Forest from peer destinations.

Make it easy for a small staff to raise awareness and attract supporters.

THOMAS JEFFERSON'S

Poplar Forest

Thomas Jefferson wrote the Declaration of Independence in 1776 at the age of thirty-three. At 64, he designed Poplar Forest, 90 miles south of Monticello. It was a three-day trip on horseback to get to his retreat, where he kept 1,200 books, played the violin, and spent time with his two granddaughters.

Thomas Jefferson's Poplar Forest retreat, nearly lost to future generations, presents us with an unparalleled opportunity to understand this exceptional person and his relentless creativity.

Lynn A. Beebe
President
Corporation for Jefferson's
Poplar Forest

Process and strategy: Poplar Forest, a modern architectural masterpiece, is relatively unknown to scholars, history enthusiasts, and the public. In 1984, after 160 years of neglect, The Corporation for Jefferson's Poplar Forest rescued the national landmark from demolition, and was in a constant "survival" mode, fundraising, buying back property, and conducting meticulous renovation, and archeological study. On the eve of 200th anniversary of Jefferson's retirement in 2009, the executive director, Lynn Beebe, and the Board were ready to start promoting Poplar Forest in a more compelling, cohesive way. Rev Group interviewed all Board members, the restoration architects, and the archeologists, as well as the Virginia Director of Tourism. The design team conducted a series of audits, visited other Jefferson-designed landmarks and other presidential sites, and examined everything from portraits of Jefferson to how the house was photographed. The new strategy was to forge an emotional connection to Jefferson's boundless curiosity, his ingenuity, and his pursuit of happiness. A new focus on Jefferson's retirement would attract both boomers and Jefferson enthusiasts.

Creative solution: Poplar Forest's brand identity system was inspired by Thomas Jefferson: his superlative ability to communicate, his creativity, his aesthetic and inimitable style. Whenever possible, Jefferson quotes and his design sensibility, which focused on simplicity and counterbalance, would be used. Another unifying principle was to use Jefferson's age, and not the year, to help visitors imagine his life at Poplar Forest. The visual identity exemplifies counterbalance by integrating hand-drawn and modern elements. Poplar Forest utilized Jefferson's handwriting from his correspondence. An iconic image of Jefferson was an interpretation of Rembrandt Peale's portrait. The direct eye contact and contemporary design create a proprietary image. A basic tool kit of applications was designed, with a special emphasis on fundraising tools. A fact-sheet system was inspired by Jefferson's information architecture in *Notes on the State of Virginia,* reprinted 18 times during Jefferson's life. Fact sheets were used both in the media room and for information kits for grant solicitation.

Results: The process refocused and re-energized the Board and the staff with a sense of possibilities. A new PR and communications person, Anna Bentson, was brought on board to assist the small staff in outreach. The new guidelines helped get funding for a new website, signage, and landscaping by presenting a more professional image, shoulder to shoulder with other presidential historic landmarks. Over the next two years, there was an increase in attendance, fundraising, and media outreach. Poplar Forest was featured in the *New York Times* with Monticello in a tribute to the 200th anniversary of Jefferson's retirement.

TiVo's overriding philosophy is that all people, no matter how busy, deserve the opportunity to enjoy the home entertainment of their choosing, at their convenience.*

In 1997, TiVo was founded by two Silicon Valley engineers, Mike Ramsay and Jim Barton. Now a public company, TiVo has created a seismic shift in the experience of television viewers, allowing them to record, pause, replay, and create their own playlists of their favorite shows. The technology has caused ripples in the advertising world, since it is easy for the user to fast forward through advertising right to the programmed content.

Goals

Name a company that aspired to change the rules of home entertainment.

Design an identity that appeals to users in the digital living room.

Create an icon as recognizable as Disney's mouse ears.

Focus on the user's desire for fun, convenience, and control.

Create a name that could have brand extensions.

*Mike Ramsay
CEO and Co-Founder
TiVo

The engineering of great products is highly creative. The team was familiar with the feelings of uncertainty that exist before an answer comes and they were comfortable that we would get it right. It's one of the benefits of an "A" level team.

Michael Cronan
Principal
Cronan

TiVo meet iPod. It sounds like a marriage made in techie heaven.
money.cnn.com

Process and strategy: In 1997, Cronan partners Michael Cronan and Karin Hibma were retained to create a new name and identity for a confidential Silicon Valley project with the code name Teleworld. Michael Cronan, principal, began by immersion into the new product: understanding its genesis, using it, watching others use it, and framing its cultural context. "Once I began to understand that it could essentially change behavior, I began to ask 'what would the next TV be like?'," said Cronan. Although his team generated over 1,600 names, once Cronan started to envision the next generation of television, he instinctively knew that the name needed to include the *T* and *V*. He looked at the visual forms of the letters, integrated an *i* and *o*, symbolic of the in and out engineering acronym, and created the fabricated name, TiVo.

Creative solution: Designing the identity was simultaneous with creating brand extensions and a new TiVo culture. Cronan aspired to design an icon "as recognizable as the mouse ears are to Disney." His early sketches were stick figure drawings with television bodies and rabbit ears. An early morning bumper sticker sighting of a Darwinian fish with human legs made Cronan realize the icon needed legs. "Everyone started nodding, and we started thinking about the TiVo identity as a mascot," said Cronan. Explorations into the look and feel of TiVo generated color palettes and other graphic elements. Once there was agreement about the name and the character, an animation team began the work of breathing life into the mascot.

Results: TiVo has become the most popular DVR in the U.S., and cites that its technology fueled "one of the most rapid and enthusiastic adoption rates in the history of consumer electronics." Consumer research has revealed that subscribers fall in love with TiVo, and would sooner disconnect their cell phone than unplug their TiVo. TiVo has recently formed an alliance with Apple and Sony to download television content to mobile devices. Although the business category is being saturated by bigger players, TiVo will always have the first mover advantage.

The first time I used TiVo in my own home, I clicked the button to pause live TV when Karin walked in with the kids. I began to feel, like most TiVo users do, that I wish I could use TiVo's feature set in life outside the box.

Michael Cronan
Principal
Cronan

Unilever's mission is to add vitality to life. We meet everyday needs for nutrition, hygiene, and personal care with brands that help people feel good, look good, and get more out of life.*

Unilever sells 400 food, home care, and personal care products, many of them local brands that can be found only in specific countries. Unilever's portfolio of familiar brands includes Birds Eye, Dove, Hellmann's, Knorr, Lipton, and Ben & Jerry's.

Goals

Work with leadership to articulate what One Unilever stands for.

Identify a core brand idea for a diverse business model.

Design a brand identity aligned with the vision.

Engage the employees, customers, and other stakeholders.

Build an online brand center to tell the story.

*Anthony Burgmans
Niall FitzGerald
Chairmen
Unilever

Vitality brings the opportunity to build a great company: one that seizes the most exciting opportunities, leads on important issues, and succeeds as a result.

Patrick Cescau
CEO
Unilever

Process and strategy: While the conglomerate reduced its brand portfolio from 1,600 to 400 brands in 1999, it has remained a vast organization. Unilever, the brand behind the brands, was largely invisible to consumers, known primarily to the investment community. Wolff Olins began working early in 2002 to articulate what the business stood for and to identify an anchor and touchstone for the future. "Through a process of workshops and discussions with the leadership team, the concept of 'vitality' emerged as the idea to build the Unilever brand on," said Ian Stephens of Wolff Olins. It has been captured in the new Unilever mission: "Adding Vitality to Life." The company identified vitality as a consumer motivation for buying Unilever products that help them feel good, look good, and get more out of life. Vitality symbolizes Unilever's commitment to social and environmental responsibility, recognizing that today's consumer examines the behavior of the company behind the brand.

Creative solution: Wolff Olin's creative team designed a new U symbol, composed of twenty-five individual marks, which embodies the vitality theme on many levels. The fish represents products like fish fingers, as well as Unilever's sustainable fish policies. Bees create honey, an ingredient in many food products, and symbolize nature and the environment. Wolff Olins consulted many experts as the brand developed. Religious experts advised changing what was a six-pointed star into the seven-pointed star. Cultural advisors suggested clarifying the hand next to the flower so it could not be mistaken for the sole of a foot, which would cause offense in Thailand. The team checked to see that even seen upside down or reflected in a mirror, none of the icons could be misread as offensive in any language or culture. They worked to obtain the buy-in of hundreds of stakeholders: business leaders worldwide, employees, external opinion makers, investors, and consumers.

Results: The vitality mission and new identity were launched at an annual shareholder meeting, followed by leadership forums around the world. An eighteen-month plan was developed to put the Unilever name and logo on products in supermarkets. Every Unilever business, from China to Argentina, has embraced the vitality idea. Unilever is using the idea to determine which businesses to invest in, which to exit from, and where to innovate, and now spends almost €1 billion a year on vitality-driven innovation.

If Unilever is truly to stand for vitality and if Unilever's employees are truly to embrace the new mission, then the idea has to weave its way into everything that Unilever does: the decisions people make, the new ideas they create, and the future commitments they make.

The new vitality-inspired Knorr Vie drink, for example, has sold 60 million bottles since launch.

Workplace

Packaging

Training Center

Vanguard's trusted heritage of indexing and low costs is now available to financial advisors and their clients with the launch of Exchange Traded Funds (ETFs).

Vanguard is one of the world's largest investment management companies, and oversees over 1 trillion in assets (2008). The company introduced the first index mutual fund for individual investors in 1976. Vanguard's Financial Advisor Services (FAS) provides investment products and services to Vanguard's financial advisor clients, including broker/dealers, asset managers, bank trust departments, registered investment advisers, and insurance companies.

Goals

Position Vanguard Exchange Traded Funds as the premier ETF choice.

Build trust and sustainable relationships with the financial advisor and broker channel.

Make it easy for Vanguard's sales force to build awareness and achieve results.

Apply consistent guidelines across marketing and communications channels.

Work collaboratively with internal and external creative partners on process and strategy.

We are founded on the principles of trust and candor. As we grow new channels for our business, we stay committed to those principles.

F. William McNabb
CEO/President
Vanguard

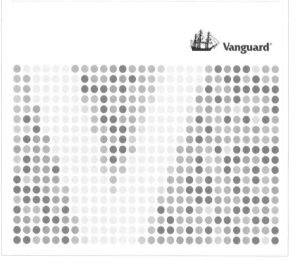

ETFs allow you to concentrate on what matters: your business

Vanguard®

A stream of fresh ideas and value-added resources reinforced Vanguard's commitment to financial advisors and their clients.

Bert Dalby
Principal of Institutional Marketing and Communications
Vanguard

Process and strategy: Vanguard's top business priority was to make its ETF products available to financial advisors. Vanguard needed to demonstrate a high level of commitment to gain credibility and visibility since there was the perception that Vanguard was not a major player in the advisor space. In addition, internally, a significant cultural shift to a more sales-driven attitude was needed.

Vanguard established a multidisciplinary team representing marketing, sales, research, editorial, design, web, public relations and legal. External experts Carla Hall Design Group and Y&R partnered with Vanguard's marketing and sales strategy, advertising, and creative concept. Interviewing stakeholders and researching their trigger-points led to creating a value proposition of Vanguard as the "Indexing Authority."

A three-step strategy was developed: 360-degree advisor experiences first built brand and product awareness via the web, advertising, direct mail, conferences, events, and PR. Interest was cultivated through communicating reasons to consider Vanguard's ETFs. Fact sheets made purchasing ETFs easy.

Creative solution: The Vanguard business heads, sales force, and marketing teams approved the value proposition of "indexing authority" supported by Vanguard's indexing expertise, low costs, and trusted name. A meta team of internal and external creative resources developed creative briefs for each project so marketers, writers, and designers could create on-target solutions together, then test them with the sales force for ease of use.

Authenticity was the unifying concept that positioned Vanguard as the "clear choice" for brokerage firms, financial advisors, and their clients. Language, tone, and clear strategic communications reinforced Vanguard's reputation for trust and candor. A bold, ever-changing graphic *V* for Vanguard imaginatively wove all media together across print, animation, and advertising, and became the leitmotif for the program. The communications framework was designed to introduce new ideas and continually migrate into a sophisticated network of mediums to communicate cohesively with the target audience.

Results: For the first time, clients working with their advisors could access Vanguard products, thus tripling Vanguard's market share and increasing advisor awareness. Vanguard ETF assets, as of year-end 2008, were over $45 billion—a ten-fold increase since the initiative was launched in late 2005. Four of Vanguard's ETFs were among the top 20 best-selling ETFs in the industry in 2008. The average expense ratio of Vanguard ETFs in 2008 was 0.14% vs. 0.58% for competing products. This communication framework proves that a creative team made up of internal and external partners can stay connected to brand consistency guidelines yet continue to inspire smart and innovative solutions that help grow the company.

We needed to position Vanguard as an indexing authority and trusted partner.

Martha Papariello
Principal of Financial Advisor Services
Vanguard

VANGUARD INTERMEDIATE-TERM BOND ETF

VANGUARD EMERGING MARKETS ETF

VANGUARD EUROPE PACIFIC ETF

Velfina is dedicated to developing the most innovative solutions in the field of medical products and to responding to the most exacting demands of our clients.*

Velfina, a Romanian medical company previously known as Actimed Emergency Systems, provides both branded and private label medical products to European and international markets. Its products are used in the treatment and prevention of wounds.

Goals

Create a brand that supports company growth.

Conduct consumer and competitive research.

Create a new name, brand identity system, and architecture.

Target a new global market.

Perform ongoing brand management activities.

*Costi Braga
CEO
Velfina

It is extraordinary to work with a client that never takes a step without asking what the impact on the brand would be. And, therefore, it is as extraordinary to watch the brand value and the client business grow.

Marius Ursache
Chief Creative Officer
Grapefruit

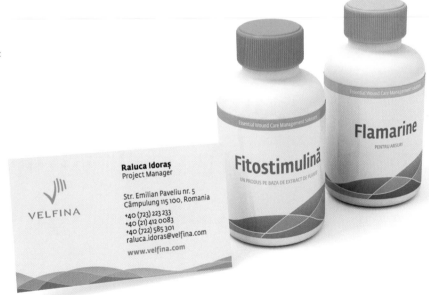

Raluca Idoraş
Project Manager

Str. Emilian Paveliu nr. 5
Câmpulung 115 100, Romania
+40 (723) 223 233
+40 (21) 412 0083
+40 (722) 585 301
raluca.idoras@velfina.com

www.velfina.com

Process and strategy: Grapefruit, a branding firm in Romania, was hired to help Actimed Emergency Systems revitalize its brand to support the growth of the company in new markets. Grapefruit assessed the existing brand and identified opportunities and risks inherent in a launch into the European market. Working closely with the CEO, Grapefruit identified a new set of key values for the brand: innovation, efficiency, and fast response. Following a brand audit and preliminary legal research, Grapefruit discovered that Actimed was already a registered trademark in most of the European Union member states, as well as in the United States, mandating a name change. Grapefruit proposed a name that would communicate the key features of the brand: gentleness and superior care. Following linguistic, cultural, and legal research, Grapefruit suggested more than 150 names that were ultimately short-listed to fit the strategic needs of the brand. Since the target market was multilingual, the final choice needed to be easy to pronounce in a range of languages. Velfina, a fabricated name, is inspired by "velum" meaning veil, or bandage, and "fine," which stands for the ultimate ideal of quality and excellence.

Grapefruit identified the phrase "Professional Wound Care Management" as Velfina's core competency. Communicating a clearly defined niche market helps the company differentiate itself from competitors. Articulating this specialization enabled Velfina to meet demanding market expectations.

Creative solution: Velfina's new logo is the result of extensive creative exploration of symbols in medical research. The chosen symbol represents the brand's niche in wound care management: the caring hand with the veil-like fabric used to make bandages. Grapefruit chose shades of teal and orange to differentiate the brand from Velfina's competitors, which used shades of cool whites. The firm developed Velfina's brand architecture, as well as created a new name (Flamarine), for a subbrand that is an innovative burn-care product. After designing a series of applications, including stationery and marketing collateral, Grapefruit began to design a packaging system. The repetitive pattern on the packaging communicates a young, cutting-edge, and optimistic positioning dramatically different from the competition. The packaging also makes the products look proprietary and not generic.

Results: Although the program is relatively new, the client is tracking income and monitoring the sales of Velfina-branded versus private label sales. Since early 2004 when the new brand was introduced, Velfina's turnover has experienced a 250% yearly growth rate to $2 million in 2004 and an estimated $5 million in 2005 from around $0.8 million in 2003.

Vueling is straightforward and fast forward. It's not just about low price; it's about being down to earth and one step ahead—in everything we do.

Vueling Airlines SA offers flights between various Spanish cities and locations in Portugal, Italy, France, Belgium, Greece, and the Netherlands. The company was founded in 2002 and is headquartered in Barcelona, Spain.

Goals

Envision and name a new brand.

Create a category-bending, envelope-pushing, new generation airline.

Design an integrated visual, verbal, and behavioral identity.

Delight the customer.

Vueling has become what we designed it to be: a new generation airline combining low prices, high style, and good service.

Juan Pablo Ramírez
Brand Strategist
Saffron Brand Consultants

Process and strategy: Vueling began as an idea for the first budget airline that would compete nationally in Spain and southern Europe from a hub in Barcelona. Public opinion of the low-cost airline category was characterized by disappointment, mistrust, and mixed feelings. Conceived jointly by founder Carlos Maños and Saffron Brand Consultants, the challenge was to reinvent the category and prove that cheap flights didn't have to mean lower standards of service, comfort, and style. Saffron began by creating the name. In Spain, Spanglish is hip. In Spanish, *vuela* means to fly, ergo, Vueling. The URL was available—vital for a service that sells mostly online. Saffron proceeded to design a new experience for customers: direct, simple, unexpected, and down to earth with low prices and great service. All brand expressions would embody *espíritu* Vueling, doing things the Vueling way. Online transactions would be as easy as 1, 2, 3. New planes, not old, would fly from major, not secondary, airports.

Creative solution: Saffron created the name and an entire identity system—not only visual and verbal but also behavioral—from nose to tail, from staff-customer contact to online interface to music and menu planning. Straightforward and fast forward, *espíritu* Vueling inspired all customer touchpoints to feel fresh, cosmopolitan, and cool. Voice was first. Saffron engineered a cultural shift from formal to informal. All brand communications speak informally by using *tu*, not *usted*. Airbus even had to rewrite the onboard signage for Vueling's planes. From the beginning, Saffron and Vueling management agreed that as a service brand, the people are paramount. The identity work informed the airline's HR policies, and has been reinforced subsequently by leading many employee training sessions. After the core brand engagement was complete, Saffron continued to keep *espíritu* Vueling alive though training, and working on their brand committee.

Results: At launch, Vueling achieved the highest capitalization to date by a new airline in Europe. It reached its full-year revenue target of 21 million euros within the first six months. In less than a year, Vueling had carried more than 1.2 million passengers on 22 routes between 14 cities. In 2008, Vueling announced it would merge with Clickair, another low-cost airline that is 80% owned by flag carrier Iberia. The decision to name the merged company Vueling is supported by surveys that confirmed the superior strength of the brand among customers and employees.

The Wild Center is alive. As the Natural History Museum of the Adirondacks, it is a base camp for exploring a 6-million-acre collection. Its living collection is the Adirondacks themselves.

Situated on a 31-acre campus in Tupper Lake, New York, the museum's main exhibit follows a river to the summit of a snowcapped mountain and includes waterfalls, a lake exhibit, forests, and streams. Two hundred live animal species inhabit this living museum. The museum's Great Hall is dominated by a towering ice wall, and its core contains a forest populated with high-definition interactive media.

Goals

Work collaboratively to define the museum's vision, brand and voice.

Determine positioning and naming strategy.

Design the brand identity.

Write the mission, master plan and exhibit text.

Our mission is to inspire a broad public understanding of the natural systems that shape and sustain life in the Adirondacks.

The Adirondacks are unique in the world. Surrounded by people, they house great expanses of nature interspersed with small towns and communities. They can be a model for a future where man and the rest of the natural world find better ways to coexist.

Donald K. Clifford, Jr.
President
The Natural History Museum of the Adirondacks

The museum team included:

Museum project manager and staff

Board of Trustees

HOK, a global architectural practice that specializes in innovation in the built environment, and designs museums, wayfinding, and exhibits

Chedd-Angier-Lewis, museum media design and production

ConsultEcon, economic research and management consultants

Points North, communications and branding firm

288

Process and strategy: Points North Communications worked closely with the project manager, museum staff, Board of Trustees, the architectural and exhibit design team, and the market research group. Points North interviewed board members, scientists, experts on the Adirondacks, and museum staff, and examined the successes and failures of similar institutions. In addition to looking at natural history subjects and Adirondacks-related material, the Points North team interviewed tourism leaders and read their research. The team traveled repeatedly to the Adirondacks to hike and boat to see what the museum would cover. The team also sat in on every meeting the architects had with the Board to shape the vision of the museum.

Points North was engaged to write the master plan and the mission, and to direct the visual identity program and naming. The firm subsequently was hired to do all marketing and communications, and to write the text for all the museum's exhibits. "The exhibit work gives us a chance to speak to the visitor inside the Center, and the marketing work gives us the chance to speak to them before they step inside," said President Howard Fish.

Creative solution: The dynamic symbol design embodies the fundamental essence of nature always changing. The museum logo, drawn by WoodPile Studios, is a fish changing into an otter, to suggest part of life's endless process. In nature, when the otter dies, it will feed the river, which illustrates the connection between the land and the water.

The symbol captured the spirit of the museum and was subsequently used as a guide in the naming process. Originally named the Natural History Museum of the Adirondacks, the team felt that the words "museum" and "history" misrepresented the engaging experience. The New York State Constitution created the forest with a commitment to being "forever wild." The team wanted a name that could be easily said and remembered by visitors from around the world. The Wild Center would be distinguished from other national and world museums and institutions.

Results: The crowd for the groundbreaking ceremony in 2004 was bigger than the crowds for the 1980 Lake Placid Winter Olympics groundbreaking. The museum has exceeded all fundraising targets. Initial surveys suggest that The Wild Center will become the most recognizable brand in the Adirondacks. It is the most successful nonprofit start-up in the history of the Adirondacks.

We were defining the brand while it was still evolving. We had to come up with a solution that would clearly define the museum but not constrict it in the future.

Howard Fish
President
Points North Communications

The symbol also mirrors an aerial view of the museum's location on an oxbow on the Raquette River. The color of the symbol changes with the seasons.

Xohm users experience a new level of mobile internet freedom, downloading movies, watching video, and playing games, whenever and wherever they want.

Xohm is a new nationwide WiMAX wireless broadband network launched by Sprint Nextel in 2008. Sprint Nextel offers a comprehensive range of communications services, bringing mobility to consumer, business, and government customers. The company is widely recognized for developing, engineering, and deploying innovative technologies. Its history goes back to 1899 with the founding of the Brown Telephone Company.

Goals

Launch a new nationwide brand.

Transcend the competition in the mobile WiMAX sector.

Attract new customers and strategic partners.

Design a comprehensive brand identity system.

Rebrand the Sprint monorail station for CES 2008 in Las Vegas.

Express connection and speed.

The public access area to the largest consumer electronics show in the world was the ideal location to launch Xohm and gain first mover advantage.

Rodney Abbot
Senior Partner
Lippincott

Photography: © Peter Aaron/Esto

Process and strategy: When Sprint announced plans to build a new nationwide WiMAX wireless broadband network, named Xohm, Lippincott was asked to work with the brand management group to determine how the brand should go to market. The team began by examining key moments in the customer experience for both Sprint and non-Sprint customers. After making the decision to create a new brand, Lippincott set out to design a brand identity system for this mobile service of the future. The long-term success of the new network would depend on the brand's ability to attract strategic ecosystem partners like Google and Intel, and mobile communications providers like Samsung; the largest consumer electronics show in the world, CES 2008 in Las Vegas, provided the ideal location to launch Xohm and gain first mover advantage. The Sprint monorail station at the Las Vegas Convention Center was selected as a venue that would serve as both a primary point of public access to the show and a briefing center where Xohm executives could conduct meetings and entertain guests.

Creative solution: The new identity captured a dynamic of connecting people, places, and devices. The bold, iconic movement combined attraction and radiance. The design solution for the monorail station used the simple, graphic dot language of the symbol to connect the indoor and outdoor spaces. Lippincott's challenge was to maximize visibility for the brand at the monorail station, cutting through the clutter in an environment overrun with competing imagery and messages. The imaginative use of color, shape, and light helped create intrigue surrounding the Xohm launch. Mixed-use spaces and interior meeting areas were created using a distinct combination of furnishings. Animation and video content on numerous digital platforms explained Xohm's story. The straightforward tone combined with oversize scale and bold color reflected a playful spirit that set Xohm apart from the hi-tech hoopla usually associated with a new technology launch.

Results: Tens of thousands of techies, key influencers, and decision makers passed though the branded space and were introduced to the new brand. Following CES 2008, there was a great deal of buzz within the technology world and positive reviews by key technology writers. Sprint took the lead in committing to build a new nationwide WiMAX wireless broadband network, and has attracted more strategic partners to provide customers with the largest and most dependable 4G network in America.

Bibliography

Aaker, David A. and Erich Joachimsthaler. *Brand Leadership.* New York: The Free Press, 2000.

Aaker, David. *Brand Portfolio Strategy.* New York: The Free Press, 2004.

Adams, Sean, Noreen Morioka, and Terry Stone. *Logo Design Workbook: A Hands-On Guide to Creating Logos.* Gloucester, MA: Rockport, 2004.

Adamson, Allen P. *BrandDigital: Simple Ways Top Brands Succeed in the Digital World.* New York: Palgrave Macmillan, 2008.

Adamson, Allen P. *BrandSimple: How the Best Brands Keep It Simple and Succeed.* New York: Palgrave Macmillan, 2006.

Advertising Metrics, www.marketingterms.com.

AIArchitect, "Best Practices, Center for Health Design Releases Findings on How Design Can Improve the Standard of Care in Health-Care Facilities," February 2005.

Baker, Stephen. "Looking for a Blog in a Haystack," *BusinessWeek,* July 25, 2005.

Beckwith, Harry. *Selling the Invisible.* New York: Warner Books, 1997.

Blake, George Burroughs and Nancy Blake-Bohne. *Crafting the Perfect Name: The Art and Science of Naming a Company or Product.* Chicago: Probus Publishing Company, 1991.

Bruce-Mitford, Miranda. *The Illustrated Book of Signs & Symbols.* New York: DK Publishing, Inc., 1996.

Brunner, Robert and Stewart Emery. *Do You Matter? How Great Design Will Make People Love Your Company.* Upper Saddle River, NJ: Pearson Education, 2009.

Buell, Barbara. "Can a Global Brand Speak Different Languages?" *Stanford Business,* August 2000.

Business attitudes to design. www.design-council.org.uk.

Calver, Giles. *What Is Packaging Design?* Switzerland: RotoVision, 2004.

Carlzon, Jan. *Moments of Truth.* New York: Harper Collins, 1987.

Carter, David E. *Branding: The Power of Market Identity.* New York: Hearst Books International, 1999.

Carter, Rob, Ben Day, and Philip Meggs. *Typographic Design: Form and Communication.* New York: John Wiley & Sons, Inc., 1993.

Chermayeff, Ivan, Tom Geismar, and Steff Geissbuhler. *Trademarks Designed by Chermayeff + Geismar.* Basel, Switzerland: Lars Muller Publishers, 2000.

Conway, Lloyd Morgan. *Logo, Identity, Brand, Culture.* Crans-Pres-Celigny, Switzerland: RotoVision SA, 1999.

"Crowned at Last: A Survey of Consumer Power." *The Economist,* April 2, 2005.

DeNeve, Rose. *The Designer's Guide to Creating Corporate I.D. Systems.* Cincinnati, OH: North Light Books, 1992.

"A Discussion with Chris Hacker," *Enlightened Brand Journal,* www.enlightenedbrand.com.

Duffy, Joe. *Brand Apart.* New York: One Club Publishing, 2005.

Ehrbar, Al. "Breakaway Brands," *Fortune,* October 31, 2005.

Eiber, Rick, ed. *World Trademarks: 100 Years,* Volumes I and II. New York: Graphis U.S., Inc., 1996.

"Fighting Dragons and Lightening Skin; Two Companies Go to Asia." Minnesota Public Radio, May 16, 2005.

Friedman, Thomas L. *Hot, Flat, and Crowded: Why We Need a Green Revolution–and How It Can Renew America.* New York: Farrar, Straus and Giroux, 2008.

Gardner, Bill and Cathy Fishel. *Logo Lounge: 2000 Identities by Leading Designers.* Gloucester, MA: Rockport, 2003.

Gilmore, James H. and B. Joseph Pine II. *Authenticity: What Consumers Really Want.* Boston: Harvard Business School Press, 2007.

Gladwell, Malcolm. *The Tipping Point: How Little Things Can Make a Big Difference.* New York: Little, Brown and Company, 2000.

Glaser, Milton. *Art Is Work.* Woodstock, NY: The Overlook Press, 2000.

Gobe, Marc. *Emotional Branding, The New Paradigm for Connecting Brands to People.* New York: Allworth Press, 2001.

Godin, Seth. *Tribes: We Need You to Lead Us.* New York: Portfolio, 2008.

Godin, Seth. *Purple Cow: Transforming Your Business By Being Remarkable.* New York: Portfolio, 2003.

Grant, John. *The New Marketing Manifesto: The 12 Rules for Building Successful Brands in the 21st Century.* London: Texere Publishing Limited, 2000.

"Graphic Design and Advertising Timeline," *Communication Arts* 41, 1 (1999): 80–95.

Hart, Susannah and John Murphy, eds. *Brands: The New Wealth Creators.* New York: Palgrave, 1998.

Hawken, Paul. *Blessed Unrest: How the Largest Social Movement in History Is Restoring Grace, Justice, and Beauty to the World.* New York: Penguin Books, 2007.

Heath, Chip and Dan Heath. *Made to Stick: Why Some Ideas Survive and Others Die.* New York: Random House, 2007.

Heller, Steven and Elinor Pettit. *Graphic Design Time Line: A Century of Design Milestones.* New York: Allworth Press, 2000.

Heller, Steven. *Paul Rand.* London: Phaidon Press Limited, 1999.

Hill, Sam and Chris Lederer. *The Infinite Asset: Managing Brands to Build New Value.* Boston: Harvard Business School Press, 2001.

Hine, Thomas. *The Total Package: The Evolution and Secret Meanings of Boxes, Bottles, Cans, and Tubes.* Boston: Little, Brown and Company, 1995.

The History of Printmaking. New York: Scholastic Inc., 1995.

Holtzschue, Linda. *Understanding Color: An Introduction for Designers.* New York: John Wiley & Sons, Inc., 2002.

Javed, Naseem. *Naming for Power: Creating Successful Names for the Business World.* New York: Linkbridge Publishing, 1993.

Joachimsthaler, Erich, David A. Aaker, John Quelch, David Kenny, Vijay Vishwanath, and Mark Jonathan. *Harvard Business Review on Brand Management.* Boston: Harvard Business School Press, 1999.

Kawasaki, Guy. *Reality Check: The Irreverent Guide to Outsmarting, Outmanaging, and Outmarketing Your Competition.* New York: Portfolio, 2008.

Klein, Naomi. *No Logo.* New York: Picador, 2002.

Kerzner, Harold. *Project Management: A Systems Approach to Planning, Scheduling, and Controlling.* New York: Van Nostrand Reinhold, 1989.

Kuhlmann, Arkadi and Bruce Philip. *The Orange Code: How ING Direct Succeeded by Being a Rebel with a Cause.* Hoboken, NJ: John Wiley & Sons, Inc., 2009.

Landa, Robin. *Designing Brand Experiences: Creating Powerful Integrated Brand Solutions.* Clifton Park, NY: Thomson Delmar Learning, 2005.

Lippincott Mercer. *Sense: The Art and Science of Creating Lasting Brands.* Gloucester, MA: Rockport, 2004.

Lipton, Ronnie. *Designing Across Cultures.* New York: How Design Books, 2002.

Lubliner, Murray J. *Global Corporate Identity: The Cross-Border Marketing Challenge.* Rockport, MA: Rockport Publishers, Inc., 1994.

Maeda, John. *The Laws of Simplicity: Design, Technology, Business, Life.* Cambridge, MA: The MIT Press, 2006.

Man, John. *Alpha Beta: How Our Alphabet Shaped the Western World.* London: Headline Book Publishing, 2000.

Mau, Bruce. *Massive Change.* London: Phaidon Press Limited, 2004.

Meggs, Philip B. *A History of Graphic Design.* New York: John Wiley & Sons, Inc., 1998.

Mok, Clement. *Designing Business: Multiple Media, Multiple Disciplines.* San Jose, CA: Macmillan Computer Publishing USA, 1996.

Mollerup, Per. *Marks of Excellence: The History and Taxonomy of Trademarks.* London: Phaidon Press Limited, 1997.

Napoles, Veronica. *Corporate Identity Design.* New York: John Wiley & Sons, Inc., 1988.

Neumeier, Marty. *The Dictionary of Brand.* New York: The AIGA Press, 2004.

Neumeier, Marty. *The Brand Gap: How to Bridge the Distance between Business Strategy and Design.* Berkeley: New Riders, 2003.

Neumeier, Marty. *ZAG: The Number One Strategy of High Performance Brands.* Berkeley: New Riders, 2006.

Neumeier, Marty. *The Designful Company: How to Build a Culture of Non-stop Innovation.* Berkeley: New Riders, 2008.

Newark, Quentin. *What Is Graphic Design?* Switzerland: RotoVision, 2002.

Ogilvy, David. *Ogilvy on Advertising.* New York: Crown Publishers, 1983.

Olins, Wally. *On Brand.* New York: Thames & Hudson, 2003.

Olins, Wally. *Corporate Identity: Making Business Strategy Visible Through Design.* Boston: Harvard Business School Press, 1989.

Paos, ed. *New Decomas: Design Conscious Management Strategy.* Seoul: Design House Inc., 1994.

Pavitt, Jane, ed. *Brand New.* London: V&A Publications, 2000.

Pentagram. *Pentagram Book Five.* New York: Monacelli Press, 1999.

Perry, Alicia with David Wisnom III. *Before the Brand: Creating the Unique DNA of an Enduring Brand Identity.* New York: The McGraw-Hill Companies, 2003.

Peters, Tom. *Reinventing Work: The Brand You 50.* New York: Alfred A. Knopf, Inc, 1999.

Phillips, Peter L. *Creating the Perfect Design Brief.* New York: Allworth Press, 2004.

Pine II, B. Joseph and James H. Gilmore. *The Experience Economy.* Boston: Harvard Business School Press, 1999.

Pink, Daniel H. *The Adventures of Johnny Bunko: The Last Career Guide You'll Ever Need.* New York: Riverhead Books, 2008.

Pink, Daniel H. *A Whole New Mind: Why Right-Brainers Will Rule the Future.* New York: Riverhead Books, 2006.

Remington, R. Roger. *Lester Beall: Trailblazer of American Graphic Design.* New York: W. W. Norton & Company, 1996.

Ries, Al and Laura Ries. *The 22 Immutable Laws of Branding.* London: Harper Collins Business, 2000.

Ries, Al and Jack Trout. *Positioning: The Battle for Your Mind.* New York: Warner Books, Inc., 1986.

Rogener, Stefan, Albert-Jan Pool, and Ursula Packhauser. *Branding with Type: How Type Sells.* Mountain View, CA: Adobe Press, 1995.

Roush, Wade. "Social Machines." *MIT's Magazine of Innovation, Technology Review,* August 2005.

Rubin, Jeffrey and Dana Chisnell. *Handbook of Usability Testing: How to Plan, Design, and Conduct Effective Tests.* Indianapolis: Wiley Publishing, Inc., 2008.

Scher, Paula. *Make It Bigger.* New York: Princeton Architectural Press, 2002.

Schmitt, Bernd. *Customer Experience Management.* New York: John Wiley & Sons, Inc., 2003.

Schmitt, Bernd and Alex Simonson. *Marketing Aesthetics: The Strategic Management of Brands, Identity, and Image.* New York: Free Press, 1997.

Sharp, Harold S. *Advertising Slogans of America.* Metuchen, NJ: The Scarecrow Press, 1984.

Spiekerman, Erik and E. M. Ginger. *Stop Stealing Sheep & Find Out How Type Works.* Mountain View, CA: Adobe Press, 1993.

Steffen, Alex, ed. *World Changing: A User's Guide for the 21st Century.* New York: Abrams, 2006.

Sweet, Fay. *MetaDesign: Design from the World Up.* New York: Watson-Guptill Publications, 1999.

Thaler, Linda Kaplan and Robin Koval. *The Power of Nice: How to Conquer the Business World with Kindness.* New York: Currency Doubleday, 2006.

Traverso, Debra Koontz. *Outsmarting Goliath: How to Achieve Equal Footing with Companies That Are Bigger, Richer, Older, and Better Known.* Princeton, NJ: Bloomberg Press, 2000.

Vogelstein, Fred. "Yahoo's Brilliant Solution." *Fortune,* August 8, 2005.

Williams, Gareth. *Branded? Products and Their Personalities.* London: V&A Publications, 2000.

Yamashita, Keith and Sandra Spataro. *Unstuck.* New York: Portfolio, 2004.

Index

A

@issuejournal.com, 153

Aaker, David A., 10, 48, 117

AARP, 21

Aase, Lee, 69

Abbot, Rodney, 176, 290

abbreviations, letterhead, 147

ABC Carpet & Home, 245

abstract marks, 51, 60–61

ACLU (American Civil Liberties Union), 84, 115, 196–97

AC Nielsen, 213

acquisitions. *See* mergers and acquisitions

acronym names, 21

Actimed Emergency Systems, 284, 285

actions, brand strategy, 12

Adams, Sean, 127, 148–49

AdamsMorioka, 127, 148–49

Adamson, Allen, 8

advertising, 95, 162–63

Aeron chair, 33

Aeschines, 162

AFLAC Insurance and AFLAC duck, 65, 135

A Hundred Monkeys, 20, 122

Aicher, Otl, 256

AIDS, 266–67

Ailey, Alvin, 54

Aldi, 76, 77

Alina Wheeler, 61

Allemann, Hans-U., 124

Allemann Almquist + Jones, 56–57, 59, 61

Allen, Harry, 205

allmyfaves.com, 39

Allstate, 25

Altman, Danny, 20, 122

Alusiv, 59

Alvin Ailey, 54

Amanresorts, 253

Amazon.com, 117, 198–99

"American Alphabet" (Cody), 53

American Civil Liberties Union (ACLU), 84, 115, 196–97

American Express, 267

American Girl Place, 18

The American Lawyer, 221

America's Choice private label, 77

Amoco, 131, 208–9

Anabliss Design + Brand Strategy, 83, 150

Anderson, Margaret, 27

Andrew Shaylor Photography, 81

animation, 136–37

AOL, 135

A&P, 77

Apotek, 200–201

Apple, 17, 25, 34, 41, 51, 132, 165, 267

Apple MacBook Pro, 58

Apple Store, 18

ARAMARK "Starman," 178–79

Archer Farms private label, 77

architecture, 164–65

Arky, David, 13

Armstrong, Mark, 256

Armstrong, Scott, 216–17

Arsentyev, Vladimir, 256

Arvin Industries, 56–57

Ask Jeeves, 65

asset management, 172–93. *See also* costs; management

brands, 11, 46–47, 48–49

brand (spirit) books, 182–83

change and innovation, 174–75

employees, 178–79, 182

internal design teams, 180–81

launch examples, 179

launch requirements, 176–77

metric system, 192–93

online tools, 187–89

process measurement, 92–93

reproduction files, 190–91

standards and guidelines, 184–87

Association of Danish Pharmacies, 132, 200–201

Assurant, 97, 202–3

Atari, 41

AT&T, 41

audio architecture, 134–35

audit readout, research, 114–15

audits

audit readout, 114–15

competitive audit, 110–11

language audit, 112–13

marketing audit, 108–9

Aunt Jemima, 65

authenticity, 31, 36–37

automobiles, 166–67

Avarde, Susan, 88, 99

avatar, 136

Aveda Uruku, 29, 204–5

Axelrod, David, 255

B

Bach, Amanda, 86

Bacher, Rick, 212–13

Bacon, Quentin, 183, 252

Baker, Stephen, 69

Baldridge, Patricia M., 175

Balkind, Aubrey, 42

Ballard Spahr Andrews & Ingersoll, 144

Bank of New York, 82

Barnet, Kim, 135

Barneys, 245

Barthlomew, Matthew, 133

Barton, Jim, 278–79

Bass Ale, 41

Batman, 273